The
Domestic
Herbal

The
Domestic
Herbal

Plants for the Home
in the Seventeenth Century

MARGARET WILLES

Bodleian Library
UNIVERSITY OF OXFORD

DISCLAIMER This book is not intended to provide medical or other health advice for readers, and none of the remedies included here is recommended for use without expert advice.

First published in 2020 by the Bodleian Library
Broad Street, Oxford OX1 3BG
www.bodleianshop.co.uk

ISBN 978 1 85124 513 0

Text © Margaret Willes, 2020
All images, unless specified on p. 219,
© Bodleian Library, University of Oxford, 2020

Margaret Willes has asserted her right to be identified as the author of this Work.

Cover design by Dot Little at the Bodleian Library
Designed and typeset in 11 on 15 Janson by illuminati, Grosmont
Printed and bound in China by C&C Offset Printing Co. Ltd.
on 120 gsm Chinese Baijin pure woodfree paper

British Library Catalogue in Publishing Data
A CIP record of this publication is available from the British Library

p. i Alexanders from Gerard's *Herball*
pp. ii–iii Comfrey and daisy from the *Tudor Pattern Book*

Contents

Acknowledgements   vii

Introduction   1

Productive Gardens   17

For the Table   57

Small Beer & Strong Liquors   89

A Herbal   112

Health & Beauty   131

Care of Clothes   161

Fragrant Chambers   181

Notes   206

Select Bibliography   216

Picture Credits   219

Index   221

❋ The time.

They flower about August, and somewhat later in colde sommers.

❋ The names.

Masticke is called of the new writers *Marum* : of *Dioscorides Clinopodium*. *Dioscorides* sheweth that *Clinopodium* is δάμνον, that is to say, a little shrub : of some it is called *Cleonicum*, and of the Latines *Lectipes*.

❋ The nature.

These plants are hot and drie in the third degree.

❋ The vertues.

Dioscorides writeth, that the herbe is drunke, and likewise the decoction thereof, against the bi- A tings of venemous beasts, crampes and conuulsions, burstings and the strangurie.

The decoction boiled in wine till the third part be consumed, and drunke, stoppeth the laske, in B them that haue an ague, and vnto others in water.

Of Pennie royall, or Pudding grasse.   Chap. 211.

1 *Pulegium regium.*
Pennie royall.

2 *Pulegium mas.*
Vpright Pennie royall.

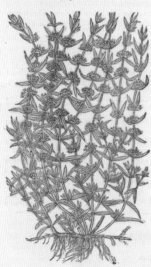 

❋ The description.

1   Pᵛlegium regium vulgatum is so exceedingly well knowne to all our English nation, that it needeth no description, being our common Pennie roiall.

2   The second being the male Pennie roiall is like vnto the former, in leaues, flowers, and smell, and differeth in that this male kinde groweth vpright of himselfe without creeping, much like in shewe vnto wilde Marierome.

3   The thirde kinde of Pennie roiall groweth like vnto Time, and is of a wooddie substance, somewhat like vnto the thinne leafed Hyssope, of the sauour of common Pennie royall.

Mm 1   3 *Pulegium*

Acknowledgements

THE INFORMATION-GATHERING FOR THIS BOOK was quite a challenge, from plant floor coverings to the use of dung in salves for wounds. A whole range of people were extremely helpful in answering my questions, to whom I would like to say a great thank you: Nancy Johnson and Ellen Shea for information on the earliest recipe books in North America, and Sara Pennell on seventeenth-century English household manuals; Catherine Sutherland at the Pepys Library, Magdalene College, Cambridge; Katy Birkwood at the Royal College of Physicians in London; Ruth Frendo at the Worshipful Company of Stationers. Much help, both information and technical rescues, was forthcoming from the staff at the British Library, the Wellcome Library and the Royal Society. All kinds of housekeeping and gardening information came from Jane Eade and Patricia Ferguson at the National Trust, and from the staff at Ham House, Rosie Fyles, Vanessa Parker and Sarah McGrady. Thanks also to Stephen Gray on the successors to strewing herbs; Claudine Merer for help on medicinal plants; Jon Stobart and Alan Crosbie for information on grocers and market gardeners; Sophie Miller and William Griffiths on the taste of lampreys; and Fiona Edwards Stuart on the use of tomatoes in the seventeenth century.

A page from Gerard's *Herball* of 1597 showing pennyroyal.

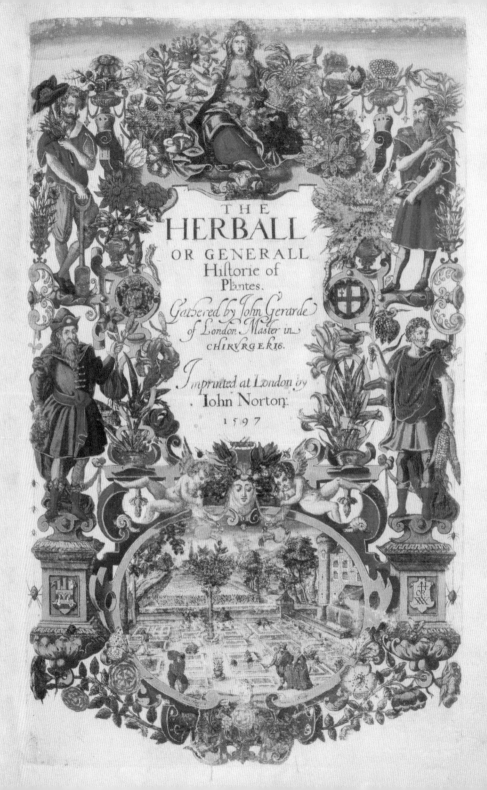

THE
HERBALL
OR GENERALL
Historie of
Plantes.

Gathered by John Gerarde
of London Master in
CHIRVRGERIE.

Imprinted at London by
Iohn Norton.
1597

Introduction

Neither is there a noble or pleasant Seat in *England*, but hath its *Gardens* for Pleasure and Delight; scarce an ingenious Citizen that by his confinement to a Shop, being denied the privilege of having a real *Garden*, but hath his Boxes, Pots, or other receptacles for flowers, plants, *&c*. ... There is scarce a Cottage in most of the *Southern* parts of England but hath its proportionable *Garden*, so great a delight do most of men take in it; that they may not only please themselves with the view of Flowers, Herbs and Trees, as they grow, but furnish themselves and their neighbour upon extraordinary occasions as Nuptials, Feasts, and Funerals, with the proper products of their *Gardens*.

T HE IMPORTANCE OF THE GARDEN for every kind of household in the seventeenth century is well summed up by the horticultural writer John Worlidge.[1] Even the most elaborate and fashionable gardens had areas set aside for herbs, fruit, vegetables and flowers for use in the house, while those of more modest establishments were vital to the survival of the household. Further sources were market gardens, gardens of herbs specifically cultivated for the use of the medical profession and, for rural households, meadows and hedgerows.

Title page of Gerard's *Herball* of 1597, from the hand-coloured version that the publisher John Norton presented to the newly established Bodleian Library in Oxford. Some of the plants featured are native to Britain; others – such as the sunflower, the head of corn and the crown imperial – were exciting new introductions from around the world.

Plants were therefore employed in every room of the house at this period, not just for the purposes of decoration, but for flavouring food, brewing and distilling, scenting rooms, washing linen, dyeing cloth, warding off pests and caring for the sick. In this book I shall take a tour of the different parts of the house, looking at how the seventeenth-century housewife or housekeeper made use of plants, starting with the kitchen and other service areas, before moving on to the chambers that we now know as living rooms and bedrooms.

The location of the kitchen introduced an architectural revolution of the early seventeenth century. Bespoke kitchens had already been a feature of aristocratic and gentry houses, usually located beyond a screens passage, as can still be seen in Oxbridge colleges. But now the plan of English domestic houses was changing from a hall, where the cooking might be undertaken on an open hearth, to a specific room, the kitchen, sharing its chimney stack with the living rooms on the same floor and in the upper storeys.[2]

A large establishment could also have a still room, where sweet waters were distilled, along with the preserving of fruit and vegetables and the manufacture of sweetmeats. In more modest houses, any distilling and preserving would be carried out in the kitchen. The results of distilling furnished not only the table, but also the medicine chest, for housewives in the seventeenth century were responsible for the care of their families, and often of the animals. Likewise, larger establishments usually had a separate brewhouse, while in more modest houses the malting and brewing would take place in the kitchen, or a room leading off it, with a cellar below for storage. The plants for flavouring these drinks were all drawn from the garden.

PREVIOUS PAGES A late-sixteenth-century depiction of spring by Lucas van Valckenborch with flowers being gathered for the still room, for strewing and for decorating the house.

Although cloth, manufactured and dyed, was available from shops, markets and travelling pedlars, it was also made at home, and both printed and manuscript books from this time include recipes for dyeing, using plants from the garden as well as exotic ingredients such as logwood and brazilwood from South America. In addition, the vigilant housewife had to look to keeping clothes and household linen clean and stored properly to prevent insect damage. For storage, sweet bags were made up from herbs and flowers to repel pests from the linen press.

The final part of my tour moves away from the kitchen and service areas of the house to the living rooms, the hall, parlour, closets and bed-chambers. Just as the kitchen could double up as a still room, a laundry or even a brewhouse, so these living rooms often had various functions. The parlour could be used as 'an eating room', the bedchamber might serve as a bed sitting room, where the diarist Samuel Pepys, for instance, used to eat his supper, while his wife Elizabeth took her dancing lessons here. In town or country alike it was a challenge to keep rooms fresh, especially in the summer months. Housewives rose nobly to this challenge and, to add luxury to necessity, imbued their rooms with the fragrance and colour of plants from the garden.

The seventeenth century was a particularly turbulent period politically in England, with a civil war, the execution of the king, Charles I, the establishment of a republic, the return of Charles II, the flight of another king, James II, during what is now sometimes known as the Glorious Revolution. Nevertheless these events do not occupy centre stage so far as this book is concerned. The Stuart monarchs make only cameo appear-ances: for example, James I's loathing of tobacco; Henrietta Maria, Charles I's French queen, planting a garden with the fashionable artichoke; and her grandchildren, William and Mary, introducing the latest technology in gardening from Holland.

Other kinds of revolution, however, can be found in the domestic life of the century. This domestic life is essentially English. Although on the death of Elizabeth I in 1603, the Scottish king, James VI, succeeded as James I, the two kingdoms remained separate until the Act of Union of 1707. In so many ways, from land holding to commerce, Scotland and England were very different. England's horizons were to change hugely during the seventeenth century. Its first colony was Ireland, with tragic consequences that are beyond the scope of this story. But the English settlers were reaching out much further, to the 'brave new world' of North America, first to Newfoundland and Virginia, and in the 1620s to what was to become New England.

The original island colonies in the Americas were Barbados, Bermuda, Nevis, Montserrat, Antigua, and a share of St Kitts and St Croix. Daniel Defoe was later to describe these West Indian islands as 'the Dregs of the Spaniards first Extraction, the Refuse Part of their Conquests, their meer leavings'.³ This dismissive view overlooks the fact that the islands were secure locations, protected from Spanish colonies to the west by the pattern of winds. Jamaica was added to this colonial portfolio in 1655, and by the end of the century the East India Company had established trading centres, or factories, in India and the East Indies, while the buccaneer William Dampier had his sights on that terra incognita, Australia.

This expansion both of colonies and of trading links brought new plants to furnish English gardens. From America, for example, came the potato and tobacco. The herbalist John Gerard noted that the potato flourished in English soil, and, though it was not welcomed onto the English table for many decades, it quickly became the staple of the Irish. Thanks to James I's hatred of tobacco, its cultivation was encouraged not in England but rather in Virginia, where Governor John Rolfe introduced the sweeter version from the West Indies. Other exotic plants could not be trans-planted to England, but the spices that they yielded, such as the nutmeg, clove and black pepper, were imported from the Middle Ages onwards. Although tobacco was the principal West Indian import, in the 1640s it was realized that Barbados in particular was suited to the cultivation of sugar cane. The English, who already had a sweet tooth with imports from North Africa and South America, avidly took to even more of this spice, so that the century could be described as the golden age of sugar.

I had assumed, when embarking on the research for this book, that households in remoter parts of England would not have had access to exotic ingredients, but have found this was quite wrong. The penetration by grocers and apothecaries, especially as the century developed, was sophisticated and extensive. Thus, for example, Elizabeth Birkett, the wife of a statesman or yeoman farmer living at Troutbeck in the Lake District at the end of the seventeenth century, had recipes in her commonplace book that required exotic ingredients. For these she would have been supplied not only by carrier from London, but also by local grocers, possibly in Kendal.

Whether ingredients were native or exotic, our principal source of knowledge about how they were used comes from herbals. Although the term 'herbal' suggests a book about herbs, in fact these volumes contained the names and descriptions of plants in general, so that flowers, fruit and vegetables are also included, with their properties and virtues. In the fifteenth century, with the invention of movable type by Gutenberg in Mainz, printed herbals were among the first books to be available to a general market – as opposed to manuscripts that could only be consulted by an individual. Such treatises were necessary not only to the herbalist or botanist, but also to the physician, the surgeon and the apothecary, for whom knowledge of medicinal plants was essential.

By the seventeenth century the herbal had also become invaluable within the domestic arena for the housewife. The first truly authoritative printed herbal in English had been compiled in the middle of previous century by William Turner, who is thus described as the 'Father of English Botany', but the two printed herbals that are central to this book are those of John Gerard and of Nicholas Culpeper. Both books are organized like encyclopaedias of the plants.

JOHN GERARD's book, entitled *The Herball or Generall Historie of Plantes*, was published in 1597. Gerard was a London barber surgeon who also acted as supervisor of the gardens of William Cecil, Lord Burghley, Queen Elizabeth I's chief minister. In addition he had his own garden in Holborn, issuing a catalogue of its contents in 1596 that listed over 1,000 plants. The following year saw the publication of his *Herball*. Gerard had been asked by the publisher, John Norton, to take over the translation of a history of plants of the Flemish herbalist Rembert Dodoens after the death of the original author commissioned to undertake the task. Gerard not only completed the translation but added much information of his own. Norton hired from a German publisher almost 1,800 woodcuts to illustrate the book. When the huge project was issued in 1597, he was so pleased by the result that he commissioned a team, probably of women and children, to colour each of the plants for a special copy to be presented to Sir Thomas Bodley for his new library in Oxford. Many of the illustrations in this book are taken from that unique copy.

Gerard's *Herball* provides all kinds of information on gardening, cooking and other domestic applications, which made it a favourite book of reference for the lady of the house if she could afford its hefty price. In the early seventeenth century, a bound copy would have cost around £1 10*s*, at a time when the annual salary of a clergyman was between £10 and £20, and that of a schoolmaster £6.[4]

NICHOLAS CULPEPER's herbal was first published in 1652 under the title *The English Physitian* but in the many subsequent editions was known as *Culpeper's Complete Herbal*.[5] His was one of the most successful books ever published in the English language and is still in print. Most of the book consists of a directory of native medicinal herbs from Adders' Tongue to Yarrow, with their appearance, location, time of picking, medicinal virtues and use, plus their astrological influences. Couched in simple, accessible language, the book was aimed particularly at women as the main providers of non-professional healthcare. Culpeper made the decision not to have illustrations in his herbal, thus keeping the price to a few pence and to reach readers who did not have the wherewithal for Gerard's book.

In addition, the expanding market in printed books in English was providing information and advice on plants for the household. In 1557 THOMAS TUSSER, a Suffolk farmer, published the first of a series of books on husbandry, *A Hundreth Good Pointes of Husbandrie*. As the title indicates, it was aimed at the man of the household, but Tusser soon recognized the importance of the housewife, publishing an expanded edition five years later with the addition of 'a hundreth good poyntes of huswifery', and a further expanded edition as *Five Hundred Pointes of Good Husbandrie, United to as many of Good Huswifery*. Tusser's books proved popular and long-lasting, going through many editions. Arranged as a calendar, they were written in simple verse, making it easier for those who were relatively unlettered to remember the information offered.

By the beginning of the seventeenth century, a range of books was available for the housewife, as suggested by their titles: for example, Thomas Dawson's *Good Huswifes Jewell* (1596) and GERVASE MARKHAM's *Countrey Contentments, or The English Huswife* (1623). Markham, of gentry stock from Nottinghamshire, published a range of books from poetry to a manual on the care of horses. He was shrewd at targeting his potential audiences, and with *The English Huswife* set out on his title page exactly what was expected of the lady of the house. He began with 'her skill in Physicke, Surgerie, Extraction of Oyles, Banqueting-stuffe, Ordering of great Feasts'. To this he added brewing of ale, along with making wines. Markham's title page also mentions as the duties of what he called 'the complete woman' the 'ordering of Wooll, Hempe, Flax, making Cloth, Dying'. Markham was aiming for self-sufficiency, which was never totally feasible, and became less so as the century proceeded.

The number of such books continued to grow. John Beale, a Somerset clergyman and expert on orchards and cider, noted in 1659: 'Our Stationers Shops have lately swarmed with bookes of Cookery.'[6] These books often had tantalizing titles, such as the *The Queens Closet Opened*, published in 1655 by 'W.M', purporting to contain recipes from Charles I's French queen Henrietta Maria that he had collected when working in the royal household. This theme continued with a collection of recipes of SIR KENELM DIGBY, produced in 1669 as *The Closet Opened*. Digby is one of the most extraordinary figures of the seventeenth century: his Catholic father was implicated and executed for his part in the Gunpowder Plot, and Digby maintained the Roman faith, despite the dangers therein. He was a privateer, a natural philosopher and an intellectual, who married the beauty Venetia Stanley; after her untimely death he retreated into his studies in Gresham College in the City of London, where he died in 1665. Four years later some of the recipes that he had collected were published as *The Closet Opened*.

The idea of letting the reader, be she a gentlewoman or a maidservant, into valuable secrets was targeting the aspirational. HANNAH WOLLEY, a widow who turned to writing to make a living for herself and her family, gave one of her books the title *The Queene-like Closet*. A chapbook produced in the 1690s went even further with its catch-all title, *The Accomplished Ladies Rich Closet of Rarities*, OR *The Ingenious Gentlewoman and Servant-Maids Delightfull Companion*. Books on gardening and cosmetics, household manuals and works containing medicinal recipes carried similar titles.

These are printed books and, apart from the works of Hannah Wolley, by male authors. Women, however, were keeping their own sources of information, handwritten books of receipts or recipes, sometimes described as commonplace books. These were not only invaluable to the original compiler but could be added to as they were handed down through the generations. Thomas Hardy describes a Victorian lady's library in which were 'books of housewifery, and among them volumes of MS. Recipes, cookery-books, and some too on surgery and medicine as practised by Ladies Bountiful of the Elizabethan age, for which an antiquarian would nowadays give an eye or a hand.'[7] Even in very recent times such recipe books continued to be kept: it is probably the wide availability of recipes in printed form and online that has rendered them a comparative rarity.

The compilers of early-seventeenth-century manuscript books had to be literate at a time when it has been estimated that a third to a half of London's population could read and possibly write. The proportion of literacy in rural areas was lower, and much lower for women. This means that inevitably the voices heard are those of the wealthier members of society, such as the country gentlewoman Lady Elinor Fettiplace; Elizabeth Birkett, wife of a substantial yeomen farmer; courtiers such as Lady Ann Fanshawe; and the Londoner Mary Doggett. I have tried whenever possible to consider the gardens and households of the less wealthy, but the book is inevitably skewed towards richer fare and practices.

There are dozens of manuscript books from the seventeenth century that have survived. I have chosen to feature a handful of these and, to provide their social context, have given details of their compilers, along with those of Hannah Wolley, as a list of dramatis personae at the end of this introduction. Sometimes these manuscript books had an order to their assembly. For example, related recipes can be grouped together, and a distinction made between culinary, medicinal and general household tips. But more often they are all mixed together, with the writer adding new recipes when she received them, and on occasion noting the source from which they came, usually members of the family or neighbours, but sometimes from 'professional' experts, such as physicians and apothecaries. Although I have in the main paraphrased their recipes in the text, at times I have reproduced them verbatim to capture the voices of the time.

Social context is also provided by diaries of the period. Although Samuel Pepys only kept his for nine years, as ever it is wonderful on all kinds of details not to be found in other diaries: what food and drink he consumed and where; the illnesses that he and his family suffered; the tribulations of wash day. In an entry for August 1663 he mentions taking a cookery book on an outing on the Thames with two friends, Mrs Turner and Mrs Morrice: 'I carried them on board the King's Pleasure-boat – all the way reading in a book of Receipts of making fine meats and sweet-meats, among others, one "To make my own sweet water" – which made us good sport.'[8] Pepys had an earthy sense of humour.

John Evelyn's diary is not as informative as that of his friend Pepys, but he was a prolific recorder of all matters horticultural during his long life. Lady Margaret Hoby is the first female English diarist. Her journal dates from the very end of the sixteenth century, and gives some details of her gardening and healing activities. Ralph Josselin kept his diary from the 1640s until his death in 1683, and provides a picture of the concerns about health in a family during this period.

Colonists took with them to their new homes plants and seeds from English gardens. When the Pilgrim Fathers set off in the *Mayflower* in 1620, the herbal of the Flemish physician Rembert Dodoens was on board, and books on gardening, cookery and medicine were to follow. The advice on the use of plants had inevitably to be adapted to local conditions, though it is hard to discover details of this because of the lack of manuscript books that might have been compiled by these first American housewives.

The book of recipes inherited by George Washington's wife, Martha, was originally compiled in England, and, as the culinary historian Karen Hess noted, 'the warp' of American cookery was English. Likewise, one kept by an anonymous lady in Virginia around the year 1700 has survived, but is remarkably like those of her English counterparts, containing many identical recipes.[9] One is for Lady Allen's Water for the 'Stomacke Small pox or Surfett'. I have come across the selfsame recipe in two English manuscripts, that of Lady Ann Fanshawe, now in the Wellcome Library, and another compiled by 'Madame Pyne', held in the library of the Royal College of Physicians in London. It is a particularly interesting recipe in

A detail from a map of the manors of Laxton and Kneesall in Nottinghamshire drawn in 1635 for Sir William Courtenay. This shows the house at the heart of the estate, with its gardens and orchards.

that it lists a large number of herbs as ingredients. Many of these could not have been available to the Virginian housewife, yet she felt it was important to list them all. Of course, the same reservation can be applied to English housewives – they had to adapt recipes to what was on hand.

HOUSEHOLD MANUALS

ELIZABETH BIRKETT (d. 1728) was the second wife of Benjamin Browne of Townend in Troutbeck, then in Westmorland. The Brownes were statesmen farmers, holding their land by 'customary tenure', a system peculiar to the border countries, meaning that the family owned everything on the land as if it were freehold, giving them an unusual degree of independence. Elizabeth's commonplace book is dated 1699, three years before she married Benjamin, and contains culinary and medicinal recipes, as well as practical household advice on dyeing and the care of clothes. Townend, with its late-seventeenth-century kitchen and 'firehouse' where visitors were entertained and family meals taken, is now in the care of the National Trust.[10]

MARY DOGGETT was the first wife of Thomas Doggett (c. 1670–1721), actor and manager of the Drury Lane Theatre in London. Apart from Mary's book of recipes, nothing is known of her: only a subsequent wife is mentioned in the *Oxford Dictionary of National Biography*. It was marriage to this second lady, a gentlewoman of means, that helped Thomas to endow the annual race on the Thames for watermen, with Doggett's Coat and Badge as the prize. Mary's recipe book, which dates from the last years of the seventeenth century, includes recipes for cooking and brewing, and for distilling waters and oils to keep the house fragrant, as well as medicinal recipes. Her 'booke of receits' is in the British Library.[11]

ANN FANSHAWE (1625–1680) was the daughter of Sir John and Margaret Harrison. At her mother's death in 1640, she took over the running of the household, but all too soon the family was caught up in the Civil War. Staunchly Royalist, they followed Charles I to his headquarters in Oxford and here Ann married her cousin, Richard Fanshawe, in 1644. Over the next few years Ann and Richard were on the move, and often apart, for he served in a diplomatic capacity for the king, including some time in Madrid. Thirteen children were born to the couple, only three of whom survived into adulthood. After Richard's death in 1666, Ann returned to England and wrote her memoirs for her sole surviving son, Richard. In addition to these memoirs, her manuscript household book has survived, providing a good picture of a courtier household. Lucy Moore has drawn upon this in her biography, *Lady Fanshawe's Receipt Book*. The original household book is in the Wellcome Library.[12]

ELINOR FETTIPLACE (*c.*1570–*c.*1647) was the daughter of Sir Henry and Anne Poole of Sapperton in Gloucestershire, who married in 1589 Richard Fettiplace of Appleton in Berkshire. Her household book, dated 1604 on the flyleaf, is one of the earliest English manuscripts to provide recipes, remedies and household tips, as well as some notes on her gardening. The recipes have been reproduced in printed form in three volumes, *The Complete Receipt Book of Ladie Elynor Fetiplace*. Hilary Spurling has put Elinor Fettiplace in her social context, and provided the historical background to her cookery in *Elinor Fettiplace's Receipt Book*.[13]

HANNAH WOLLEY (*c.*1622–*c.*1674) learnt her medical skills first from her mother and elder sisters, and then from a local noblewoman, probably Anne Maynard of Little Easton in Essex. After marrying a schoolmaster, she provided medical care for his pupils and for the local community first in Newport in Essex, and then in Hackney just to the north of London. At the death of her husband, Hannah turned to publishing at her own expense *The Ladies Directory*, in 1661, and three years later *The Cook's Guide*. She remarried; on the death of her second husband she embarked on two books, which would be highly successful, *The Queene-like Closet* and *The Ladies Delight*, the latter seeing many editions, including a German translation. Hannah Wolley was one of the first Englishwomen to make an income as an author.

A Scale of yards

NOBILISSIMO VIRO D° D° RICH:
ardo Brutono Equiti aurato et Baronetto floris:
fissimi Regis Caroli sui a Cubiculis sanctioribus,
Concessu Secretario, nec non apud Lodovicum
XIII et XIIII. Reg. Christ. Prolegato.

Hunc Cellulare
Spectaculum pro
Regis spacatissimæ
chœr loci Dux

long wanting yards
cloth
the Iland mans Isle now a Cross y ronne over x
y south grasse, and unfrequested.
be sorts mingled, and warranted for 3 yeares

mner house set but
ne of this South pale
nd about this field.
d I purpose to plant this
300 m. length.

Iland mans Isle
gh may was set

Productive Gardens

Gardens, to serve for the use of the Table whether of the poore or rich of our Countrey

John Parkinson, *Paradisi in Sole*, 1629

T HE SEVENTEENTH-CENTURY ENGLISH GARDEN came in all shapes and sizes. Some grand establishments displayed the latest fashions from the Continent: formal parterres in elaborate patterns, mazes, mounts, wildernesses, grottoes, fountains and terraces. Even these great gardens, however, had an area set aside for produce to supply the house, with kitchen gardens and orchards. For example, when the diarist John Evelyn took over the running of his father-in-law's Thames-side estate of Sayes Court at Deptford in the 1650s, he created a fine garden with features he had seen during his travels on the Continent. These included an oval parterre based on one admired in Paris, but also a kitchen or 'olitirie' garden, as he sometimes described it, close to the house, and a great orchard.

John Evelyn's gardens at Sayes Court have now gone, commemorated only in the detailed drawings that he made of their layout. But we can see

John Evelyn's drawing of the layout of his garden at Sayes Court in Deptford. It includes formal features, such as an oval parterre inspired by one that he had seen during a visit to Paris, and a grove of trees. But there are also productive areas, with the kitchen garden next to the grove, a great orchard running down the right-hand side, and a cutting garden of flowers close by the house.

a grand seventeenth-century garden at another Thames-side estate, Ham House, upriver from London near Richmond. The house was built in 1610, and extended and refurbished in the 1670s when Elizabeth Dysart, who had inherited the estate from her father, married John Maitland, Duke of Lauderdale, one of Charles II's principal ministers. The duke and duchess not only altered the interior in line with the latest fashions, but also re-organized the gardens. At the rear of the house, a long terrace was re-tained, overlooking large 'plats' or plots of smooth scythed grass and gravel walks. Beyond these was a wilderness with walks within trees. On one side ran an extensive orchard, on the other a productive kitchen garden with a 'Greene House' for the accommodation of tender plants during the winter. The National Trust has begun to plant beds in the kitchen garden with herbs, flowers and vegetables of the period.

For smaller households the kitchen garden and fruit trees were the key elements, an inheritance from monastic gardens, and continuing the tradition of the housewife's plot, certainly in the countryside, and where possible in towns. At the Weald and Downland Museum at Singleton near Chichester, a garden has been re-created around Pendean, the home of a yeoman farmer and his family, built in the early seventeenth century. It has rectangular beds for herbs, root crops and 'salad leaves', separated by paths about a foot in width to allow access for barrows and baskets. A few fruit trees represent the orchard. Another seventeenth-century house at the Museum is Walderton, with its garden re-created as for a village environ-ment. Along with beds for vegetables and salad herbs, there is a bed sur-rounded by planks to provide a simple form of hot bed, for the cultivation of pompions, or pumpkins, and melons. Although the enclosing of open

The layout of a garden proposed by William Lawson in *A New Orchard and Garden*. The house is shown at the top, with access by a bridge over a moat. Six square compartments include an orchard arranged in quincunxes, groups of five trees, a knot garden, kitchen gardens, and a horse and swordsman possibly indicate topiary. A mount at each corner supports four little houses. The upper two are designated as still houses, the lower two as standings for bees.

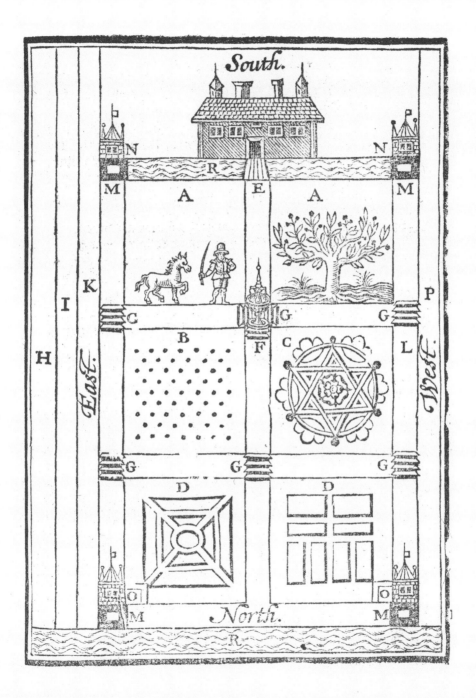

fields, where households had been able to grow their crops in common and provide pasturage for their animals, had begun in Tudor times, the movement was still at an early stage of development. Therefore the households of both Pendean and Walderton would also have fields for their wheat and barley, peas and beans, but a third house now at the museum, Poplar Cottage, was the home in the seventeenth century of a landless labourer and his family. This household was therefore entirely dependent on their garden to provide food throughout the year.

The ideal layout of a 'moderately' sized garden was suggested by William Lawson in *A New Orchard and Garden*, first published in 1618. Lawson was a Yorkshire clergyman, and his book often referred to his own experience of gardening on the banks of the River Tees. He was Puritan in his attitudes, and a friend of the pious diarist Lady Margaret Hoby (p. 12). While she, however, fretted in her diary about being distracted from her devotional reading by her gardening, he delighted in flowers, punning about knots and knotty problems, and giving away his fruit to his neighbours to avoid pilfering.

Lawson divided the contents of his book into three sections, as set out on his title page. First was the orchard, where he described 'the best way for planting, grafting, and to make the ground good'. An illustration on the title page shows gardeners at work making grafts of fruit trees and planting them. Next came the garden for the 'country housewife', looking at the 'vertues' and 'seasons' for herbs, along with a variety of knots and models for trees. Third, he looked at the husbandry of bees, 'with their severall uses and annoyances [pests], all being the experience of 48. yeeres labour'. In his layout of a garden, Lawson depicts little houses on mounts at the four corners. The two lower are designated as standings for bees, while the top ones are indicated as still rooms for the distilling of cordials

The title page of Lawson's *A New Orchard and Garden*, showing gardeners making and planting grafts of fruit trees.

A
NEW ORCHARD
and Garden :
O R

The beſt way for planting, grafting, and to make
any ground good, for a rich Orchard : Particularly in the North,
and generally for the whole kingdome of *England*, as in nature,
reaſon, ſituation, and all probabilitie, may and doth appeare.

With the Country Houſewifes Garden for herbes of common vſe, their
vertues, ſeaſons, profits, ornaments, varietie of knots, models for trees, and
plots for the beſt ordering of Grounds and Walkes.
AS ALSO

The Husbandry of Bees, with their ſeuerall vſes and annoyances, all being the
experience of 48. yeeres labour, and now the ſecond time correcked and
much enlarged, by *William Lawſon.*

Whereunto is newly added the Art of propagating Plants, with the true ordering
of all manner of Fruits, in their gathering, carrying home, and preſeruation.

Printed at *London* by *I. H.* for ROGER IACKSON, and are to be ſold at his

and medicines, although their shape suggests they could also be used as banqueting houses.

As his title implies, Lawson was particularly interested in the orchard, specifying the best uses for different fruit trees, with plum, cherry and damson for borders, while orchard squares were reserved for quince, apple and pear. He gave careful instructions on the shape to be aimed at for an apple tree to ensure health, strength and productivity. Trees should be planted about 24 feet (7.3 metres) apart to allow room for growth over thirty or forty years. In the spaces in between, he suggested creating a

nursery for the cultivation of saffron, liquorice and other herbs useful for the still room and kitchen.

Although herbals were compiled primarily to give information on the medical use of plants, they were wider in their remit, sometimes providing gardening information. John Gerard's great *Herball* is particularly interesting in this area, talking of his own experience of plants that were comparatively recent introductions to Britain. In his Holborn garden he had a dwarf fig tree that fruited in August. He noted that before

Gerard was able to grow a dwarf fig tree in his garden in Holborn. He used the fruit in a range of ways: as an ingredient of a plaster to calm swellings, in wormwood wine as a remedy for dropsy, added to honey for a sore throat. The milk of the unripe fig could also be applied to the skin, to combat roughness and freckles.

the fruit was fully ripe, it produced a white 'milk' that he recommended to be used to combat roughness of the skin, including freckles and 'small pockets' or measles. Once the fruit had matured, he compared its juice to honey, which could be used to ease sore throats and coughs. The apricot was introduced into the country in the early sixteenth century, taking its name from the Portuguese *albricoque*. Again, Gerard noted in his herbal that it grew in his garden, 'and now adaies in many other Gentlemans gardens throughout all England'.[1]

A botanical 'scoop' achieved by Gerard was the potato. In fact, he mentioned in his herbal two types of what he called potato. One, which he also referred to as 'skirrets of Peru', is what we would now call the sweet potato. 'There is not any that hath written of this plant, or saide any thing of the flowers, therefore I shall hereafter have further knowledge of the same.' He bought his roots from what he called the London Exchange, which would seem to be the bourse established in the City some twenty years earlier by Sir Thomas Gresham. Initially these roots flourished in his garden, but with the coming of winter they rotted and died. His second potato he described as from Virginia, although it originally came from further south in the Americas, from Colombia. This is a member of the *Solanum* family and what we now commonly think of as the potato. Gerard received his roots from the nascent English colony in Virginia, and reported happily they 'grow & prosper in my garden as in their owne native country'.[2]

Another plant from the Americas introduced into English gardens at this time was tobacco. The first European record of it was made by Christopher Columbus's sailors on his famous expedition of 1492. They watched Cubans and Haitians burning the leaves and inhaling the smoke through a *tobacco*, a device shaped like a two-branched catapult that fitted the nostrils. Spanish merchants brought the plant to Europe in the mid-sixteenth century, and some herbalists named it 'henbane'. Others referred to it as 'nicotiane' after the French ambassador to the Portuguese court, Jean Nicot, who was presented with the plant in 1559. Information about the qualities of tobacco was first published in English in 1577 by a London merchant, John Frampton. Translating the text from the Spanish, he gave the book the title *Joyfull newes out of the newe-found world*, explaining how regions, kingdoms and provinces had been discovered by 'our Spanyardes', thus bringing to Europe new medicines and remedies.[3]

Gerard described tobacco as 'Henbane of Peru', advising that it 'must be sown in the most fruitefull grounde that may be founde, carelessly cast abroade in the sowing, without taking it into the ground or any such paine or industrie taken, as is requisite in the sowing of other seedes'. Gerard

experimented with sowing at different times, though taking care to have stock 'lest some unkindly blast should happen after the sowing, which might be a great enimie thereunto'.[4] The association with henbane is a reminder that tobacco could not be taken internally, but if chewed it was a narcotic comparable with opium, for the treatment of toothache, migraine, a purge against poison, the scouring of old ulcers, among a long list of medical problems. He also noted that the leaves might be burnt in a pipe and inhaled.

Tobacco, or 'Henbane of Peru', had been brought to England about thirty years before Gerard compiled his herbal; it was therefore very much a curiosity. He found it easy to cultivate, and used it in a variety of ways, although he warned that it should not be taken internally.

Tobacco was regarded with implacable hostility by the Scottish king James VI. Two years after he succeeded to the English throne in 1603 as James I, he published his *Counterblaste to Tobacco*, declaiming that its omnipotent power could 'by the smoke thereof chase out devils ... it would serve for a precious relic, for both the superstitious priests, and the insolent Puritans, to cast out Devils withall'.[5] But James was also keen to encourage trade, so he eventually adopted the policy of supporting the traffic in tobacco from the English colony in Virginia while condemning the English variety as cruder and more poisonous, issuing a pronouncement to this effect in 1619. This came as a blow to English growers, as reported by a keen botanist, John Goodyer, who noted how one of his friends 'intended to plante great store thereof, and was hindered of his purpose by a proclamation sette forth by Authoritie'.[6]

John Goodyer noted a different kind of drawback in the cultivation of a vegetable that was known as the potato of Canada. This was in fact the Jerusalem artichoke, and neither an artichoke nor from Jerusalem. It got its name from the fact that it was a relation of the sunflower, described by the French Canadians as a 'girasole'. Goodyer acquired some of the

In a register of plants, *Stirpium adversaria nova,* published in London in 1570, Matthias de L'Obel and Pierre Pena included not only an illustration of the tobacco plant, but also an idea of how natives of South America smoked the leaves.

first roots to be sent to London in 1617, and found that they flourished in his garden at Droxford in Hampshire. He noted how the vegetable could be cooked: 'Their rootes are dressed divers waies; some boile them in water, and after stewe them with sack and butter, addinge a little Ginger: others bake them in pies, puttinge Marrow, Dates, Ginger, Reasons of the Sunne [raisins], Sack, etc', but he also warned that however they were prepared 'they stirre and cause a fithie loathsome stinking winde within the bodie' and that in his judgement 'they are a meat more fit for swine, than men'.[7]

Among Gervase Markham's wide range of publications was what he described as an 'augmented' version of *The Countrie Farme*, published in 1616. Originally it was a French work, *Maison Rustique*, that had been translated by Richard Surflet in London in 1600. In this were details of how to plan a kitchen garden, beginning: 'You shall dispose of your Beds in such sort as they may be in the middest of your Garden, giving and allowing unto your Turneps the largest roome and next to them the Coleworts.' A path three feet wide should then be laid to separate them from beds for spinach, beets, orach, rocket, parsley and sorrel. Another path should lead to beds dedicated to leeks, chives, garlic and different kinds of onion, and carrots. A section of the garden was to be set aside as 'a plat for sweet flowers' and another for 'your Winter pot-hearbs'. Yet more beds should accommodate a range of herbs, including marjoram, lavender, rosemary, southernwood, savory, hyssop, costmary, basil, balm, pennyroyal and camomile, 'to make seats'.

Markham recognized that the garden was often the realm of the house-wife, for it was important for her to cultivate herbs for medicinal purposes. He added that he had learnt many remedies from the experiments and observations of women skilled in healing. This is a significant remark, for we have to remember that many women at this period were not literate, but had learnt their knowledge from their mothers and other family members, and developed their skills through experience. Moreover, the valuable knowledge of women herbalists was so often not acknowledged. Markham described how these ladies laid out at the end of their kitchen garden, close to the orchard, special beds for 'physick hearbes', such as valerian, houseleek, mercury pellitory and tobacco.[8]

The first writer, in fact, to recognize the role of women as gardeners was Thomas Tusser. In his *Five Hundred Pointes of Good Husbandrie*, his verse form called upon the female gardener to get to work in September:

> Wife, into thy garden, and set me a plot
>   with strawberry rootes, of the best to be got:
> Such growing abroad, among thornes in the wood
>   wel chosen and picked prove excellent good

There was no concern about digging up wild plants. The strawberries would have been delicately sweet – the modern, plump fruit that we are familiar with are generally descended from North American plants. In the same month he advised on keeping bees, giving the term of endearment for a woman, a 'good conie' or rabbit.

> Now burn up [smoke out] the bees that ye mind for to drive,
>   at Midsomer drive them and save them alive:
> Place hive in good ayer, set southly and warme,
>   and take in due season wax, honie and swarme.

> Set hive on a plank (not too low by the ground)
>   where herbe with the flowers may compass it round;
> And boordes to defend it from north and north-east
>   from showers and rubbish, from vermin and beast.

To encourage the bees, fruit-tree blossom was recommended, along with violets, and herbs such as thyme, marjoram and rosemary.

He advised that as winter closed in the garden should be well dug over, composted using refuse from privies and covered with leaf mould. He recommended that in December strawberry plants be protected from frost by being covered with straw, while water and a dish of rosemary branches be put into the hives to nurture the bees.

For March, he encouraged the gardener to come out of her winter seclusion, with lists of seeds and herbs for the kitchen for salads and sauces, and to strew in the house. His list of vegetables to cultivate includes beans, carrots, cabbages, gourds, pompions, parsnips and peas. Peas were an important plant for the poorest households, grown to be stored and used through the autumn and winter; green – that is, immature – peas, only began to come into fashion in the second half of the seventeenth century. The landless labourer in Poplar Cottage, for example, might have grown Carlin peas, a tall variety dating back to the fifteenth century, producing a yellow pea that was dried and ground up to make a kind of flour in the absence of a supply of corn. Peas also formed the basis for 'pease pottage', the staple diet of the poor.

Tusser's advice for the garden tailed away during the late spring and summer months, when attention would be focused on work in the fields. But he advised that in August the provident gardener should save seeds. This serves as a reminder that for many countryside households this was a communal life, where shops and suppliers were not often available:

> Good huswifes in summer will save their owne seedes
> against the next yeere, as occasion needs,
> One seede for another, to make an exchange
> with fellowlie neighbourhood seemeth not strange.⁹

Tusser's arrangement of his gardening advice in months is echoed by a writer in the seventeenth century, and this remarkably was a woman. Between 1658 and 1664, Sarah Jinner published four almanacs, in which she provided meteorological forecasts for every day of the year, along with medicinal recipes of particular interest to women, and for each month 'physical observations' about the state of the world and advice on husbandry and gardening. A portrait of Sarah Jinner is reproduced on the frontispiece of each edition of the almanac, along with the description 'a Student of Astrology', and that is the sum total of what we know about her. Her writing style indicates that she was well educated, and her political commentary suggests she was critical of Oliver Cromwell's government.

One of the recipes gives details of writing letters in invisible ink, a reminder that many were involved in clandestine correspondence supporting the exiled Charles II during this period, including Elizabeth Dysart from Ham House.

Sarah Jinner's gardening advice is much briefer than Tusser's, and in prose rather than verse. For February she counselled 'Set Beanes Peas and other pulse in fresh ground. Begin the soonest. Prepare your garden, prune and trim your Fruit trees [from Moths, Cankers and superfluous branches] plash hedges, lay your quickset close, plant Rose and Gooseberry trees, and other shrub trees, and graft your tender stocks.'

For March, while predicting that on the political scene 'Flanders is much disturbed', she advised: 'Transplant all sort of summer flowers, comfort them with good earth, especially the Crown Imperial, Narcissus, Tuleps and Hyacinth.' The mention of these particular flowers is interesting, for they were all introductions from the Middle East in the sixteenth century and much prized among gardeners, and especially florists, who specialized in their cultivation. By picking them out, the author showed that she was part of a knowledgeable horticultural circle.

Her advice for May was to sow 'your tender seeds, as Cucumbers, Musmelions [melons], all sweet kinds of hearbs and flowers', and the following month she reminded the reader to get to work in the still room with whatever plants and herbs were available. August was the time for harvesting the fruit crop in the orchard – 'gather your Plums, Apples and Pears, make your Summer Perry and Cider' – and setting slips of flowers such as the gillyflower. Politically, she predicted 'the French seem to be losers'. Winter fruit should be gathered in September, and the stock of bees either sold off or prepared for the cold weather, checking that 'no Droans, Mice or other vermin be about them'. In October, the orchard trees should

OVERLEAF Lucas van Valckenborch's depiction of summer, showing the vegetables and fruit grown in the kitchen garden. The flower arrangement in the centre of the painting is in the fashion of the seventeenth century, with 'crowning' blooms – in this case lilies.

be checked, and where necessary transplanted, with winter perry and cider made, together with malt for the brewhouse. Finally, in December, 'cover your dainty fruit' and 'yr best flowers with rotten horse litter'.[10]

After 1664, Sarah Jinner falls silent, and with her the voice of a published female gardening writer: it was to be two centuries before another was to appear in print. It is frustrating that we do not know why she produced no more, for almanacs were a very lucrative area of publishing. And she stands out, along with Hannah Wolley, as one of the first professional women writers. Moreover, she provided information about the reproductive system at a time when many herbals and books of medicine excised such subjects from their texts.

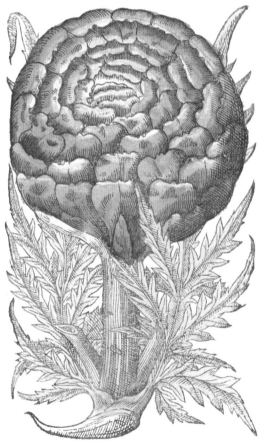

Another 'student of astrology' was Nicholas Culpeper, who once declared that he 'had courted two mistresses that had cost him dear, but it was not the wealth of kingdoms should buy them from him'.[11] These two ladies were physic and astrology. In his herbal, he wrote of the 'Herb True-Love', also known as One-Berry: 'The leaves or berries hereof are good as antidotes against all kinds of poison' and that the plant

The globe artichoke, introduced to England by the Dutch in the sixteenth century, became highly fashionable, with Charles I's queen, Henrietta Maria, setting aside a whole section of her garden at Wimbledon for its cultivation. Recipe books included instructions on how to preserve the leaves and chokes through the winter months.

should be found in every 'good Woman's Garden'.[12] His astrological beliefs convinced Culpeper that the Herb True-Love was 'owned' by Venus, as was Featherfew (feverfew) because it expelled the afterbirth and strengthened women's wombs. Pellitory, owned by Mercury, was recommended by Culpeper as one of the best purgers of the brain, as well as helping with gout and sciatica. The butterflower, with its fiery and spirited nature, was under the dominion of Mars, not to be taken internally but used as an ointment to draw a blister. Despite the enduring popularity of the herbal, his ideas drew fierce criticism from contemporaries, especially the fellows of the Royal College of Physicians, while John Evelyn dismissed him as a 'figure-flinger'.

Evelyn, however, accepted that some celestial influences might be valid, writing at one point that 'the moone, as being most neere to Earth, has great operation on Vegetables'.[13] Lady Elinor Fettiplace shared this view. Most of the entries in her book are for culinary and medicinal recipes, but she also noted some records about her garden at Appleton Manor in Berkshire. Under 'Sewing Herbs' she wrote:

> The best month is aprill in the wane of the moone, at Midsomer in the wane of the moon sow all kinds of potherbs, & they wilbee greene for the winter; also Lettice seeds sowne at this tyme and removed when they bee of a prettie bignes at the full wilbee good and hard Lettice at Michaelmas. All these seeds which you sow in the wane of the moone or last quarter in Marche, will never runne to seed. And for those you will have run to seed the last quarter of the moone in Aprill is best to sow them in.

Globe artichokes enjoyed popularity at this period, and Elinor Fettiplace recommended planting them 'in the new of the moone about our Ladie day in Lent, & cut them close to the ground, & at winter open the earth about the root, & lay some dung therein, & in frostie weather cover the root over with dung'. The religious festivals of the pre-Reformation year are reflected in her notes. 'Sow red Cabage seed after Allhallowentide [All Hallows Day, 1 November] twoe days after the moone is at the full.' Roses should be planted

33

in the new of the moone at any time after Michaelmas [29 September], until the new moone after Candlemas [2 February], then three weeks after they have done bearing the Moone being new, is the best tyme to cut them. Set any flowers about Bartholomews tyde [24 August], three days before the full, or three days after.[14]

The title 'productive garden' implies one of vegetables, fruit and herbs, but, as Markham pointed out in his layout of a kitchen garden, there should be a 'plat' for sweet flowers. These have always played an important role in providing ingredients for the kitchen and the still room, as well as furnishing the house with fragrance and colour. In larger gardens flowers were often planted en masse within small hedges as parterres. In the early seventeenth century these patterns were geometric, known as knots, as can be seen in William Lawson's ideal layout of a garden (p. 19). When Henrietta Maria arrived in England in 1625 to marry Charles I, she brought with her from France a more fluid style, *de broderie* or embroidery.

In 1629 a book was published by John Parkinson, dedicated to Queen Henrietta Maria, 'a feminine of flowers', in which he featured 'a garden of pleasant and delightfull flowers', selecting 'the chiefest for choice, and fairest for show'.[15] This book was *Paradisi in Sole,* a pun on his name, 'park in sun'. From Lancashire farming stock, Parkinson went to London to be apprenticed as an apothecary to a grocer. In 1589 he began to create his own garden in Cripplegate, in the north-eastern section of the City, but moved westwards to Long Acre to avoid the pollution from sea coal that was beginning badly to affect London. Now Long Acre is a busy shopping street in Covent Garden, but in the late sixteenth century it was an area of fields, as reflected in the names still current of the local churches, St Giles-in-the-Fields and St Martin-in-the-Fields.

Parkinson's garden in Long Acre took up about 2 acres. Here he planted beds, separated from his orchard by shrubs such as lavender and rosemary, and plashed cornelian cherry trees. Many of his friends were Flemish florists who had formed a community in Lime Street in the City. The term 'florist' first appears in English in 1623, and was applied to gardeners who specialized in the cultivation of exotic flowers such as the tulip and the carnation, as mentioned by Sarah Jinner. From these Lime Street florists he acquired plants such as a 'great white Spanish daffodil' from the Pyrenees, which grew to 2 feet in height, and a whole variety of fritillaries. He experimented with different kinds of plants to create knots, trying thrift and germander, which did not work well, and juniper and yew, which grew too big, finally alighting upon cotton lavender, a recent import from the Continent. His Flemish friends also introduced him to the 'small, lowe or dwarfe kinde [of shrub], called French or Dutch Boxe', which he found an excellent plant for outlining knots, although he also commented on its smell, which has been compared to the urine of cats.

While country housewives worked in every part of their garden, gentlewomen would expect to confine their activities to the flower garden. When Lady Margaret Hoby was living in Yorkshire, she kept a diary between 1599 and 1605. With a cantankerous husband and a domineering mother-in-law, she sought refuge in her garden. In October 1603, for example, she recorded an Indian summer, with a second blooming of white, red and musk roses. She was also a pious Puritan, so fretted over her horticultural distractions, lamenting in her diary how 'I bestowed too much time in the Garden, and thereby was worse able to performe sperituall duties.'[16]

One man who had no such qualms about spending time with his flowers was Sir Thomas Hanmer. During the Civil War he lived in France, making the acquaintance of leading florists there. On his return to Britain, Hanmer created a fine garden at Bettisfield in North Wales. We know in detail how he organized the garden because he kept garden albums, one of which was discovered and published in 1933. Like Tusser and Sarah Jinner, he wrote 'Remembrances' of what was to be done in the garden every month and a record of what plants were usually in flower.[17]

In addition he made detailed notes of his flower beds, which were either square or rectangular. Those to accommodate tulips he thought should be about 4 feet wide and raised in the centre so that all the flowers could be seen. In his great garden he recorded having four little bordered beds of tulips, all named, in the middle of a bordered knot. Colchicums and anemones were planted in the corners of these beds. In the middle of another bed he planted a double crown imperial. This was the stately cousin of the meadow fritillary, introduced into England in the 1580s from the Middle East via Constantinople. Fashionable flower arrangements in grand houses at this period were 'crowned' by dramatic flowers (see p. 30), and so too were the flower beds in the garden. Despite the prominence of his crown imperial at the centre of such a bed, Hanmer was not a great admirer of the plant, finding its orange colour 'ill dead'. More beds were planted with rows of irises, polyanthus and daffodils, again with anemones in the corners.

Hanmer's garden was very much that of a florist, with many exotics, or 'outlandish' flowers as they were sometimes described. Flowers native to England, on the other hand, could be referred to as 'vulgar'. Although often disdained in fashionable horticultural books of the later seventeenth century, they are recorded by John Worlidge in his *Art of Gardening*, published in 1677. He dedicated one of the chapters to the 'more Vulgar Flowers' to encourage 'the honest and plain Countryman'. The list runs from aconites through to toadflax, including flowers that would have provided colour such as 'blew-bottles' (cornflowers), nigella, sunflowers and candytuft. Others were ingredients in medicines and ointment, such as the lesser celandine, also called pilewort, indicating its use. Scabious was prescribed for coughs, shortness of breath, and for the drawing of splinters. Amaranthus, also known as love-lies-bleeding, was recommended for the staunching of wounds.

These were the flowers that would have been found in the majority of country gardens at this period. We get a rare glimpse of one such with the garden of Goodwife Chantrey, the wife of a Northamptonshire yeoman farmer. In addition to her herb plot, with fennel to make an infusion for weak eyes, camomile for headaches, and goat's rue to counter the plague, she grew sufficient flowers to be able to supply the Hatton family at nearby Kirby Hall in July 1658. The list includes lupins, larkspurs, scabious, sweet william and honeysuckle, along with four sorts of gooseberries – white, green, red and yellow – double currants, and 'violette plumbe'.[18]

For somebody running a still room, such as Lady Elinor Fettiplace at Appleton Manor, or John and his wife Mary Evelyn at Sayes Court in Deptford, certain plants had to be grown in considerable quantity. This particularly applied to the rose, the basis for rose water and for mixtures for 'sweet bags' that refreshed linen and clothing. It was the Damask rose that was particularly desired for its strong scent, making it 'fitter for meate and medicine' according to Gerard.[19] To obtain sufficient rose petals to distil into the oil and thus into rose water required a gathering in bulk, and this also applied to violets, again much desired for oils

The crown imperial in Gerard's *Herball*. This was a very recent introduction, arriving in England in the 1580s from Constantinople. Although handsome in appearance, its smell is not pleasant, as Gerard was quick to point out, reminding him of the pungent scent of a fox.

and conserves. For these, a range of beds must have been set aside in the garden. Reproduced below is Elinor Fettiplace's recipe for oil and rose water.[20]

John Evelyn does not elaborate in his publications on how many beds should be so reserved, but he has left us copious details of the plants that he cultivated. In particular, he made a series of lists for 'Jonathan Mosse who came to me Apprentice for six yeares 24 June 1686'. By this time Evelyn was in his late sixties, and wanted gradually to hand over the garden to his assistant. We do not know what Mosse thought about such a daunting task, made even more daunting by the great amount of information provided, but 'Directions for the Gardiner' gives us an unparalleled view of the organization and running of a late-seventeenth-century English garden.[21] Beginning with 'Termes of Art used by Learned Gardeners', he defined techniques such as lætation (dunging), repastination (shallow digging), semination (sowing) and plashing (cutting a branch nearly half through to make it supple for layering). The seasons are given: vernal (spring), estival (summer), autumnal and hyemal or brumal (winter). To these are attached the times for fruit and flowers: præcoce (early blossoming and

Elinor Fettiplace's Recipe for Oile of Roses Sweet

Take a faire earthen pot of a gallon, or twoo, for the quantitie els wil bee verrie small, & when the time of the yeare serveth, cut the white [the base of the petals] of the roses of, & put them in the earthen vessel, stuffing them as hard as you can, then put as much cuminn water as will cover the roses, covering the bung hole with some cloth to keep out the rayne, but not the ayre, and so let it stand a summer & a winter, & then when you find the leaves rotten take it out some & some, & put the rotten leaves & the water into a still of glas, & so let it rise in balneu[?]; first you shall have with a soft fine the spirit, & then the water & oile, the oile will swim like a thin fat, or greace on the top, which you must continually take of.

ripening), median (middle term, applied particularly to tulips), and serotine (late flowering and ripening).

The relationships between the garden and the offices of the house are explored. This, of course, was important for all households, but here it is a sizeable establishment:

> The Gardner, is every night to aske what Rootes, sallading, garnishing, &c will be used the next day, which he is accordingly to bring to the Cook in the morning; and therefore from time to time to informe her what garden provision & fruite is ripe and in season to be spent.
>
> He is also to Gather, & to bring in to the House-Keeper all such Fruit of Apples, peares, quinces, Cherrys, Grapes, peaches, Abricots, Mulberies, strawberry, Rasberies, Corinths [currants], Cornelians, Nutts, Plums, & generally all sort of Fruite, as the seasone ripens them, gathering all the windfalls by themselves: That they may be immediately spent, or reserved in the Fruite & store-house. ...
>
> He is to give his Mistris notice when any Fruites, Rootes, Flowers, or plants under his care are fit to be spent, reserved, cutt, dried, & to be gathered for the still house and like uses, & to receive her directions.

Evelyn included another stipulation:

> He may not dispose of any the above said Fruite nor sell any Artichock, Cabbages, Aspargus, Melons, strawberries, Rasberies, Wall, or standard & dwarfe fruite, Roses, Violets, Cloves or any Greenes, or other flowers or plants, without first asking, and having leave of his Master or Mistress; not till there be sufficient of all garden furniture for the Grounds stock and families use.

This shows that many gardeners did regard it as one of their 'perks' to sell what in their view was surplus produce, and the plants mentioned would certainly attract a market. Significantly the precious roses and violets are included in the list.

For the borders and parterres, Evelyn set out a list of what he called 'coronarie' flowers. Evelyn, as can be seen from the terms mentioned earlier, loved long and complicated words. In the case of 'coronarie', he is talking of a crown shape, suitable for garlands, wreaths and ornate flower arrangements. The list includes florists' flowers such as the tulip, narcissus, anemone and the crown imperial. But it also has flowers that are 'vulgar', such as candytuft, nigella, larkspur and foxglove. The more exotic flowers needed to be raised in the hotbed. At this period this would have consisted of a deep pit lined with brick, filled with dung, which could be topped up with tan bark. It was usually covered with glass, looking like today's cold frame. According to Evelyn, flowers that needed this particular care included a lily from Japan and the tuberose from Mexico.

Technology, however, was being developed to enable tender exotics to survive Britain's winters. During the reign of Elizabeth I, Sir Francis Carew devised a way of doing this at his garden at Beddington Place in Surrey. He proudly showed the queen how he had extended the season for

his cherries by putting a canvas cover over the trees. He also imported lemon, pomegranate and orange trees and planted them in the ground, again protecting them with makeshift shelters and stoves. The first English orangery was probably built for James I's queen, Anne of Denmark, at Somerset House in London in 1611–12, sparking a fashionable trend. During the winter, the fruit trees would be wheeled in their pots

Strawberries in the sixteenth and seventeenth centuries grew wild and would be transplanted into gardens in September or February. Shakespeare has the Bishop of Ely getting strawberries from his Holborn garden in *Richard III*. John Gerard's garden was located nearby.

into the orangery, where a heated stove had been installed, to maintain a temperature of around 8°c.

John Evelyn, however, was concerned about the impure air emanating from such stoves, warning that 'Plants ... rarely pass'd their Confinements, without Sickness, a certain Langour or Taint discoverable by their Complexions.'[22] In 1685 he paid a visit to the Chelsea Physic Garden, laid out by the Society of Apothecaries for the instruction of their apprentices upriver from the City of London. He was pleased to note that, rather than stoves, the head gardener was providing subterranean heat in the conservatory. This had been described by the physician Hans Sloane as

> a new contrivance (at least in this country), viz. he [the gardener] makes under the floor of his greenhouse a great fire-place with grate, ash-hole &c., and conveys the warmth through the whole house by tunnels, so that he hopes, by the help of weather-glasses within, to bring or keep the air at what degree of warmth he pleases, letting in upon occasion the outward air by the windows. He thinks to make, by this means, an artificial spring, summer and winter, &c.[23]

Evelyn, after his visit, noted how effective this had been, even though the winter of 1683–4 had been exceptionally harsh.[24]

The ingenious Dutch had also taken the idea of glass frames over hotbeds to another level by enlarging those frames and turning them into glasshouses, combining the heat from the sun's rays with heat from underground furnaces. When William and Mary ascended the English throne in 1688, they introduced this technology to the gardens of Hampton Court Palace. Their glass cases, three in all, were breathlessly described in a letter from Mary Evelyn to her husband in 1691. They were, she wrote,

> filled with the most rare plants of the Indies things wonderfull in the kind some with leaves ¾ of a yard long and a quarter broad others of different forms not to be described easily the name I know not ... I wish you there a day with all my heart and hope you will go the gardners are holanders.[25]

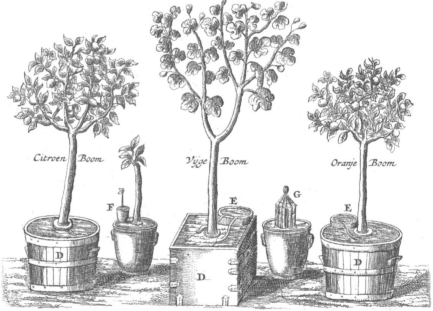

A greenhouse with a free-standing stove for the cultivation of tender citrus plants, from Jan van der Groen's *Den Nederlandsten Hovenier*, published in Amsterdam in 1683.

It was now possible to eat oranges and lemons grown in England, rather than imported from Spain and the Mediterranean. But this was a luxury for the rich – the cost of maintaining heat throughout the winter months was exorbitant. And even the royal gardeners were unable to raise fruiting pineapples, perhaps the most desirable fruit of the period. From the middle of the seventeenth century pines, as they were often called, were imported from the English colony of Barbados. John Evelyn was offered a slice from the plate of Charles II in 1668, but recorded in his diary how it fell 'short of those ravishing varieties of deliciousness' voiced by writers.[26] This was hardly surprising as the fruit had endured a long sea journey. The first person to succeed in producing a ripe pineapple from her hothouse was a wealthy Dutch lady, Agneta Block, on her estate near Amsterdam in 1687. This was not replicated in England until the beginning of the eighteenth century, so no recipes for pineapple dishes appear in contemporary recipe books.

Despite these developments in technology, there would always be ingredients derived from plants that had to be imported. Self-sufficiency was the key for the very poorest, and the garden vital in providing this. But for most households in the seventeenth century, garden produce was supplemented from other sources for domestic use. The traditional purveyors of these exotic ingredients were the grocers, so called because they sold in gross or bulk. In 1375 the Company of Grocers of London was formed, taking as the symbol for its coat of arms the clove, one of the precious spices that they imported from the East. Although this Company was peculiar to the City of London, similar arrangements were put in place in provincial towns. In 1447 the Company successfully petitioned Henry VI for a wide range of goods to be brought under its care, arguing they were the men who could properly look after the sifting and cleaning of spices, and their preparation for sale. They also added to their remit dried fruits, oil and ingredients for medicines – usually handled by apothecaries, their name derived from *apotheca*, a store for spices and herbs. The garden writer John Parkinson, for example, was an apothecary who served his apprenticeship with a grocer.

Jon Stobart in his study of the grocers' trade has found seventeenth-century records, especially inventories, that show the penetration of their market in England.[27] Foreign merchants had traditionally provided grocers with their spices and other exotic ingredients, but in 1600 the East India Company of London was founded, becoming their chief supplier, along with other trading bodies, such as the Turkey Company and the Muscovy

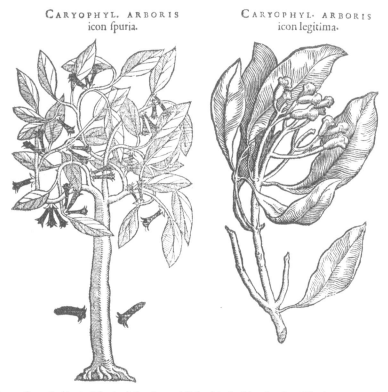

CARYOPHYL. ARBORIS
icon fpuria.

CARYOPHYL· ARBORIS
icon legitima.

Cloves from India, in Clusius' *Exotica*, published in Leiden in 1605. Clusius was anxious that his readers, apothecaries and physicians, should know what this very precious spice looked like, so has reproduced an *icon spuria* from an earlier book alongside the correct image, *icon legitima*.

Company. The Grocers' Company would then act as wholesalers, selling on to grocers and apothecaries throughout Britain. An example of a town grocer was Lawrence Newall of Rochdale in Lancashire. His inventory of 1648 reflects the range available: pepper, sweet soap, starch, red lead and bayberries. The total combined value of these items was a modest 17s 3d. Much more valuable was his stock of sugar loaves, £4 2s; tobacco, £3 5s 1d; and the dye indigo, £10 4s. He also had a valuable stock of cloths, yarn and thread.[28] The items may have travelled up to Rochdale by carrier, or by ship to north-west ports such as Liverpool, Preston and Lancaster.

Grocers, moreover, were not confined to towns. The early-seventeenth-century inventory of Peter Harries, from the Warwickshire village of Grandborough, lists a series of spices: pepper, mace, nutmeg, cloves, ginger, turmeric, liquorice, sugar candy and loaves. It also details ingredients for dyes – the very expensive logwood for black, verdigris for green and indigo for blue – along with brimstone, soap, candles, wax and tobacco pipes.[29]

Some retailers operated through fairs. Although the inventory of Robert Bennett, who died in 1606, gives no occupation, the substantial list of his goods covers textiles, haberdashery, hardware and groceries. He does not seem to have had a shop, but traded in a series of fairs across Cornwall, for boards, trestles and a fair pole are recorded in his house in Tregony, four more poles in Helston, five in Probus, and three kept with a Mr Cowling in Madron, in the far west of the duchy. The groceries included almonds, raisins, currants and figs, all requiring a regular turnover to keep fresh. As Jon Stobart points out, this harks back to earlier times when the stewards of large households would go to buy at fairs, and Cornwall was less urbanized than most parts of the country.[30]

This surprisingly wide range of imported ingredients available in the early years of the seventeenth century is reflected by William Shakespeare in his play *The Winter's Tale*, first performed in 1610–11. Ostensibly set in Bohemia, the play in fact provides a glimpse of English rural life of the time, along with a calendar of the flowers to be found in gardens in contrast to the hybrids created by some florists. In the fourth act of the play, preparations are under way for a summer shearing feast. The shepherd's son lists the grocery goods that he has been instructed by his adopted sister, Perdita, to buy from the pedlar Autolycus: 'Three pound of sugar, five pound of currants, rice'. Here he pauses to ask what she might want with rice. Then he continues, 'I must have saffron to colour the warden pies; mace; dates, none – that's out of my note; nutmegs, seven; a race or two of ginger – but that I may beg; four pound of prunes, and as many of raisins o' th' sun.' Wardens were hard pears that were baked in 'coffins' of pastry, and saffron was traditionally used to give them colour, just as today we sometimes poach pears in red wine.

Not only were all these goods familiar to Shakespeare's London audience; they would not have seemed improbable as part of a country celebration. In Autolycus, however, Shakespeare has produced a complex and questionable character. As the pedlar cheerfully admits, he was a snapper up of unconsidered trifles, including household linen that had been left out to dry. Margaret Spufford in her studies of itinerant salesmen of the period found that there were some who specialized in ballads, almanacs and chapbooks, hence chapmen. Others carried linen garments, haberdashery and trinkets. Shakespeare's Autolycus would appear to be an amalgam of these, for he offers ballads, but also

Lawn as white as driven snow,
Cyprus black as e'er was crow,
Gloves as sweet as damask roses,
Masks for faces, and for noses;
Bugle-bracelet, necklace amber,
Perfume for a lady's chamber;
Golden coifs and stomachers
For my lads to give their dears;
Pins and poking-sticks of steel,
What maids lack from head to heel.[31]

Title page from the first herbal to be printed in Hungary in 1573. This shows the apothecary gathering his plants in his garden, ready to be turned into waters and oils in his still room.

HERBARIVM.
AZ FAKNAC FVV
EKNÉC NÉVEKRÖL, TÉRMÉSETEK-
ról, és haßeairól, Magyar nyelwre, és ez
rendre hoßta az Doctoroc Könyueiböl
az Hothi Meltus Peter.

Nyomtattot, Colofuárat Heltai Gafpárnc
Mûhellyébé, 1. 5. 73. Eßtendöben.

What Margaret Spufford did not find was any reference to chapmen and pedlars carrying food items that were liable to perish and were also bulky. This suggests that either Autolycus was charged with a special commission for the shepherds to get these items from the shop of a grocer or a trader like Robert Bennett, mentioned above, or else he was conning them.[32]

The ingredient that consistently appears in grocers' inventories, and on the list given to Autolycus, is sugar. In the Middle Ages it was imported into Britain from North Africa and later from Brazil and the West Indies. Originally it was regarded as a spice, sold by grocers in grades according to the degree of refining, the coarsest being in large cones or loaves. Like spices, it was treated in cooking as a seasoning, often sprinkled on a dish just before serving. It could also be used in medicines, and physicians thought it preferable to honey. Wealthy Elizabethans enthusiastically followed this advice. A German visitor, Paul Hentzner, noted that even Queen Elizabeth's teeth were black from decay, 'a defect the English seem subject to, from their too great use of sugar'.[33]

For many people, sugar was beyond their means, and honey was the universal sweetener, but this was to change in the seventeenth century. First, with the establishment of the East India Company at the beginning of the century, London was no longer reliant on foreign merchants for the trade in exotics. Second, in the 1620s, while the Spanish were preoccupied in fighting the Dutch, England began to gain its first island colonies in the Americas, including Barbados. As noted earlier, although tobacco was the island's first successful export, in the 1640s it was discovered that Barbados was particularly well suited to the cultivation of sugar cane. By the following decade exports from Barbados alone were worth more than £3 million per annum, making it the wealthiest place in the English-speaking world. The acquisition of Jamaica in 1655 just added to the potential for the trade in sugar. Spices from the East remained expensive commodities, but sugar became more affordable for households across the country. This shift can be seen in the recipes given in the next chapter, with sugary creams and custards, cakes and preserves embraced with gusto. Little wonder John Beale described the island of Barbados as the fairest garden in the world.

In the early seventeenth century apothecaries sought to break away from grocers, sending a petition to the king, James I, in 1614. Their argument was that their part of the trade was a specialized one, and that false and corrupt medicines were being made up 'to the imminent danger of your subjects healths and lives which abuses by your said subjects remaining one body politic with the Company of Grocers, hath not hitherto nor cannot receive any due reformation'.[34] With the support of influential men, such as the natural philosopher Sir Francis Bacon and the royal physician Sir Theodore de Mayerne, their petition was successful and the Society of Apothecaries duly created in 1617.

There were, however, such fine lines of distinction between the two institutions that this did not end the arguments. After an early dispute, a schedule was drawn up as to who could sell what. Apothecaries were licensed to make and sell medicines, to sell flower seeds and roots used for medicines, along with distilled waters, pills, syrups, conserves and ointments. Grocers were permitted to continue to sell sweets, scents, spices, wax, tobacco for worming, and colouring materials for painters and dyers.

For the ingredients for medicines that could be grown in England, apothecaries often kept their own gardens. John Parkinson described his garden in Long Acre as his laboratory, taking instruction from the Flemish herbalist Matthias de L'Obel on how to organize it in a methodical way, and taking on the challenge of identifying the seeds, roots and bulbs that he received from his contacts. Making his way to Somers Quay on the Thames, he met up with the captains of foreign ships when they arrived in London with their exotic cargoes.

The apothecary Nicholas Culpeper likewise had his garden in Spitalfields, to the north-east of the City. This is long gone, but at the Geffrye Museum in nearby Hoxton a garden of herbs for medicine, the kitchen, dyeing and brewing has been planted in his honour.

The Physic Garden in Chelsea was founded by the Society of Apothecaries in 1673 on a site that offered various benefits. Well away from the pollution of the City, the garden was used to train up apprentice apothecaries in surroundings that contributed to the well-being of both students and plants. From here, the apprentice apothecaries could set out on 'herborizing' expeditions to nearby Battersea and Putney Heath. And last, but not least, the Society's barge could be kept here ready for use on ceremonial occasions such as the procession of the new Lord Mayor.

The Physic Garden was originally laid out in an ornamental fashion. A visitor in 1691 described how it had 'a great variety of plants both in and out of greenhouses: their perennial green hedges and rows of different coloured herbs are very pretty: and so are the banks set with shades of herbs in the Irish stitch way'.[35] It was in the eighteenth century that the garden was arranged in a more scientific way, during the curatorship of the formidable Philip Miller, echoing the style of the botanic gardens that had been established by European universities from the early sixteenth century. The first botanic garden in Britain was created for the University of Oxford in 1621, followed by the Edinburgh Botanic Garden in 1670. These were laid out in a series of rectangular beds containing families of plants. This was a time when botanists were seeking a satisfactory classification, which was finally achieved with the binomial system created in the eighteenth century by the Swedish naturalist Carl Linnaeus.

These gardens were being enriched by plants coming from all over the world. And in the case of North America, the trade was two-way. When colonists made the perilous sea voyage to the colony that became New England, they took with them herbals and plants. The Rev. Francis Higginson, who arrived in Salem in 1629, wrote a rapturous account the following year, which was published in London. In it he described how 'Our Turnips, Parsnips and Carrots are here both bigger and sweeter than is ordinarily to be found in England. Here are also store of Pompions, Cowcumbers, and other things of that nature which I know not of.' He went on to list a wide range of herbs, including two that could be woven into cloth, roots and berries that the Indians used for dyes, and Damask roses, so much sought after for distilling. The governor of Salem had planted green peas, as good as any in England.[36]

The governor of Boston, John Winthrop, created a garden that flourished on a rocky island in the harbour. In 1631 his son, also John, returned with a substantial supply of plant seeds for the garden, and for the gardeners of the young community. These seeds were purchased from the London grocer Robert Hill, who traded from the Three Angels in Lombard Street; the bill for these has survived. In alphabetical order they run from Alexanders to wallflowers, with 'hartichockes' added perhaps as an afterthought. They include seeds for vegetables, such as colewort, lettuce, pumpkin and skirrets; herbs such as angelica, dill and savories, winter and summer; and flowers, such as bugloss, hollyhock and violets.[37] It is not only a fascinating record of what was taken over to America at this early date, but also the range that grocers could offer.

Robert Hill must have got his supplies of seeds from nurserymen or from market gardeners who were developing their trades around the fringes of the City. Similar market gardeners were located around cities throughout England. A list of the supplies of a gardener of Liverpool, Matthew Pluckington, dated 1692, includes not only vegetables and fruit trees, but also seeds for a wide range of plants, such as lettuces, onions and cucumbers. These seeds he could sell both to householders, for their gardens, and to local grocers.[38]

Today, we think of market gardeners as supplying fruit and vegetables for the table and flowers for decoration. In the seventeenth century there were certainly these, but in addition there is evidence of the cultivation of a wider range of plants for practical use. For example, the records of St Thomas' Hospital in London dating from the early years of the century show that a herb-woman was employed to provide the raw materials for the medicines and ointments prescribed by the chief medical officer, the apothecary, for his patients. While the apothecary in 1629 was paid an annual salary of £60, the surgeon £35 and the doctors £30, the herb-woman received a mere £4. Since the apothecary was expected to pay for the ingredients for his drugs out of his salary, the herb-woman may have received additional money on top of her modest wages.

This woman supplied in bulk, with wormwood calculated by the horse-load, other herbs by the lapful, bundle, bag or flasket, which suggests she cultivated her herbs in the style of market gardening to supply the demand. More details are available for sellers in London after the Great Fire of 1666, when herb markets were established in various places within the City and in the West End at Covent Garden. Names of women renting stalls begin to appear, along with the locations of their gardens. They form a ring around the City, in places such as Bermondsey, Bethnal Green, Vauxhall, Camberwell and Stepney.[39] It is possible that one of these herb-women may also have supplied herbs in quantity for special occasions in the City. In the records of the Worshipful Company of Stationers are the expenses for a feast every August in the late seventeenth century at the Company's hall in Ave Maria Lane. Alongside entries for food items such as venison and umble pies, payments to the herb-woman are duly noted for moderately substantial sums of between 10s and £1 5s. The size of these payments suggests that she provided the herbs not only for the dishes of the feast, but also for strewing the hall.[40]

We do not know the size of these herb gardens supplying the London markets, but some may have been extensive, rented from farmers and possibly using hired labour. A study made by Ann Robey of an Essex village from 1550 to 1610 provides just such an example. The village, Stock, with a population of around 300, was located just a few miles away from the main road running from Colchester to London. The economy of the village was mixed, with some industry, making tiles, bricks and pottery, including the galley pots used by both gardeners and housewives, and a diversity of farming. The land had been enclosed, with farmers combining cash crops of wheat and oats with animal husbandry. But also they were growing plants for dyestuffs, such as rose madder and weld, and herbs for the London market, with the owners of smaller holdings hiring themselves out to the larger farmers, although it was also possible to make a viable living from plots of less than 10 acres.[41]

Market gardens of this type were growing around other urban centres. A reference in the papers of the Leicester family of Tabley Hall in Cheshire notes how the household bought supplies from a herb-woman in the early eighteenth century.[42] This might have been a trader like the herb-women of London, growing her herbs in bulk, and either selling them at market or bringing them to the house. It is a tantalizing glimpse of what might have been a common practice all over the country.

John Gerard gives us clues to other cash crops. He described how grocers had in their shops barrels of dried marigold petals to be sold

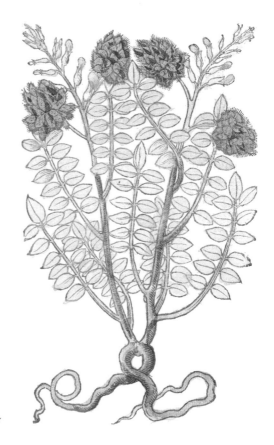

Liquorice from Gerard's *Herball*. Although liquorice is a native of the Mediterranean area, he found that it flourished in his garden. It became a cash crop in the north of England, especially around Pontefract where the roots of the plant could be boiled and made into sweet cakes that were soothing for coughs.

'by the pennie more or lesse'. The orange petals were used in medicines as they were thought to strengthen the heart, and for colouring. Cheaper than saffron, they could be used in cooking. He also described the cultivation of liquorice: 'These plants do grow in sundry places of Germanie wilde, and in Fraunce and Spaine, but they are planted in gardens in England, whereof I have plentie in my garden.' There are two types of liquorice plant: the wild form grows in rough grassland, but it is the cultivated form to which Gerard was referring, native to south-east Europe and western Asia. He noted how the latter type was grown as a cash crop by poor people in the north of England, who applied plenty of manure, and replanted every four or five years. The industry was particularly located around Pontefract in Yorkshire, with the roots of the plant boiled up to produce a thick, sweet confection. Gerard illustrated his entry on liquorice with two moulded cakes that apothecaries made by adding ginger as a remedy against coughs. These were the ancestors of the confectionery known as Pontefract cakes, although today the liquorice comes mainly from Turkey, and the Yorkshire enterprises are a just a memory.[43]

For the manufacture of rose water, apothecaries and some private house-holds must have got their petals in bulk from market gardeners, as implied by Hugh Platt in his book *Delightes for Ladies*, first published in 1602. Platt was the son of a rich London brewer, enabling him to devote himself to his fascination with science and topics from mechanical inventions to alchemy, and to gardening. He advised that the ladies, for whom he was presenting all kinds of delights, should buy up rose petals at bargain prices: 'This way you may distill Rosewater good cheape, if you buy store of Roses, when you find a glutte of them in the market, whereby they are sold for 7 pence or 8 pence the bushell, you then engrosse the flower.'[44] A bushel was the equivalent of 8 gallons or 36.4 litres, while engrossing was buying wholesale.

In the reign of Elizabeth I, the Bishop of Ely was 'persuaded' to lease out his London palace and extensive garden to the queen's favourite, Sir Christopher Hatton. Although he ceded Ely Place in Holborn to Hatton, he insisted on retaining the right to gather from his garden 20 bushels of roses a year, a substantial amount. The bishop must have wanted this quantity of rose petals either to be distilled in his episcopal still rooms, or to sell to apothecaries. Not only were the petals used to make rose oil and rose water, but apothecaries sold on the petals for culinary purposes and making up sweet bags and pot pourris. In *Romeo and Juliet* Shakespeare described the shop of an apothecary visited by Romeo in Mantua, but it could equally have been found in an establishment in London. As it was a rather down-at-heel shop, among the stock were old cakes of roses.

Saffron was also a potentially valuable cash crop, with the yellow dye coming from *Crocus sativus*, with its deep purple flowers. In the sixteenth and seventeenth centuries the English centre of cultivation was based around Saffron Walden, although the flowers were also grown in other parts of Essex and in south Cambridgeshire by gardeners with small amounts of land in what were described as closes or garths. At Foxton in Cambridgeshire the crocuses were grown in open fields, in plots ranging in size from half a rood (one-eighth of an acre) to 2 acres.

William Harrison in his *Description of England*, published in 1577, explained how in September 'the flowers were gathered in the morning before the rising of the sun, which would otherwise cause them to welk or flitter [dry up or wither].' They were then dried in little kilns over a gentle fire and pressed into cakes. 'In good years we gather fourscore or an hundred pounds of wet saffron of an acre, which being dried doth yeild [*sic*] twenty pounds of dry and more.'[45] Harvesting was skilful business, with pickers, usually women and girls, using their nimble fingers to extract the tiny stamens from the flowers. All this care reaped rich dividends, for the saffron was used in medicine, as a poultice to relieve itching, and internally to strengthen the heart. In cooking, it provided a flavouring for cakes and biscuits and a colouring, as in pies of warden pears (mentioned on p. 46). In addition saffron was made into a dye for silk and for lace to make them look as if they were made from gold thread, a style of clothing very much in fashion during the reign of James I.

Gardens, domestic, professional or commercial, thus provided a wide range of plants and products derived from plants for use in households in the seventeenth century. We shall now take a tour of the home to show their use in various rooms, painting an intimate portrait of the social life of the time. In his translation of the *Maison Rustique*, published in London in 1600, Richard Surflet wrote 'the first foundation of a good House must be the Kitchin', and that is where we shall begin.[46]

THE
QUEENE-LIKE CLOSET
Or
RICH CABINET

Printed for Rich: Chiswell
And Tho Sawbridge 1684.

For the Table

In Marche, and in Aprill, from morning to night:
  in sowing and setting, good huswifes delight,
To have in their gardein, or some other plot:
  to trim up their house, and to furnish their pot.

                Thomas Tusser, *A Hundreth Good Pointes of Husbandrie*

T HESE LINES EMPHASIZE THE IMPORTANCE of the garden in providing ingredients for the kitchen. The author goes on to specify
some of the ingredients for furnishing the pot:

Have millons [melons] at Mihelmas, parsneps in lent:
  in June, buttred beanes, saveth fish to be spent.
With those, and good pottage inough having than:
  thou winnest the heart, of thy laboring man.[1]

We get here a glimpse of the modest kitchen. The pottage that won the
heart of the labouring man was the daily diet of a substantial proportion
of the population in the seventeenth century, particularly in rural areas.
This dish consisted mostly of herbs, thickened by 'pease', dried peas such
as Carlins, and, if lucky, with some meat. One herb used particularly for

The title pages of the 1684 edition of Hannah Wolley's *Queene-like Closet*, showing
different domestic tasks. While the maids undertake boiling, roasting and cooking over
a chafing dish, as well as baking in ovens, the lady of the house, wearing rather grander
clothes, is working in her still room.

pottages was Good King Henry, and its close botanical relative, fat hen, which went by the alternative names of 'bacon weed' and 'lamb's quarters'. The young shoots and flowering tops of these herbs when boiled resemble spinach. Their names suggest a wistful desire for the presence of meat.

In strong contrast comes Sir Kenelm Digby's recipe for 'an ordinary potage'. He suggested taking the fleshy and sinewy part of a leg of beef, scrag end of neck of veal and mutton, and boiling them in water from six o'clock in the morning to be ready by noon. 'At a fit distance, before it be ended boiling, put in a store of good herbs, as in Summer, Borrage, Bugloss, Purslain, Sorel, Lettice, Endive, and what else you like; in Winter, Beetes, Endive, Parsley-roots, Cabbage, Carrots, whole Onions, Leeks, and what you can get or like, with a little Sweet-marjoram and exceeding little Thyme.' Further flavour could be obtained by adding a hen or capon during the cooking, and the pottage was finished by beating in some eggs. The dish is what the Spanish call *olla podrida*, the English the anglicized 'pot pourri', and the French *pot-au-feu*.[2]

Digby's recipe reflects the rich diet of Stuart court circles. The one thing that it has in common with the pottage consumed by the poorest households is that it uses garden produce; in Digby's case, a profusion of herbs and vegetables. Our information about this period is skewed by what has been recorded and published, the recipes of the literate and leisured. As mentioned earlier, we have the manuscript recipe books compiled by women. We also have printed cookery books of 'professional' writers, all of them men, with the exception of Hannah Wolley, who is one of the first English women to make an income as an author.

Added to these are the rare survivals of chapbooks, little publications produced for sale for a few pence, such as the almanacs of Sarah Jinner, introduced in the previous chapter. Among the collection of chapbooks made by the diarist Samuel Pepys are four principally concerned with culinary recipes, and one with medicinal remedies.[3] Categorized by Pepys as 'Penny Merriments', these were collected in the 1680s for their form rather than their content, for he recognized that printing was moving on from 'black letter' or Gothic with woodcut illustrations to 'white letter' with metal engravings, and sought to keep a record of the old technology.

Although the books were probably not used by Pepys's own cookmaids, they provide a picture of the information sought by housewives, house-keepers and servants, able to read, in 'middling' households of the later seventeenth century. From these various sources come the recipes given in this chapter, selected to show the different methods of cooking, and the styles in food that dictated what would be grown in attached gardens or plots, or bought at markets.

Three meals per day were produced in most seventeenth-century households. Breakfast was usually a repast of bread served with ale or wine, although cheese, fish or cold meat might be added in wealthier establishments. At the beginning of the century the main meal, dinner, was eaten around midday, but as the century progressed the fashionable hour for dining in wealthy households moved later. Dinner was normally of two courses, with on special occasions a third course of rich sweet dishes and wines known as a banquet. Supper was again a simple meal, taken at no fixed time.

Cooking was based around the open hearth of the kitchen. Spits installed in the wide space enabled roasting, while boiling and stewing were organized in a kettle or cauldron suspended over the fire, or in a pot on a trivet, set in hot ashes. Cookery recipes of the period assume an oven would also be available, lined with brick, heated by a fire within, with ashes swept out and the floor cleaned before baking. Frying could be undertaken in a pan over the fire. Alternatively, if the establishment was sufficiently large and prosperous, chafing dishes might be used on charcoal stewing stoves that were set near windows to ensure proper ventilation and allow the noxious fumes to escape.

All these operations are shown in the frontispiece to Hannah Wolley's *Queene-like Closet*, with women performing the different tasks. In most homes, the kitchen had always been the realm of the housewife, but in medieval times in large establishments it was run by men, from the cook to the humble scullions. In the sixteenth century the scene changed, so that by the following century only grand aristocratic households and royal residences had a male cook. A gentlewoman would have paid servants to work in the kitchen and to prepare everyday meals, while she presided over the still room, where a better-dressed woman with a collar of lace is shown sealing a jar of conserves. Maidservants or female members of the family might help with work in the still room, where the sweetmeats and other dishes for the third course, the banquet, were made and medicines prepared.

The kitchens of large houses were traditionally set near the hall on the ground floor. This arrangement can be seen at Hardwick New Hall in Derbyshire, built in the late Tudor period. The kitchen is tall and airy, with a stone-flagged floor and whitewashed plastered walls. In the seventeenth century, however, the style developed to design grand houses with a high ground floor, set over a storey for the kitchen and domestic offices, as at Ham House in Surrey, built in 1610.

An example of a yeoman's kitchen of the early seventeenth century can be seen at Pendean, a house in the Weald and Downland Museum. The ground floor of the farmhouse is largely taken up by the kitchen and the hall, separated by a central chimney stack, with the domestic offices – the bakehouse, the brewhouse and the milkhouse or dairy – clustered around in 'outshoots'. The housewife here would not have had a still room, using her kitchen instead to make her conserves and medicines.

Seventeenth-century recipes show that the culinary herbs most often used were parsley, sage, rosemary and thyme, as celebrated in the traditional ballad 'Scarborough Fair'. If not grown in the garden, these could be bought at market or from itinerant sellers: among the Cries of London a woman selling sprigs of rosemary and bay is sometimes depicted (see pp. 62–3). Gervase Markham, in his *The English Huswife*, advised that the housewife's diet for her family should 'proceed more from the provision of her own yarde [garden] then the furniture of the markets', but this extolling of the virtues of self-sufficiency was simply not practical for those living in larger towns, and especially in London.[4]

Parsley, with its sweet taste, was particularly good with delicate meats such as rabbit. In Shakespeare's *The Taming of the Shrew* a cookmaid is mentioned going to the garden for parsley to stuff a rabbit. Just such a stuffing is noted in a late-sixteenth-century cookery book using a coney, an adult rabbit. It was briefly parboiled before the stuffing was put in its belly, well buttered, with a handful of parsley, a few sweet herbs and the yolks of hard-boiled eggs chopped together, some currants and pepper. The coney was then put into a pot of mutton broth with some vegetables and boiled well together before being served with sops, pieces of bread.[5]

Recipes for cooking meats often refer to sweet herbs, sometimes gathered as a faggot, rather than specifying individual names, though the collection would probably have included parsley, thyme and rosemary. A recipe for shoulder of mutton gives a herb stuffing as well as herbs to rub on the joint before roasting:

Gerard described various types of parsley. This image is of what he called 'garden parsley', which he grew for both culinary and medicinal purposes.

61

When you kill a sheepe, take some of the blood and mince in sweete
herbes, and a little suit [suet], and cromes of bread; mingle it altogether
and stuffe the motton in every place with it, then spitt the mutton and
when you lay it on the fire, rubb it all over with the blood and hearbes,
so rost it and bast it with butter, sett a dish under it to save the gravie,
when it is rosted put some wine vinigere to the gravie and a litle butter
and make it hott and powre it on the mutton and so serve it in.[6]

Sage, still today combined with onion for stuffing for pork, was the
herb used by Mary Doggett in 'To Collar Pig'. She 'small minced' the sage
with pepper, salt, nutmeg and ginger, and rubbed this mixture over the
pork before it was rolled up and sewn in a cloth. This was boiled with a
stock made of bones and a faggot of sweet herbs until tender. White wine,
vinegar and bay leaves were then added to the liquor, and the pork left
in this to stand until cold. One of Pepys's chapbooks contains a recipe for
boiling a loin of pork, using sorrel rather than sage. The accompanying
sauce was composed of bread, yolks of hard-boiled eggs, mustard and salt
with white wine. The recommended garnish for this dish was an attractive
arrangement of parsley, marigold flowers and the leaves of violets.[7]

These boiled meats could be served alongside meats roasted, as Samuel
Pepys recorded in his diary. His household employed a cookmaid to work
with his wife Elizabeth in the kitchen, and some were wanting in their
skills. But in 1663 a maid was hired with a salary of £4, and she proved a
good investment. Pepys noted on 4 April of that year: 'Very merry before,

The Cryer?   Kitchin=Stuff.   The Fidler's Goodmorrow.   Waintfleet=Oysters.   Chimney=Sweep.   Rosemary & Bays.

Part of a sheet of Cries of London, from the collection of ephemera made by the diarist Samuel Pepys. The series, dating from the early seventeenth century, shows a procession through time from the town-crier at daybreak. The figure on the far right is a seller of bay and rosemary, two important culinary herbs for the kitchen.

at, and after dinner, and the more for that my dinner was great and most neatly dressed by our only mayde.'[8] Among the dishes produced was a leg of mutton boiled, three carps in a dish, a great dish of a side of lamb, a dish of roasted pigeons and a dish of four lobsters.

Also on the Pepys household menu was a fricassee of rabbit and chicken. The idea of frying small pieces of meat had been introduced from France. A late-seventeenth-century recipe book provides advice for using chicken, rabbit or pigeon. Whatever was the meat of choice, it should be cut into small pieces, and the bones lightly bruised. The pieces were first fried with sweet butter, then put back into the pan with onion water, and cooked until the meat had become white. To this mixture was added anchovies dissolved in white wine, egg yolks, grated nutmeg, lemon juice and 'some sweet herbs shred small'. Fried balls of veal and forcemeat could be added at the last moment, with the dish garnished with slices of lemon.'[9]

Sweet herbs were used in another dish from France that involved frying, 'Scotch Collops'. The name is rather mysterious and it is often described as a Scottish dish: maybe it was taken there from the French court by Mary, Queen of Scots? Collop Monday was established in the sixteenth century

63

as the day when slices of bacon were consumed before the general clear-
ing of the larder on Shrove Tuesday in preparation for Ash Wednesday,
marking the commencement of Lent and of fasting. The herb of choice
for Elizabeth Birkett's dish of collops was thyme, which she added to
thin slices of veal, with orange peel. A sauce was made from egg yolks
and wine and added to the cooked meat, served with slices of lemon.[10]
Although Elizabeth Birkett lived in the Lake District, the Browne family
had connections in London, and books were regularly dispatched to them
by carrier. The fashionable recipe for Scotch Collops may have travelled
up to her in this way, while a local grocer, possibly in Kendal, could have
provided her with the more exotic ingredients.

Boiled suet puddings became popular following the development of the
pudding cloth, enabling them to be suspended in a cauldron to cook. At
the end of the seventeenth century, the French traveller François Misson
blessed its invention, describing with excitement how the English boiled
their puddings with meat, making them in fifty different ways. His account
reaches a crescendo with the observation 'Ah! l'excellente chose qu'un
English Pudding. To comme in Pudding-time, venir à l'heure de *Pudding*, c'est-à-
dire, venir à point nommé, le plus heureusement du Monde.'[11]

Winter savory, with its biting flavour, was chosen by Elinor Fettiplace
to make her 'Bagge Pudding'. She mixed thick cream that had been gently
heated with eggs well beaten. To this mixture she added the savory and
some parsley, finely chopped, nutmeg, sugar and a little salt, thickening
it with breadcrumbs and flour to achieve a consistency that was thicker
than that for pancakes. This batter mixture was put in a bag that had been
soaked in cold water, before being put into the boiling water of the cauldron. Monsieur Misson noted that bag puddings could be boiled alongside
meat, but Elinor Fettiplace did not like this practice, ending her recipe, 'yt
must not bee boyled wth meate but alone in fayre water'.[12]

Set alongside puddings on the dinner table were pies, baked in the
oven. Tusser's description of a Tudor Christmas feast includes 'shred pies

of the best', to be enjoyed alongside 'brawne, pudding and souse', and all kinds of meat and fowl with 'good bread and good drinke, a good fier in the hall'. One seventeenth-century version of shred pies, which we would call mince pies, took a leg of veal, parboiled, with beef suet and pared apples. These were all chopped up together, seasoned with currants, mace, sugar, dates, candied lemon peel, rose water and dry white wine, and then baked rather than boiled, taking only quarter of an hour to cook through.[13]

The *pièce de résistance* of Pepys's feast in 1663 was a lamprey pie, 'a most rare pie'. Lamprey is a primitive vertebrate that fixes upon its fishy prey with its sucking mouth. It enjoys an uncertain reputation: King Henry I was said to have died as a result of eating a surfeit, but it was obviously much prized by Pepys. His description of it as most rare is borne out by the fact that recipes for lamprey do not often feature in cookery books. Hannah Wolley, however, gives one using bay leaves, for the richness of the lamprey required a strongly aromatic herb.

> Take your Lamprey and gut him, and take away the black string in the back, wash him very well, and dry him, and season him with nutmeg, pepper and salt, then lay him into your Pie in pieces with Butter in the bottom, and some Shelots [shallots] and Bay Leaves and more Butter, so close it and bake it, and fill it up with melted Butter, and keep it cold, and serve it with some Mustard and Sugar.[14]

Lampreys are still rarely eaten in Britain, but the report from an intrepid gastronome who has recently tasted them in Spain is that the flavour is rather meaty, with the blood mixed into the stew.

Turning from products of the herb garden to the vegetable plot, there are two vegetables that are now very common in our cuisine, but remarkably absent from English recipes of the seventeenth century: the tomato and the potato. They are in fact related, members of the *Solanum* family, and were both introduced from the Americas. These clues may explain the reluctance with which they were originally taken into the kitchen, for another relative is deadly nightshade, so they were thought to be narcotic and possibly poisonous.

The tomato, from Mexico, was called the 'love apple', and credited with aphrodisiac qualities. In his *Herball* Gerard includes a reference under the heading 'apples of love'. He noted that they grew in Spain, Italy and 'such hot countries, from whence my selfe have received seedes for my garden, where they do increase and prosper'. He also provided suggestions for eating them, 'prepared and boiled with pepper, salt and oile', or made into a sauce to be eaten with meat, 'even as we in these cold countries do mustarde'. But he came to the conclusion that they provided little nourishment. The monks in Spain arrived at a very different view, rating them highly as food for the sick. In the summer of 1608, tomatoes were documented as on the menu at the women's Hospital de la Sangre in Seville, funded by lay Franciscans.[15] The English, however, remained firmly suspicious, and the tomato really only begins to appear in cookery books in the early nineteenth century. In Charles Dickens's *Pickwick Papers*, when Samuel Pickwick is accused of breach of promise to Mrs Bardell, the lawyer points out that the two shared a plate of chops *with tomato sauce*, suggesting sexual undertones.

The development of culinary interest in the potato runs slightly differently. *Solanum tuberosum* was first described and illustrated by John Gerard in his herbal in 1597. Although Sir Walter Raleigh is often credited with introducing the potato into Britain, it was probably Francis Drake who deserves the accolade, having brought it from Cartagena in Colombia. Gerard, who misleadingly called it the Virginian potato, reported how it prospered in his garden, recommending that the root should be 'boiled and eaten with oile, vinegar and pepper, or dressed any other way by the hand of some cunning in cookerie'.[16]

Raleigh's role in the history of the potato was to introduce it on to his Irish estates; within fifty years it had become the principal staple of the island. But the rest of the British Isles did not embrace it with the same

The Virginian potato, a 'botanical scoop', for Gerard was the first person in England to show an illustration of the vegetable that Sir Francis Drake brought back from South America. Although Gerard provided advice on how to cook the potato, it did not catch on as a product for the table until late in the seventeenth century. The illustration of the flowers and berries is a reminder that it is a member of the *Solanum* family, and therefore a relation of deadly nightshade.

enthusiasm. Like the tomato, it was credited with aphrodisiac qualities, so that Shakespeare made Sir John Falstaff call upon the sky to rain potatoes, along with another foreign introduction, the root of the sea holly known as eringo, as he prepared for a romantic assignation with one of the merry wives of Windsor in the fifth act of the play. Yet another objection raised by seventeenth-century writers was that the taste of potato was bland.

An interesting theory that has been put forward for the slowness of the potato to catch on is connected with the cutlery available. Although forks had been introduced from Italy for the spearing of sweetmeats and candied fruit as part of the banquet course, and large forks were used to hold joints of meat during carving, the table fork only became part of the canteen in the later seventeenth century. Before this, food was eaten with a knife and spoon, making the idea of the meat-and-two-vegetable menu unfeasible, so the potato did not flourish.

In the 1660s advocates of the potato began to give voice. In *The Whole Body of Cookery Dissected*, published in 1661, William Rabisha presented a recipe for potato pie that contained more than enough flavour. Nutmeg, cinnamon, ginger, sugar, bone marrow, raisins, dates, candied orange and citron peel, and, ironically, eringo root, were all added, with a sauce of vinegar, sack (dry white wine), sugar, egg yolk and butter. Three years later, John Forster published a treatise devoted entirely to the potato, *Englands Happiness Increased*. His subtitle, *A Sure and Easie Remedy against all succeeding Dear Years*, indicated that he was trying to provide sustenance for the poor, although his recipe suggestions, which included potato custards and cheesecakes, would suggest a more extravagant cuisine.

The potato may have been slow in finding its way into seventeenth-century recipe books, but the globe artichoke enjoyed vegetable stardom there. Introduced by the Dutch during the reign of Henry VIII, by the Stuart period they had become very fashionable. Queen Henrietta Maria had a garden devoted entirely to their cultivation at her manor in Wimbledon, while John Evelyn described them as noble thistles. To ensure that this delicacy lasted over winter, recipes were noted for their storage.[17]

After harvesting her artichokes, Elinor Fettiplace ensured they would last over the winter by boiling a mixture of water and verjuice with salt, and two strong-flavoured herbs, fennel and hyssop. This was reduced to a 'good sharp brine' into which the artichokes were thrown, briefly scalded and removed. Once the brine was cold, it was put in stone jars with artichokes laid in it on their bottoms with the herbs on top, ensuring the brine covered them entirely.[18] They were then ready for use in pies and salads. Verjuice was an important element in cookery at a time when lemons were expensive and not easily available outside urban markets. It was made from the mashing of crab apples, an important autumnal task for gardeners, either using a mill or mashing with wooden mallets into a trough, extracting the juice.

Sometimes recipes refer to thistles. These were probably the cousin of the artichoke, the cardoon. One recipe gives details of how to make a salad by taking the longest stalks of a young thistle, scraping and washing them, boiling in salted water until tender, draining and pouring butter over them. This suggests that they were eaten like asparagus.[19]

The term 'salad', or often 'sallet', covers a wide range of dishes, and an even wider range of ingredients. The first salad recipe in English appears in the *Forme of Curie* compiled by Richard II's cooks at the end of the fourteenth century. It represents a garden on the plate, taking parsley, sage, green garlic, spring onions, onions, leeks, borage, mints, fennel, cress, rue, rosemary and purslane. These were all washed, chopped and mixed together with oil, vinegar and salt.

HUGH PLATT'S RECIPE FOR STORING ARTICHOKES

In a mild and warme winter about a moneth or three weekes before Christmas, I caused great store of Artichokes to bee gathered with their stalkes in their full length as they grew, and, making first a good thicke laye of Artichoke leaves in the bottome of a great and large vessel, I placed my Artichokes one upon another as close as I could couch them, covering them over, of a pretty thicknesse with Artichoke leaves; these Artichokes were served-in at my table all the Lent after, the apples [chokes] being red and sound, only the tops of the leaves a little vaded, which I did cut away.

By the seventeenth century, for the courtly palate this idea had developed into a 'compound salad' with many exotic components, as in the following recipe:

Take a good quantity of blanched almonds cut coarsely. Then take as many raisins of the sun clean-washed and the stones pikt out; as many figs shred like almonds; as many capers; twice as many olives, and as many currants washed clean as all of the rest. Add a good handful of small, tender leaves of red sage and spinach. Mix these all together with a good store of sugar. Lay them in the bottom of a dish, then unto them vinegar and oyl. Then take oranges and lemons and cut them into thynne slices. Then with those slices cover the salat over. Cover the oranges and lemons with thinne leaves of red cole-flower, then over

these red leaves lay another course of old olives and the slices of well-pickled cucumbers together with the inward hearts of cabbage lettice cut in slices.[20]

This recipe, with its consideration of colour in the ingredients, represents the acme of luxury so far as salads are concerned, but housewives would have produced simpler combinations, which often included flowers. One such recipe advises 'As for Salads, they are various, according to the Season; as Corn, Salads and Pickles with Endive and French Grand Salads in Winter; and Lettice, Spinage, Purslain and Salads of Flowers in Summer.' Another recipe was for pickling clove gilliflowers 'for salleting all the year'. The clove carnation was often described as a gillyflower, or July flower, blossoming at the end of the summer. It was only with the arrival of exotic flowers, such as dahlias and chrysanthemums, that colour in the flower garden continued through into autumn. This recipe suggests interleaving layers of clove gilliflowers with layers of sugar in a gallipot, and then pouring on claret wine to cover them. A thin board was then laid over the top, and tied close, to 'let them stand a month in the Sun, and use them as you have occasion'.[21]

Ideas for a bewildering number of recipes are provided by John Evelyn in his remarkable work devoted entirely to the subject of salads, *Acetaria*. It was the last of a whole series of books that he wrote on gardening matters, appearing in 1699, although he had talked to one friend about publishing the information some twenty years earlier. Some have suggested that his advocacy of what he described as a 'herby diet' meant that he embraced vegetarianism. Although arguing against cruelty to animals, he enjoyed eating both meat and fish. His message in *Acetaria*, conveyed in flowery language punctuated by classical allusions, often makes it difficult to follow, but basically he was arguing that vegetables represented a healthy addition

PREVIOUS PAGES A kitchen scene painted by Bueckelaer in 1566, with some of the vegetables and fruit to accompany the dishes of meat and game. In centre stage are globe artichokes, the fashionable vegetables of the time.

to the diet, and, with more than a hint of modern thinking, he discussed what made for good food. He pointed out that 'Men in the Country look so much more healthy and fresh, and commonly are longer liv'd than those who dwell in the Middle and Skirts of vast and crowded Cities, inviron'd with rotten Dung, loathsome and common Lay Stalls.' On the other hand, good practice brought with it improved taste, 'most powerfully in Fowl, from such are nourish'd with Corn, sweet and dry Food'. In contrast to his prolix general style, he provided clear instructions on how to cultivate a wide range of vegetables, native and exotic, along with herbs and fruit. The book ends with an appendix of recipes for salads and dressings 'from an Experience'd Housewife': undoubtedly his wife Mary, who was celebrated for her skills in the still room.

In the kitchen garden at Ham House some of Evelyn's salad vegetables are now being grown. One is what he called 'viper-grass', scorzonera, and its relation, salsify. These Evelyn felt were good for palpitations of the heart, fainting and obstruction of the bowels, but also provided 'a very sweet and pleasant Sallet; being laid to soak out the bitterness, then peel'd, may be eaten raw, or Condited [pickled]; but best of all stew'd with Marrow, Spice, Wine &c'. He also suggested baking, frying or boiling them, concluding that 'a more excellent Root there is hardly growing'. Another 'salad vegetable' now to be found in the beds at Ham is sea kale, or 'ancient Crambe' as Evelyn describes it. This is one of the many cabbages that he recorded, claiming rather surprisingly that brassicas were introduced less than a century earlier.

Evelyn provides a long list of things that might be pickled. Artichokes, unsurprisingly, are on his list, but there are several unexpected ideas. He advises gathering young ash keys, boiled four times to remove their bitterness, and then boiling them 'on a very quick Fire' with a sauce of white wine vinegar, sugar and a little water. The result was green-coloured keys 'fit to be potted so soon as cold'. Other pickles unusual to modern tastes are the buds of the elder tree, and buds and pods of the broom plant. Yet another intriguing concept is 'Mango of Cucumbers'. Taking cucumbers that were particularly green, Evelyn advised that the seeds be scooped out and replaced by a small clove of garlic, or seeds of rocambole, a species of leek. The cucumbers were put into a glazed earthenware or glass jar, and a mixture of spices such as peppers, cloves and mace should be boiled up with white wine vinegar and poured over them. The following day they were to be transferred to a skillet with dill and brought to the boil before being returned to their jar. When cold, mustard should be added and the container well sealed. The result was a pickle which resembled that produced by the Malaysian fruit the mango, hence its name. Evelyn finished by recommending the pickle be removed from the jar with a spoon, and not the fingers.[22]

Cooks took full advantage of the plants in their gardens, and from hedgerows and meadows, for the ingredients of the tarts that featured so strongly on the seventeenth-century menu. Flowers, for example, were used, as in a recipe for borage tart in an Elizabethan recipe book. The parboiled flowers were added to egg yolks and sweet curds before being baked in a short pastry case. The author of the recipe suggested that the borage flower could be replaced by marigolds, primroses or cowslips.[23]

Sweetness combined with the savoury was much appreciated, as found in this recipe for a spinach tart:

> Take a good quantity of spinage and boyle it, and when tis boyled, put it into a Cullender, that the water may run out from it, then shred it very small, and season it with good flow of sugar, and a pretty quantity of melted butter, then put in yolks of Eggs and beat them altogether. Then make a sheet of paste very thin, and put it upon a Dish; so put your Tart stuff upon it, then another sheet to cover it.[24]

A still room from John Evelyn's translation of *Le Jardinier François*, published in London in 1658 as *The French Gardiner*. Some of the equipment of such a room is shown, including a pestle and mortar, chafing dishes, stills and bottles.

Other cooks added dried fruit, almonds, and even macaroons, and sometimes iced the tart with rose water and sugar.

Such rich tarts would be served towards the end of the meal and may have been prepared and baked in the still room of larger establishments. Here essences could be extracted, ointments concocted, cordials distilled and preserves made. A good idea of the appearance of a late-seventeenth-century still room can be had at Ham House. While most of the 'lower offices' are located in the basement, the still room is on the ground floor, with a door leading to the garden. Here the Duchess of Lauderdale could work with her maids. The floor is partially laid with black-and-white chequered marble, partly with stone flags. Under the window charcoal stoves have

been re-created: the originals would have allowed cooking at different temperatures. The room is furnished with a work table, and tall, shelved cupboards that back on to the chimney breast of the kitchen, and thus would have been gently warmed. The Ham inventory dating from the 1670s lists a considerable battery of equipment: pestles and mortars, braziers, scales, presses, bains-marie, graters, strainers, sieves and glass funnels. In smaller establishments,

The Damask rose. Distilled rose water was an essential for so many recipes, and the Damask rose was considered the best for this. Gerard explained, 'the especiall difference consists in the colour and smell of the flours: for these are of a pale red colour, of more pleasant smel, and fitter for meat and medicine'.

without the opportunity for a bespoke still room, the housewife could use pans, gallipots, bottles and even a sunny windowsill to do their distilling.

One essential for so many seventeenth-century recipes was water distilled from roses. Ralph Josselin in his diary reported how his wife distilled roses from their Essex garden at the very end of May. Lady Margaret Hoby in Yorkshire followed suit rather later, noting in her journal for 22 July: 'I was busie with Roses.' We have seen Elinor Fettiplace's recipe for making rose water on p. 38. While the concentrated oil derived during the process could be used in perfume and in lotions and creams, the rose water provided a luxurious ingredient in cookery, in medicinal recipes and in 'sweet waters' for washing.[25]

Hilary Spurling, in her book about Elinor Fettiplace's cookery, remarks on the substantial amount of petals required for rose water, and wonders whether she furnished some of her requirements from commercial growers, as mentioned in the last chapter.[26] To obtain rose water made up by the apothecary was expensive. Mary Doggett, who lived in London, noted its purchase: we do not know the quantity, but the cost was £1.00, a significant sum. Orange-flower water, which had to be imported from Spain, set her back £2.00.

Lady Ann Fanshawe, as noted in the Introduction, spent most of the tumultuous years of the English Civil War on the move around Europe. Nevertheless, she was able to use a still room in the intervals that she was in England. In her book of receipts she copied out 'conclusions and rules to be used in stilling, and the ordering of each hearbe or flower before they can be distilled' (see right and over).

First a soft Fire maketh sweete water and sweetnes to continue long.

2 ndly Coales still the best Water.

3 Wash nothing that you will still: but wipe it with a cleane Cloth.

4 All Hearbs Flowers and Seedes must be gathered when the Dew is of them.

5 That which you will Still must lye at the least six hours before you still it.

6 All Spices corrupt your Water, except Amber Gris, Civett & Muske.

7 Scumm your water well.

8 Keep your Still very cleane.

9 Wash your Stille but not often, then dry it with a dry Cloth.

10 A Glasse Still is best.

11 Borrage must be distilled the hearbe with the Roote chopped together.

12 Hysope the leaves stripped from the Stalkes, when it bares blew flowers.

13 Camomile in the midst of May the hearbe and Flower being chopt together.

14 Dill the Hearbes in the beginning of May.

15 Fumitory the whole substance chopped in the End of May.

16 Mint either red or other; the Hearbe stalke and Leaves in the middle of May.

17 Roses cutting away the white endes of the Flowers.

18 Rosemary the Flower Budds and Leaves stripped from ye Stalke in May in the Flowering.

19 Centory the Hearbes and Flowers chopped at the end of June.

20 Violet Flowers in Aprill.

21 Woodbynd the Flowers in the beginning of June.

She acquired this information from a book published in 1627 by John Partridge, *The Treasurie of Hidden Secrets*. We know very little about John Partridge, but he certainly could make close association between the garden and the house, and his instructions sometimes specify the times of the year for harvesting the herbs and flowers. The only alteration Ann made to the text was to omit Partridge's modest alternative to the glass still, in tin, earthenware and lead.[27]

Just as it was recommended, if possible, to set aside garden beds specially for the cultivation of roses for waters and syrups, the same applied to other fragrant flowers for distilling: primroses in spring, and violets and gillyflowers in summer. Elinor Fettiplace's syrup of violets required careful separation of the flowers from the white bases of the petals. They were put into a thick sugar syrup that had been clarified, and left for twenty-four hours at a low temperature. The flowers were strained out of the syrup and a new batch put in: this process was repeated another four times, and

The garden violet from Gerard's *Herball*. Like the rose, it was a mainstay of the still room in the seventeenth century, and beds were set aside in the garden for its cultivation as the recipe for violet water required a huge number of petals.

then the syrup was simmered for 'a good while'. Lastly lemon juice was added, before the syrup was strained ready for use.

She also had a recipe for 'balles of Violetts', where she cut off the white parts, and ground the rest of the flowers on a perfuming stone. This stone may have resembled the glazed tiles used by apothecaries to roll their pills, examples of which are on show at the Apothecaries' Hall in London. Once the grounds were 'so small that you cannot see what they are', she stood them on a window out of the sun to stiffen sufficiently. Grinding them again, she added sugar to enable her to mould them into little round balls or confits. When Falstaff called upon the heavens to rain down potatoes and eringoes (p. 67), he also called for kissing comfits that would have sweetened his breath.

Violets could be used as colouring. Elinor Fettiplace described how she took sugar plate, a kind of uncooked fondant, and coloured some of it blue with the juice of violets, some yellow with cowslips, and some she left white. She would then make layers and roll it into various marbled shapes.[28] Hugh Platt went even further with his ingenuity in his *Delightes for Ladies*, describing how to make a complete sugar-plate dinner service of saucers, bowls and so on, as a spectacular feature of the banquet. This he complemented with a suggestion in his gardening book, *Floraes Paradise*, that guests at a banquet should go into the garden and pick flowers that had been candied as they grew. The flowers were to be dipped in gum water 'as strong as for Inke, but made with Rose-water' at around ten o'clock in the morning on a hot summer's day, and then shaken. An alternative was to use a soft pencil and shake over the flowers a sugar powder using a box with a sieve of fine lawn. After three hours, the candy would have hardened 'so you may bid your friends after dinner to a growing banquet'.[29] It must have been fun to have dinner with Platt.

With the coming of autumn, work in the kitchen and the still room built up as fruit was brought in from the orchard; seventeenth-century correspondence refers to the frantic pace of work at this time of the year. Fruit could be candied in syrup; the results were often referred to as suckets or succades. The peel of oranges and lemons was often used for wet suckets, boiled in water again and again until it was 'sodden' and the bitterness eliminated. A syrup was made from rose water and sugar, boiled on a 'soft fire', and then the peels were dropped in while the syrup thickened. Once cold, the suckets could be kept in a stone jar. For dry suckets, also known as chips, the fruit would be removed from its syrup and put in sugar that had been boiled to candy height. The fruit was then shaken so that the candy stuck to them. Alternatively, boiled candy might be poured over the fruit, and the process repeated for several days, until 'they begin to sparkle as they lie'; at which point they should be dried.[30] The results could be stored in boxes to be given as presents, ready to be served at banquets during the winter months, or offered to guests as informal snacks. The decorated lacquer boxes in which sweetmeats were kept are still to be seen at Ham House.

Fruit was also made into preserves that required an adjustable heat. This could be made easier with chafing dishes heated over charcoal stoves.

The fruit would be gently softened over a low heat and mashed to extract the juices. Elinor Fettiplace had the following recipe for quinces:

> Take to every pound of quinces, a pound & somewhat better of sugar, beat it & put it into a deep silver basin or pewter, to every pound of sugar & quinces take half a pinte of faire water, so boyle your syrup first, then pare & core your quinces as fast as you can, so put them in rawe into your syrope & two or three of the cores loose, then lay a pie-plate in upon them, so let them boyle verie softlie, & never take out your quinces, but let them boyle as long as the syrup, when the syrup comes to bee iellie, then they are done.[31]

She suggested that the same recipe could be used for 'wardens', hard green cooking pears. Other fruits treated in this way included barberries, raspberries and cherries.

Some manuscript books contain recipes for fruit pastes, others for marmalades. In fact, the two were basically the same. Today we associate marmalade with oranges, but the word is derived from the Portuguese *marmelado*, which in turn comes from *marmelo*, or quince. Although oranges were grown in England from the sixteenth century, they had to be protected from winter cold by being wheeled in their pots into orangeries, and were thus a great luxury. Seville oranges were imported into the country from the beginning of November, Allhallowtide, through to the following spring. Again, however, they were expensive, literally the preserve of the wealthy, and the trade was liable to disruption through war.

English housewives therefore made pastes from the fruit that they had in their gardens and orchards. One recipe for apricot paste runs:

> Take your Apricocks and pare them, and take the stones out of them put them into a Pot and cover them close, sett them into a Kettle of Watter, and let them stand infusing in it 2 or 3 hours, then take them and strayne them through a Sieve, then put to a pound of your Pulpe of boyled Pippins, then clarify a pound of Sugar, and boyle it to a candy height, and put your Pulpe of Pippins and Apricocks into it. Keep it stirring

over the fire till it comes cleane from the bottom of the Pan, then lay it upon plates, dry it and keep it for use.[32]

The pippins, apples, provided the pectin content, and the result was a stiff paste like the quince cheese *membrillo*, which could be cut into squares or modelled into decorative shapes.

Orchard and dairy came together in snows, syllabubs and creams. Egg whites were used in snows as a raising agent, beaten with thick cream, sugar and rose water until the mixture could stand up in peaks. The fruit that was often added to this was apple. One recipe for green apple snow specified that the fruit should either be good codlings or, in winter, apple johns. Codling was a general name for young, unripe apples with a sharp taste. Apple johns were withered, partly desiccated fruit kept in store through the winter and, although not attractive to look at, remaining edible when so many other kinds had completely rotted. The traditional way of serving apple snow was to lay sprigs of rosemary on a plate and pile the mixture on top. Syllabubs were confections of wine or fruit juice, seasoned with sugar and flavoured with lemon, spices or rosemary, to which cream had been added with force to produce a frothy head. Some recipes even suggested that the cow should be milked directly into the liquor. Syllabubs were often drunk from the miniature spout of a two-handled glass, while the foam was eaten with a spoon.

Fruit was used in creams to provide a sharpness of taste. Most of the cream would be boiled with flavourings, while egg white was beaten into the remaining cream and then added to the hot sauce together with a little sugar. It was then left to cool after straining, and a fruit purée added. Featuring at a banquet, creams were either spooned from the dish, or eaten

'The portingegale Quince', a painting from *The Tradescants' Orchard*, an album of watercolours of various fruits dating from the mid-seventeenth century. The Portuguese for quince is *marmelo*, and the fruit formed the principal ingredient in the seventeenth-century fruit paste known as marmalade.

The portingegale
Quince.

Henbane. Fernstonge.

with wafers or bread. This is Elizabeth Birkett's recipe for a raspberry cream:

> Take a quart of Creame put it to boyle. Beat the whites of 3 Eggs well, and when it hath boyled well, put in your Eggs with a Leafe of Mace and a slice of Lemon peel. Boyle it till it thicken, season it with sugar, then strain it, and beat it well in your dish, then haveing your Raspberryes well stewed, mix them with your Creame, stirr it with some of the juice of them, you must also put in some Amber, and serve it up.

Unusually she also had recipes for herb creams. The one for rosemary boiled its flowers in cream until thick, then added sugar and rennet, making it like a jelly. The second was for thyme, cooked with 'new milke' and lemon rind, with sugar, cream and lemon juice added. This would be cooled and let stand for at least a day, before serving.[33]

The important elements of the banquet were richness, sweetness and visual delight. In his play *The Staple of News*, first performed in 1626, Ben Jonson captures the idea of the visual element when he describes how the cook Lickfinger

> Mounts marrow bones, cuts fifty-angled custards,
> Rears bulwark pies, and for his outer works,
> He raiseth ramparts of immortal crust;[34]

The custards were baked in raised pastry cases, sometimes referred to as 'coffins'. A recipe in *The Compleat Cookmaid* in Pepys's collection of chapbooks instructed how to make a gooseberry custard by removing the stalks and eyes from the fruit and boiling them until they could be broken up by a spoon. Removed from the liquor, they were added to eggs, and

Pies laid out on a table, along with other dishes, in the *Tudor Pattern Book*. The pattern book, part bestiary, part herbal, was compiled in the 1520s in East Anglia, and may have been used by limners for ornamental lettering, and by embroiderers. The plants, always in pairs, are sometimes shown with practical household utensils. This is a particularly incongruous combination, for the dinner dishes are teamed with the poisonous herb henbane and with hart's tongue.

cooked in a chafing dish over coals, with rose water and plenty of sugar, before being put into the pastry case and served cold.[35]

To make even more of an effect at a banquet, the upper crusts of custard and other types of tarts were sometimes removed and replaced by intricately patterned puff-pastry tops that had been baked separately. The designs for these could be obtained in books, such as John Murrell's *Delightfull Daily Exercise*, published in 1621. Murrell was a teacher of cookery and comfit-making. His enterprising publisher/bookseller, Widow Helme, based in St Dunstan's Churchyard in Fleet Street, offered moulds in the patterns specified in Murrell's book. Some of these resemble the garden parterres and knots that were so fashionable in the seventeenth century, bringing an extra dimension to banquets that were held in little garden buildings (see p. 19).

Intricate patterns were also used to decorate marchpane cakes, the climax of the banquet. In his section on 'Ordering of Banquets' in *The English Huswife*, Gervase Markham wrote: 'March-panes have the first place, the middle place and the last place.' The cakes were large flat roundels made of almonds and sugar, iced, anointed with rose water. Elinor Fettiplace in her recipe explained that she gilded her cakes and decorated them with 'conceits', three-dimensional figures and shapes, and with comfits.[36]

Some of the constituents of the banquet could also be served as 'snacks', as Pepys shows in his diary. He had a sweet tooth, although this love of sugar would appear to have been shared by most of his fellow countrymen and women if they could afford such a luxury. In the summer of 1663 he recorded drinking sugared beer with his booksellers at their stall in Westminster Hall, before going to visit his merchant friend Mr Bland, where he was offered 'a collacion of cheesecakes, tarts, custards and such-like, very handsome'. He also records a visit to Abingdon, then in Berkshire, to the custard fair, which lasted a week in June. Here he spent the goodly sum of 5 shillings consuming custards and listening to music.[37]

As an antidote to all this richness, Pepys also records more meagre fare. On the first day of February 1660 he noted returning home at noon from the office to dine with Elizabeth on pease porridge, 'and nothing else'. Observations of fasting in Lent are noted throughout his diary, including a Good Friday dinner, again of pease porridge, this time leavened with apple pie, followed that evening by a supper of wiggs, sweet buns, with ale.[38]

But it has to be remembered that for many of the poorest, pease pottage or porridge was the customary fare, dinner or supper, in or out of Lent, as recalled in a traditional rhyme:

Pease Porridge hot,
Pease Porridge cold,
Pease Porridge in the Pot
Nine days old

The ingredients for this dish, the peas and the herbs, could all have been grown in the garden, and for special occasions a rasher of bacon might be added if the household was able to keep a pig. Pottage was washed down by drink brewed with herbs, and the manufacture of this is where we shall begin the next stage of our tour of the seventeenth-century house.

Small Beer
& Strong Liquors

Water is not holsome sole by it selfe, for an Englysshman.

Andrew Boorde, *Dyetary of Helth*, 1542

WATER CARRIED THE THREAT of all kinds of diseases, so it was much safer to drink liquors that had been fermented by brewing, and thus resistant to infection. Andrew Boorde's *Compendious Regiment, or Dyetary of Helth*, published in 1542, was one of the first printed books on diet in English. Although adopting a patriotic tone, Boorde was making a valid point.

Brewing was traditionally the work of women, as Gervase Markham made clear in his *The English Huswife*: 'for it is a house-work, and done altogether within doors, where generally lieth her charge'. Men might grow the grains and bring them home, 'but for the art of making the Malt, and the several labours appertaining to the same, even from the Vat to the Kiln, it is only the work of the Housewife, and the Maid servants to her appertaining'.[1]

In smaller establishments brewing could be carried out in the scullery or back kitchen. This arrangement can be seen at Pendean, the yeoman's

Ale could be heated and drunk warm as a posset, served in a special handled cup such as the lead-glazed earthenware example shown here, made in Staffordshire and dated 1688.

Alehodde   Addirtonge

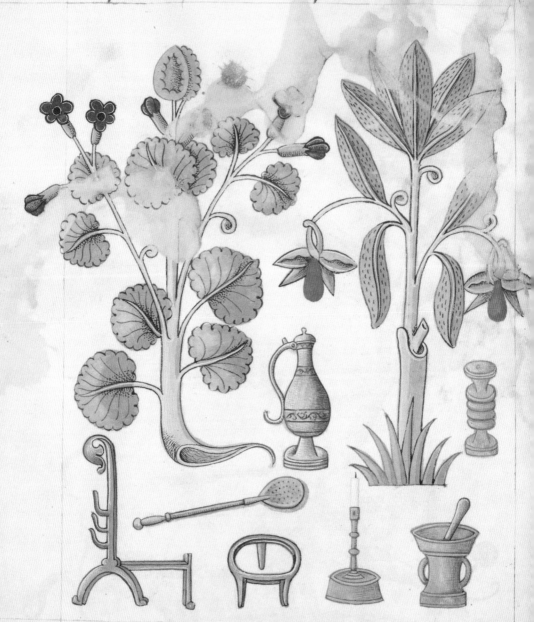

house dating from the first decade of the seventeenth century now in the Weald and Downland Museum. The brewhouse would seem to be part of the original building, with an exterior door, and another leading from the kitchen. An adjoining cellar was added slightly later. In larger households, the brewhouse might be a completely separate building. When Sir William Sharington acquired the dissolved nunnery at Lacock Abbey in Wiltshire in the 1540s, he installed in a service courtyard a brewhouse located next to the bakehouse. Brewing ale and baking bread were traditionally linked, using similar ingredients such as grain and yeast, and thus sometimes having shared chimney stacks and stores.

Whatever the scale of establishment of the enterprise, the essential equipment was a copper for boiling up the water. The hot liquid would be run off into a barrel or mash tun and the malt added. Malting was a winter task: steeping the grain in water, spreading and turning for at

Alehoof, or ground ivy, shown here in the *Tudor Pattern Book* in combination with adder's tongue. Alehoof, as the name implies, was a 'gruiting' herb used in brewing, and as an 'opening' herb for medicines. Here too is a mixture of utensils, including an andiron, a candlestick and a pestle and mortar.

Another gruiting herb was alecost, as seen in this image from Gerard's *Herball*. Apart from its usefulness in the brewhouse, alecost or costmary was an ingredient of medicines, could be put in clothes presses to ward off moths, and interleaved in books to absorb the smell of mildew.

least three weeks before being baked in a kiln and ground. Markham explained in his book that there were really only two suitable grains for the malt, barley and oats, though he added that it was also possible to make it from peas, lupins and vetches. The mashing of the malt would take several hours, while the starch of the grain gradually converted into sugar, known as wort. This would then be returned to the copper and boiled again.

Ale was the general term given to the fermented drink that resulted from the malted grain and water. As this could deteriorate fairly rapidly and develop a sour taste, aromatic herbs, known as gruiting, were often added to give flavour. The origin of the word gruit is rather a mystery, not appearing in the *Oxford English Dictionary*. However, it would seem to come from an area located in what is now part of the Netherlands, Belgium and westernmost Germany, where the sale of gruit was a monopoly, and as such a tax on beer.

Housewives would set aside a patch in the garden to grow their gruiting herbs, which could include sweet gale, mugwort, yarrow, horehound and heather. Ground ivy, which also went by the name of alehoof, might be planted, although the horticulturally minded would have been careful to avoid it becoming rampant. Another gruiting herb was alecost or costmary: the 'cost' part of its names refers to costus, a spicy plant from Kashmir, related to ginger. It was introduced into England from central Asia in the sixteenth century. Spices such as ginger, nutmeg and cinnamon might also be added to the brew.

Gerard was particularly keen on sage ale, writing that no man needed to doubt its wholesomeness. He explained that it was brewed from a series of herbs: sage itself, of course, but also betony, scabious, spikenard (mountain setwall or nardus), squinath (camel's hay), costmary and the seeds of fennel. The resulting brew was good for 'provoking urine' and for hardness of the womb.[2]

Yeast would be introduced, possibly from the bakehouse. There was an art in keeping the yeast well, maintaining warmth but at the same time providing regular doses of air. A besom or brush of twigs was used to stir the fermenting tun. When not in use, the besom could be hung out so that the sticky yeasts that were adhering to the twigs got plenty of air until next required. The besom would be made up of twigs from strongly scented shrubs such as bog myrtle, rosemary or sweet briar.

Hopped beer, introduced from the Low Countries, was regarded by some with deep suspicion, and this time comments were chauvinistic. Boorde wrote that it made men fat and inflated their bellies, being the natural drink of the Dutch. A century later John Taylor, who was known as the Water Poet because he was a Thames waterman, wrote a diatribe against beer, describing it as 'a Dutch Boorish Liquor, a thing not knowne in England, till of late dayes an Alien to our Nation, till such times as Hops and Heresies came amongst us, it is a saucy intruder in this land ... And now in late days it is much used in England to the detriment of many Englishmen.'[3]

Despite such opposition, hopped beer grew in popularity, for it enjoyed an important advantage over ale: hops had a preservative quality. They could be grown in gardens alongside gruiting herbs. Sir John Oglander, a landowner on the Isle of Wight, recorded in his commonplace book in 1632 how he not only planted a hop garden, but also made good money from it:

My hop-garden was the first in the Island that was made according to art. I brought 2 men from Farnham to plant mine and I have had in it 1000lbs in a year being not full an acre of ground. A hop garden, if it be in good ground, well-ordered and dunged, will return a great profit. I have often made £50 on an acre of ground according to the proportion.[4]

Although experts recommended that brewing ideally should take place in March, housewives, often referred to as 'ale wives', brewed regularly. The strength of their ale depended on how long it was left in the tun. 'Small beer' was the weakest, drunk almost at once as everyday consumption, including for children. The strongest brew was often described as March beer. John Aubrey, in his life of Sir Francis Bacon, wrote: 'His Lordship would often drinke a good draught of strong beer (March-beer) to-bedwards, to lay his working Fancy asleep, which otherwise would keepe him from sleeping great part of the night.'[5]

Stronger ales could be brewed for special occasions, and stored in the cellar. Recipes for 'bragget' or 'bragot', with the addition of honey, often appear in seventeenth-century manuscript books. One such recipe contains strongly flavoured ingredients:

> Take a firkin of good ale when tis 3 days old, take 3 pints of good stone honey, and put it into a pan, put thereto 2 or 3 quarts of wort or new ale and stir ym in ye panne together and set it on ye fire to clarify, as it boyles, take of ye scum till it looks as cleere as Syrup.
>
> Then take three quarters of beaten liquorish, as much curry seeds beaten. Put in an ounce of cloves, an ounce of pepper beaten with a score of nutmegs, all being well beaten, put in ye clarified honey. Set it over the fire.[6]

Liquorice comes from the root of a small perennial legume, *Glycyrrhiza glabra*, with flowers of a bluish purple, that grows wild in southern Europe and the Middle East. As noted earlier, in his *New Orchard and Garden* William Lawson recommended the space between apple trees be used as a nursery for the cultivation of liquorice roots, along with other flowers and herbs that would be useful for the still room and the kitchen. The juice from the root would have been concentrated by boiling.

This ale, with its highly flavoured additions, would then be bottled. The middle Sunday of Lent was celebrated as Bragget Sunday in many parts of the country. Perhaps the tastiness of the drink was intended to keep observants going until Easter? Pepys certainly thought that wigs (sweet buns) and ale constituted a good Lenten supper.

At the end of the year ale was added to crab apples, as recorded by Shakespeare in the song that concludes *Love's Labour's Lost*. The singer sets the wintry scene: 'When icicles hang by the wall, / And Dick the shepherd blows his nail.' This is the time when 'roasted crabs hiss in the bowl' and 'nightly sings the staring owl'.[7] In their raw state crab apples are inedible, but, as noted earlier, they would be mashed in autumn. They could also be roasted in the hot coals of the open fire and added to liquor to make a hot drink, lamb's wool. For a version made in Sussex, mashed crabs were added to ale, pressed through a sieve, and sweetened with ginger and nutmeg.

Lamb's wool was drunk as a wassail cup. The word comes from the Old English *wes hal*, meaning 'Be of good health'. During the twelve days of celebration at Christmas, apple trees in the orchard would be wassailed to ensure a good crop in the year to come. Even today in some parts of the West Country a little wassail is poured around the roots and a piece of toast, soaked in wassail, is placed in the forks of the trees. One version of the accompanying song runs:

> Here's to thee, old apple tree,
> That blooms well, bears well.
> Hats full, caps full,
> Three bushel bags full,
> An' all under one tree.

Another warming drink using ale was posset. What was described as a 'good herby posset' was included in Elinor Fettiplace's recipe book. Marigolds, agrimony and borage, along with sugar, were added to her basic recipe. She recommended this for a member of the household who was not well, to drink before going to bed. Possets were served in special handled cups with the thick liquid spooned from them. An early-eighteenth-century recipe specifies that it has froth at the top, custard in the middle and clear liquid at the base.[8]

Samuel Pepys mentions drinking possets on several occasions in his diary. At Twelfth Night in 1668 he described a party at his home in Seething Lane, with dancing and singing until midnight, when 'we had a good sack-posset … and an excellent Cake' cut into twenty pieces for the ritual of choosing a king and queen. Most of the references are to drinking a posset when he had a cold or felt generally unwell. On 3 December 1662 he ended his entry in typical Pepysian manner: 'and so home and had a posset, and so to bed'.[9]

Honey was the basic constituent of the drinks known as meads and metheglins. Metheglin was the Welsh cousin of mead; so in *The Merry Wives of Windsor* Shakespeare has the Welsh parson, Evans, describe Sir John Falstaff as having a 'belly [that is] all putter [butter]', 'given to fornications, and to taverns, and sack, and wine, and metheglins'.[10]

Sir Kenelm Digby would seem to have been a devoted connoisseur of meads and metheglins: in his collection he had no fewer than 110 recipes, making no distinction between the two. For the queen mother, Henrietta Maria, he made a particularly weak version of mead, which he called 'Hydromel', of eighteen parts water to one of honey. Another of his recipes was for white metheglin 'of my Lady Hungerford, which is exceedingly praised'. The recipe begins 'Take your Honey, and mix it with fair water, until the Honey be quite dissolved. If it will bear an Egge above the liquor, the breadth of a groat, it is strong enough; if not, put more honey to it, till it be so strong; Then boil it, till it be clearly and well skimmed.' The next step was to raid the garden for the flavouring herbs, which included strawberry and violet leaves, sorrel, rosemary, lemon balm, hart's tongue, liverwort, thyme and red sage. With the addition of these, the mixture was to be boiled for another hour, poured into a wooden vessel and allowed to stand until quite cold. Once put in the barrel, it was time to add spices: 'Take half an Ounce of Cloves, as much Nutmeg, four or five Races of Ginger, bruise it, and put it into a fine bag, with a stone to make it sink, that it may hang below the middle; Then stop it very close.'[11] Lady Hungerford informed Digby that she made this metheglin at the end of summer, when she had collected her honey. It would be ready to drink the following Lent.

Digby not only noted recipes, but also recorded his thoughts on honey. In his opinion, 'the Honey of dry open Countries, where there is much Wild-thyme, Rosemary and Flowers, is best. It is of three sorts, Virgin-honey, Life-honey and Stock-honey'. His grading is reminiscent of that applied to olive oils. 'The Virgin-honey is of Bees, that swarmed the Spring before, and are taken up in Autumn; and is made best by chusing the Whitest combs of the Hive.'[12] He warned that honey that was forced out of the combs would always taste of wax. Hampshire honey was most esteemed in London, though Norfolk was also famous for it.

Just as Lady Hungerford included many garden herbs and flowers in her recipe, Digby provided a long list in his considerations for the making of both mead and metheglin, advising that the brewer could use what herbs and roots she wanted according to her taste. But he noticed that bitter and strong herbs, such as rosemary, bay, sweet marjoram and thyme, would conserve the mead better and longer, 'being as it were in stead of hops'. He also warned not to boil the mixture too much, for this will lose the 'Volatil pure Spirit'.[13]

Rosemary was the herb of choice in Elinor Fettiplace's recipe for lemon mead. She took ten quarts of water to one of honey, three pounds of 'ye best powder'd sugar' and having mixed them together, set them on a fire. This mixture was constantly skimmed as it boiled. After three quarters of an hour the spices and herbs were added: 'Six penniworth of Cloves & Mace, one Race of Ginger sliced, & as much of Rosemary'. The brew should be boiled for a further quarter of an hour and then allowed to cool. Six lemons, cut in half, were then added to the liquid along with brown toasts spread with yeast. Once fermentation was complete, the liquid was sealed up for a week before being put in bottles with a lump of sugar in each. It was then ready for drinking.[14] If the availability of sugar presented a problem, Elinor advised adding more honey.

Apples have long been the main ingredient of cider, but interest in the cultivation of the fruit, along with other orchard trees, was particularly developed in the mid-seventeenth century. This is shown in an account that has come down to us in the autobiography of Leonard Wheatcroft, a Derbyshire 'jobbing' gardener: remarkable for a man of his comparatively low status to have written. The first reference to gardening comes in 1651 when he planted an orchard for a local rector, and thereafter there are notes of orchards created for various members of the county's gentry.[15]

Several books of fruit husbandry were produced at this time, including *A Treatise of Fruit-Trees* published in 1657 by the Puritan divine Ralph Austen. In this he advocated that profit should be combined with pleasure, and the practical with the spiritual. Of a very different religious persuasion was Sir Kenelm Digby. Nevertheless, when he was able to turn his attention from his meads and metheglins, he provided thoughtful information on cider and the kind of apples that should be grown in the orchard for its manufacture. His recommendation was Pearmains, Pippins, Golden Pippins, but he thought the best cider apples of all were codlings. This was the general name for a young, unripe apple. In *Twelfth Night*, Shakespeare has Malvolio describe somebody as 'Not yet old enough for a man, nor young enough for a boy; as a squash is before 'tis a peascod, or a codling when 'tis almost an apple.'[16]

To keep the apples ready for cider-making, Digby recommended covering them with hay or straw in the cellar during freezing weather, In 'open weather' they should be moved to another part of the cellar and stood upon the bare ground or pavement. In hot weather they should be set in sand. His recipe for making cider was to

> take a Peck of Apples, and slice them, and boil them in a barrel of water, till the third part be wasted; Then cool your water as you do for wort, and when it is cold, you must pour the water upon three measures of the grown Apples. Then draw forth the water at a tap three or four times a day, for three days together. Then press out the Liquor, and Tun it up; when it hath done working, then stop it up close.[17]

John Evelyn was also an enthusiastic proponent of cider, in 1664 attaching to his book on forest trees, *Sylva*, the annex *Pomona: or An Appendix concerning Fruit-Trees in Relation to Cider; the Making and several ways of Ordering it.*

The title page of Ralph Austen's *A Treatise of Fruit-Trees*, published in Oxford in 1657. A Puritan divine, Austen combined spiritual concepts with practical information on the planting of fruit trees for the making of ciders and perries.

Profits   Pleasures.

A Treatise of
FRVIT=TREES

Shewing the manner of Grafting, Setting, Pruning, and Ordering of them
in all respects: According to divers new and easy Rules of experience;
gathered in y^e space of Twenty yeares.

Whereby the value of Lands may be much improued, in a shorttime, by
small cost, and little labour.

Also discovering some dangerous Errors, both in ye Theory and Practise
of ye Art of Planting Fruit-trees

With the Alimentall and Physicall vse of fruits.

Togeather with

The Spirituall vse of an Orchard: Heldforth in divers Similitudes betweene Naturall & Spirituall Fruit-trees: according to Scripture & Experiēce.

By RA : AUSTEN.

Practiser in ye Art of Planting

A Garden inclosed is my sister

my Spouse: Thy Plants are

an Orchard of Pomgranats, with

pleasant fruits: Cant. 4. 12. 13.

The second Edition   with many additions.

Oxford printed for.   Tho: Robinson 1657.

Dismissing hops as a medical rather than an 'alimental' vegetable, and accusing those who advocated wine as putting up with the 'Sophistications, Transformations, Transmutations, Adulterations, Bastardizings, Brewings, Trickings [and] Compassings of this Sophisticated God they adore', he declared 'Give me good Cider'.

He waxed lyrical about apple blossom perfuming the air. The inhabitants of Herefordshire, he claimed, enjoyed 'constant Health and Longevity' by using their orchards to shelter 'their Habitations and wet Recesses from Winds and Winter invasions, the heat of the Sun, and his insufferable Darts'. He also pointed out that the apple trees 'harbour a constant Aviary of sweet singers, which are here retain'd without a charge of Italian wines'. He ended this paean of praise on a patriotic note: 'That if at any time we are in danger of being hindred from Trade in Forreign Countries, our English Indignation may scorn to feed at their Tables, to drink of their Liquors, or otherwise borrow or buy of them … so long as our Native soyle does supply us with such excellent Necessaries.'[18] John Evelyn was not averse to hyperbole.

His familiarity with the orchards of Herefordshire arose from his correspondence with John Beale, a West Country clergyman with a particular interest in the cultivation of apples. Beale supplied him with his personal favourite apple varieties. From Herefordshire, he singled out the Red Strake or Streak, a pure wilding. From Gloucestershire, he recommended the Bromsbury Crab, which 'affords a smart winy liquor, and is peculiarly hardy, it being not ripe in hot Land till the end of Autumn, nor fit to be ground for Cider till Christmas, lying so long in heaps and preparation'. For London 'and the more Southern Tracts', like Kenelm Digby he recommended 'the Pepin, and especially the Golden'.

'An Early ripe Apple and good in taste' from *The Tradescants' Orchard* (see p. 104). This is the only apple featured in the album; it was known in the seventeenth century as a 'finger' because of its cylindrical shape.

127

An Early ripe Apple
and good in taste.

August 22

Pear trees are also included in *Pomona*:

> Concerning Perry, the Horse-pear and Bare-land-Pear are reputed of
> the best, as bearing almost their weight of spriteful and vinous Liquor.
> The Experienced prefer the tawny or ruddy sort, as the colour of all
> other most proper for Perry: They will grow in common-fields, gravelly,
> wild and stony ground, to that largeness, as one only Tree has been
> usually known to make three or four hogsheads [large barrels of 52½
> gallon capacity].

The fruit of the Bosbury was so tart that it was safe from both pigs and
human thieves.

Just as all kinds of ingredients were added to ale at this period, so they
were put in cider and perry. Among these additions, Evelyn lists juniper
berries, ginger, sprigs of rosemary and bay, and even mustard. He recommends a cordial with clove gillyflowers, and a summer drink of cider with
raspberries called bonella.[19]

Evelyn continued his patriotic theme by recommending that gluts of
plums and cherries be made into fruit wines. His disdain for Continental
grape wines was, however, rather exceptional. In London, Rhenish wines
were landed in barrels at the Steelyard, originally the headquarters of the
merchants of the Hanseatic League, while other wines from Europe and
the Levant would arrive at Vintners' Wharf near London Bridge. These
wines were neither clarified nor matured before sale, but drunk young. As
such, they were treated in a way that we would consider cavalier, often
with the addition of sugar, herbs and fruit. Sack, according to Shakespeare
the favourite tipple of Falstaff, was 'secco', a dry white wine from Spain,
to which the fat knight added sugar so much as a matter of course that
one of his companions referred to him as 'Sir John Sack and Sugar'. In his

'The grete winter peere' from *The Tradescants' Orchard*. The great art collector of the
early seventeenth century, Lord Arundel, was described by a contemporary as a winter
pear, meaning a late developer.

The great winter
peare.

Toe Make Sirrope of any Hearbe or Flower

Fill an Earthen Jugge full of herbes or flowers you will make sirroppe of, then ad to yt as much springe water as your Jugge will receive, so let yt stand where yt may bee kept warme 2 howers, then straine yor licoure from the rest very hard, then to that licoure put more of the herbes or flowers, and lete yt stand 2 howers as you did before, thus you must doe 3 times strayninge out the licoure and putinge in fresh herbes the last time ad to every pinte of licoure 2 pound of suger smale beaten, set yt in your Jugge againe in a pott of warm water tille your suger bee dissolved but cover yt not until yt bee cold.

diary, Pepys recorded drinking wine with the addition of the bitter herb wormwood. On 10 January 1661, for instance, he noted taking wormwood sack at the Hoop Inn by London Bridge, and on occasion drinking wormwood wine with friends at the Steelyard.[20]

The wormwood may have just been steeped in the wine: there has long been a tradition of adding it in vermouths and other aperitifs. But more mysterious is Pepys's reference to 'raspberry sack', which he consumed along with some sausages on an outing with his wife to watch a puppet performance of Ben Jonson's *Bartholomew Fair*. After this meal, in November 1661, they returned home 'very merry'.[21] The possibility is that raspberry syrup may have been added to the wine.

A raspberry syrup is included in Elinor Fettiplace's collection of recipes, as shown here. She used her garden to good effect. In this all-purpose recipe, she focused on rosemary and on purple clary, a herb related to sage. If a syrup of strawberries, raspberries or other small fruit was

The Tradescant Cherry. The connection between the Johns Tradescant, father and son, and the album that bears their name is rather mysterious, but it is thought that the watercolours contained within it were used as a kind of catalogue for them to show to customers at their nursery garden in Lambeth.

The Tradescant Cherry
June the 21

required, they should be put whole into a jug and left to stand without any liquid over a gentle fire for two hours. Once they had become liquified, two pounds of sugar was added for each pint and left in a pot of warm water until the sugar had dissolved. The resultant liquid was then poured through a jelly bag ready for use.[22]

Her syrups could be used in a refreshing summer drink, julep. The word comes from the Persian *gulab*, meaning rose and water, and is used for drinks that are cooling. While Elinor's versions are non-alcoholic, a favourite and famous drink from the American South is mint julep, with the addition of brandy, whiskey or other spirits. Samuel Pepys noted in his diary in late June drinking 'a can of good Julipp' at a tavern, so this may well have had an alcoholic ingredient.[23]

Elinor used as a base what she described as French barley water, home-grown barley corn soaked, beaten with a wooden 'beetle' in a sack, then rubbed, winnowed and wetted. To this she added violet syrup and red rose water. Red rose water could be produced by steeping the petals in a stoppered container with distilled water, which would otherwise have been colourless. Finally she added citron syrup, produced by boiling sugar and squeezed citron juice. This would all be stirred together to make a refreshing drink, 'and when you are dry or in your burning heate drinke 2 or 3 spoonffulls at a time as ofte as you please'.[24]

Another cooling drink was almond milk, again based on barley water. Mary Doggett's recipe book contains several almond milks. For one of these recipes she took the leaves of violet and strawberry plants, adding liquorice and sebastians (a plum-like fruit from the cordus tree). These were boiled in fresh barley water, and, when reduced by a third, blanched almonds, pounded fine, and sugar were added. The liquid was strained through a cloth, and rose water could be added. 'This milk is good for cooling ye liver and ye inward parts at any time being fever-ish inwardly.'[25] Almonds from Spain and Italy could be bought from grocers' shops.

With the coming of autumn, housewives would use surplus crops from the orchard to make their own wines. A wide range of fruit were used, from raspberries and strawberries through to black- and whitecurrants.

The most powerful liquors – what we would describe as spirits – were known in the seventeenth century as 'strong waters'. It is thought that the taste for these was brought to England in the reign of Elizabeth I by soldiers returning from the Low Countries. By 1621 two hundred strong-water houses were recorded in London, mainly selling a spirit from fermented grain, while Dutch gin, French brandy and Irish whiskey (uskebaugh) were imported. In 1638 the Distillers' Company of London was given its royal charter by Charles I. A prime mover in this was the king's Swiss physician, Sir Theodore de Mayerne, who had already been instrumental in establishing the Society of Apothecaries (p. 48). The Company's coat of arms has a Russian figure as one supporter, the Baltic being a principal source of rye and barley, and an Indian as the other, a reminder of the herbs and exotic spices which were important ingredients. By the mid-century apothecaries often offered these strong waters for sale for their medicinal properties.

Strong waters could also be produced domestically, in the still room, with recipes described as 'Imperial Waters' and *aqua mirabilis*. For one of her *aqua mirabilis* recipes, Elinor Fettiplace again made full use of her garden for ingredients. The basis for the drink was white wine imported from Malaga, 'Angelico strong water', brandy wine and the juice of celandine flowers. To this liquid she added the flowers of cowslips, rosemary and borage, along with mint and balm, and spices such as cinnamon, nutmeg, ginger, cloves, cubeb, cardamom and saffron. The flowers, herbs and spices were bruised and then mixed together before 'being drawen in a cold still stopped close with course paste' and then put over a gentle fire. After distillation she added even more taste by steeping a bag containing sugar, musk and ambergris. The highly aromatic result was used as a medicine to comfort patients suffering from a range of complaints, including ulcerated lungs, heartburn, melancholia, poor circulation and failing memory. Brandy wine was also used in her recipe for ratafia, where apricots were cut into quarters and their kernels crushed and added to the brandy in a wide-mouthed glass. This was set on a windowsill in the sun for two or three weeks depending on the weather, and then strained and bottled.[26]

Non-alcoholic drinks that we might call herbal teas were more usually known at this time as 'ptizans', from the Greek for peeled barley, which was often the base ingredient. We would now use the term 'tisane'. The Duchess of Lauderdale's 'Ptizan for a Consumption' took maidenhair fern, liverwort, coltsfoot and liquorice, all boiled together in water, from which she recommended drinking half a pint every morning.[27] The term 'tea' also begins to appear for herbal drinks of a medicinal nature. John Evelyn in his *Acetaria*, for example, describes how pennyroyal, if 'discreetly dried', could make 'a most wholsom and excellent Tea'.[28] However, the normal application of the term was to the dried leaves of *Camellia sinensis*, first imported from the Far East in the middle years of the century. It was one of a trio of exotic beverages – coffee, tea and chocolate – whose ingredients could not be cultivated in gardens in Britain, but which radically changed drinking habits and the social scene.

Coffee arrived from the Middle East via Holland. John Evelyn must have been one of the first to record its arrival in Oxford while he was an undergraduate. He noted in his diary how in 1637 a fellow student from Greece, Nathaniel Conopius, was 'the first that I ever saw drink Caffè, not heard of then in England, nor til many yeares after made a common entertainment all over the nation'.[29] Two decades later, a group of students and fellows of the University persuaded an apothecary, Arthur Tillyard, to prepare and sell coffee for their consumption, recognizing that the drink was able to keep them awake and alert. Tillyard's house, next to All Souls College in the High Street, became a meeting point for the Oxford Coffee Club, which included leading scientists such as Robert Boyle. This informal club was therefore one of the groups that evolved into the Royal Society.

The first coffee house in London was opened in 1652 by Pasqua Rosee, the Armenian servant of a Levant merchant. His premises, just off Cornhill in the heart of the City, was soon followed by many similar establishments. Broadsheets were published highlighting coffee's health benefits. One described it as a sober and wholesome drink, with 'Incomparable Effects in Preventing or Curing Most Diseases incident to Humane Bodies'. But it was the conviviality of the coffee houses that really attracted the clientele, places where men – and it was exclusively men who frequented them – could read newspapers, discuss politics and cultural events, and conduct business.

While coffee was a drink usually consumed in these houses, tea became the fashionable drink to be consumed within the home. This beverage arrived from the Far East into Europe in the early seventeenth century on the ships of the Dutch East India Company. Samuel Pepys in his diary for September 1660 described how in the middle of his working day he 'did send for a Cupp of Tee (a China drink) of which I never had drank before'. He makes no further reference to taking tea himself, but does mention, seven years later, how he returned home from work to find his wife Elizabeth 'making of Tea, a drink which Mr. Pelling the pothecary tells her is good for her cold and defluxions'.[30]

Apothecaries and grocers both stocked tea. One of their best customers must have been the scientist Robert Hooke. Obsessed with his health, he started each day with a dish, buying it in 15 lb boxes at the bargain price of 5s 6d per pound. He defined no less than twenty qualities for tea, from purifying the blood and vanquishing heavy dreams to sharpening the wit and strengthening 'the use of benevolence'.[31] Recipes involving tea do not appear in contemporary recipe books, either printed or manuscript, save for one for a caudle from Sir Kenelm Digby, always the exception to the rule. Caudle was a drink closely related to posset: a syrupy gruel, often with spices, wine and ale added.

Digby's source for his recipe was a Jesuit priest returned from China, who warned him against letting the hot water 'remain too long soaking upon the Tea, which makes it extract into it self the earthy parts of the herb. The water is to remain upon it, no longer than whilst you can say the *Miserere* Psalm very leisurely'. The recipe ran:

> Take two yolks of new-laid eggs, and beat them very well with as much fine sugar as is sufficient for this quantity of liquor; when they are very well incorporated, pour your Tea upon the Eggs and Sugar, and stir them well together. So drink it hot. This is when you come home from attending business abroad, and are very hungry; and yet have not conveniency to eat presently a competent meal.[32]

Coffee house proprietors also dealt in tea, and served it in their establishments. But it was principally drunk by women in their own homes, and a whole trade grew up providing the paraphernalia to accompany the tea ceremony. The tea was usually green, although a minimal quantity of black, known as bohea, was also being imported. It was drunk with the addition of sugar; right at the end of the seventeenth century, references appear for 'milk bottles'. At Ham House, the Duchess of Lauderdale took tea with general visitors in her White Closet, furnished with japanned or lacquered tables and chairs, dispensing water from what is described in the inventory as an Indian furnace, or kettle, into a silver tea set. For her most intimate friends, she used her boudoir or private closet, again furnished with lacquer work, including a 'Japan box for sweetmeats and tea'.

The third beverage, chocolate, came from New Spain in the Americas. The Aztec emperor, Moctezuma, offered it as 'the food of the gods' to the conquistador Hernán Cortés, serving it cold, without sugar, although sometimes honey was added along with spices such as chilli and vanilla. Having acquired a taste for chocolate, the Spanish tried to keep the processing of the beans from the cacao tree secret, but the monopoly was broken in the early seventeenth century by an Italian traveller. Chocolate arrived in London in the 1650s, advertised as 'an excellent West India drink', with curative properties. Pepys in an entry in his diary for April 1661 noted: 'Waked in the morning with my head in a sad taking through the last night's drink, which I am very sorry for. So rose and went out with Mr Creed to drink our morning draught, which he did me in chocolate to settle my stomach.' The draught was taken with wine in a tavern.[33]

The aim with drinking chocolate was to produce a froth. The Aztecs achieved this by pouring the liquid from one vessel held aloft into another. The Spanish, finding this time-consuming and awkward, invented the *molinillo*, a little swizzle stick of wood. When Sir Richard Fanshawe was appointed English ambassador to Spain by Charles I in 1647, his wife Ann sketched a *molinillo* in her book of receipts, along with a chocolate pot. She noted that, apart from the Indies, the best chocolate was to be found in Seville, and added a recipe for dressing chocolate, which is the earliest known in English. Unfortunately it was subsequently crossed out and is illegible. However, recipes for chocolate do begin to appear in late-seventeenth-century cookery books. Mary Doggett has four recipes, including one for making chocolate almonds, in which she grated the chocolate, sieved it and added double the quantity of sugar. Oil of almonds was added, with gum arabic that had been steeped in water. The mixture was beaten well and then poured into moulds.[34]

These exotic beverages were in their infancy in seventeenth-century England, but they signal the beginning of a revolution in the nation's drinking and eating habits. By the end of the century, other changes were taking place. Gin was becoming a very popular drink, and, with the removal of duties on its import, available to the poor, with the results that Hogarth was to spell out clearly in his engravings in the eighteenth century. Meanwhile Gervase Markham's image of the ale wife producing her home-grown brews was also receding. Gruiting herbs were left untouched in the garden, as commercial enterprises took over the manufacture of beer.

A Herbal

I HAVE MADE A SELECTION OF FIFTY HERBS that were used by seventeenth-century housewives. This is a fraction of what were available. I have chosen three groups: those that were particularly versatile, such as rosemary and bay; some that are less familiar to the modern reader; and some that provide an insight into the cultural context of the time. The botanical names in italics are Linnaean, and would not have been used by John Gerard or Nicholas Culpeper.

ALECOST (*Tanacetum balsamita*) is an attractive perennial herb of the *Compositae* or daisy family. 'Cost' refers to the spicy Kashmiri plant, costus, which has a slightly similar, gingery flavour. As its name suggests, it was used to flavour ale. Another common name is 'costmary', a reminder of its traditional association with the Virgin Mary. Culpeper attributed it to the dominion of Jupiter, with a whole range of medicinal properties, including an astringent for the stomach and a blocked nose. The beautiful pale silver leaves were interleaved in bibles to disperse the smell of mildew, and it was also used in clothes presses to ward off moths.

ALEHOOF or ground ivy (*Glechoma hederacea*) has long purplish blue flowers that run along the ground. Yet another name is 'tunhoof'. Gerard described it as being the herb of choice for brewing in Wales and the Borders, even after hops arrived in Britain. Bitter in taste, it was used as an 'opening' herb in medicines, and as a remedy for problems with eyes and ears.

ALEXANDERS (*Smyrnium olusatrum*) are coastal plants from the Mediterranean, with glossy leaves (left). In the seventeenth century the different parts were variously used: the young flower buds were pickled; the leaves were used in soup to help digestion during the fish diet of Lent; while the pungent roots could be stewed or eaten raw with vinegar. This made the herb a mainstay of the cottage garden.

ALL-HEAL, also known as self-heal (*Prunella vulgaris*), has roots that are hot and biting, bitter hairy leaves and little yellow flowers. According to Culpeper, it is in the dominion of Mars, curing a whole range of medical problems including gout, aching joints, vertigo, stones in the kidneys and bladder, and the bites of mad dogs and venomous creatures. Gerard pronounced that there was no better wound herb to be had.

ANGELICA flourishes in streams and damp woods as *Angelica sylvestris*, with tall, pink and purple stems topped by umbels that look as if they are dipped in claret wine. Their fragrance is similar to that of the garden variety, *Angelica archangelica*, which is often referred to in seventeenth-century recipes as Archangels. Culpeper suggested combining it with the 'blessed thistle' (see overleaf) and treacle as an antidote to the plague, although he disapproved of such holy epithets. The stems have tradition-ally been candied for decoration of confectionery.

BAY (*Laurus nobilis*) is an aromatic evergreen with green glabrous leaves that give a strong taste in cooking. According to both Gerard and Culpeper, the leaves acted as an opening herb, provoking urine, and when the bark and roots were drunk in wine they could break up stones in the bladder. Planting a bay tree was thought to protect the household from all kinds of evil, including witchcraft, while the leaves were used against stings and venomous bites, and to protect the house from meal moths and flies. As an evergreen, it was one of the decorations brought in for Christmas, and would be burnt, alongside rosemary, to scent rooms in winter.

BETONY (*Stachys officinalis*) is a member of the deadnettle family, with spiked heads of reddish purple flowers (left). It favours established grassland and heath, and the edges of woods. In the Middle Ages, betony was regarded as a talisman against wicked spirits and witches, and an antidote to poison. Culpeper noted the herb was 'most fitting to be kept in a man's house both in Syrup, Conserve, Oyl, Oyntment, and Plaister'.

CARDUUS BENEDICTUS (*Cnicus benedictus*) came originally from Southern Europe. It has a stem about 2 foot in height, and bears pale yellow flowers. Its name of 'blessed thistle' reflects the belief that it had supernatural powers, although the nonconformist Culpeper wrote that he supposed it was so named by those who had little holiness in themselves. It was used to treat headaches and migraine, to stimulate the liver, and to strengthen the heart.

CLARY is a member of the large salvia family. The wild version, *Salvia horminoides*, has crinkled leaves and small violet flowers that bloom from June to the end of August. This version comes with a warning to gardeners, for once introduced to the garden it spreads rapidly. The garden version, *Salvia sclarea*, has square stalks and similarly wrinkled leaves of a hoary green. The herb was sometimes known as clear eye, because the seeds, when soaked in water, swelled up to form a frogspawn-like jelly, which could be put into inflamed eyes to sooth them.

COMFREY (*Symphytum officinale*) is a bushy perennial that likes damp conditions (right). It has bristly, spear-shaped leaves and pink-purple flowers hanging in clusters like bells, although a white version, taken to New England in the seventeenth century, went native. Its alternative names of 'knitbone' and 'bone-set' reflected its use as a poultice for sprains, bruises and abrasions (it contains allantoin, which promotes healing in connective tissues). In spring the roots were lifted and grated, to be spread over the affected part. Gerard also recommended that the slimy substance from the root could be made into a posset of ale to relieve back pain.

Cuckoo pint (*Arum maculatum*) enjoys a huge number of other names, including 'lords-and-ladies' and 'Jack-in-the-pulpit'. For Hannah Wolley, the leaves could be added to rose water to cleanse the face. For Gerard the roots made a clear white starch, though he warned that they could blister the hands. The roots, baked and ground, could also provide a form of arrowroot under the name of 'Portland sago'.

Dyer's greenweed (*Genista tinctoria*) resembles broom, with bright yellow flowers. As its name suggests, it was used as a dye, providing the yellow base for a green cloth: an alternative name is 'woadwise', reflecting the addition of the blue of woad. Taken by early colonists to America, it was described by John Josselyn in his 1672 *New-Englands Rarities Discovered* as

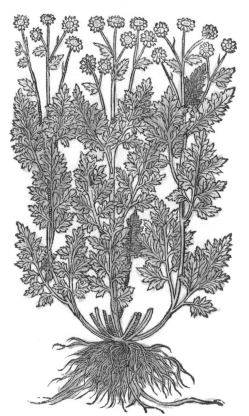

'Woodwax, wherewith they dye many pretty Colours'. For the cloth industry in Gloucestershire poor women, known as wood-waxers, harvested the wild crop by pulling the plant up by the roots.

Fennel (*Fœniculum vulgare*) Medicinal qualities were attributed to the roots, leaves and seeds. Gerard credited the bulb-like root as a prime opening remedy: 'The decoction of Fennell drunke easeth the paines of the kidneis, causeth one to avoideth the stone and provoketh urine.' It was also used in drinks and broths. The feathery leaves of the cultivated form are sweet, tasting like aniseed, and highly decorative, so were used in garlands and flower arrangements.

FEVERFEW (*Chrysanthemum parthenium*) has little white flowers with yellow centres, which may be why it is sometimes known as bachelor's buttons (see opposite). The herb was introduced into England from the Balkans in the Middle Ages. When the golden green leaves, pungent and bitter in taste, were made into a syrup it was used as a remedy not only for fighting fever, but also to treat headaches and depression. Feverfew's reputation as 'the aspirin of the herbal era' has been upheld in modern times, as it is believed to be efficacious in treating migraine.

GOOD KING HENRY (*Chenopodium bonus-henricus*) has tall spire-like flowers of greenish yellow, and triangular leaves (right) rather like spinach, which it resembles in taste: Culpeper in fact found it tastier. It served as a very useful pot herb in pottages, with its glaucous texture: the names of its close relations, 'fat hen' and 'lamb's quarters' reflect this use in place of meat. It was used medicinally to treat scurvy.

GREATER CELANDINE (*Chelidonium majus*) with its bright yellow flowers is from the poppy family, and not related to the lesser celandine. It derives its name from *chelidon*, the Greek for swallow, and Gerard describes it as the swallow-wort, which was the name adopted in New England when it was taken there by men and women from the West Country. Like the poppy, celandine exudes a latex, which was used in the seventeenth century for various eye conditions, often in conjunction with the daisy, or 'day's eye'.

HEMP (*Cannabis sativa*) provided the fibre that was one of the main sources of clothing and household linen in the seventeenth century. But it was the medicinal uses of the plant upon which Culpeper concentrated, for its narcotic qualities were known ever since it arrived in England from the Middle East. Culpeper noted that the seeds could be used as a remedy against jaundice, ague and diarrhoea. A decoction from the roots was employed against gout and pains in the joints, while fresh root mixed with oil and butter could be applied to burns.

HOUSELEEK (*Sempervivum tectorum*) is a native of mountainous regions of Europe. Its name *tectorum* is thought to have derived from the Norse god Thor, and it was traditionally grown on roofs as a magical protection against lightning, especially on thatch. The sap from the thick succulent leaves was made into a cooling ointment to treat scalds and burns, ulcers and severe headaches. Culpeper also recommended rubbing the leaves onto stings from bees and from nettles to assuage the pain.

HYSSOP (*Hyssopus officinalis*) This pretty herb was brought to England from southern Europe. It is a shrubby plant, about 18 inches to 2 feet in height, with long, dark green leaves and royal blue flowers that blossom from midsummer through to autumn. Both the leaves and the flowers have traditionally been used in medicines, producing a flavour that is slightly bitter, rather like rue.

LAVENDER (*Lavandula angustifolia*), with its pale purple flowers and narrow grey leaves, was introduced into English gardens from France and Spain. It is thought that the name is derived from the Latin *lavare*, to wash, as it has always been used in infusions. Herbals and recipe books sometimes refer to 'spike' (*L. latifolia*) and 'French' (*L. stoechas*). Lavender is a 'hot herb', because the flowers have time to mature through spring into summer, so that the extracted oil is powerful in its effect. Gerard warned against 'divers rash and overbold Apothecaries, and other foolish women', who made it too strong. The antiseptic quality of lavender made it an effective strewing herb, while its pretty flowers were used in sweet bags and potpourris (right).

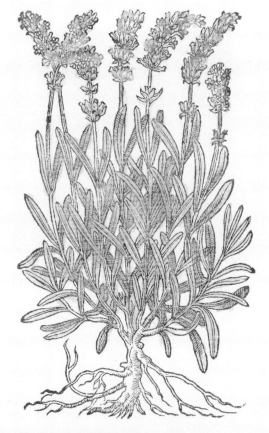

LESSER CELANDINE (*Ranunculus ficaria*), with its shiny yellow flowers, is a member of the buttercup family, and not related to the greater celandine. An alternative name is 'pilewort', for according to the doctrine of signatures the knobbly root tubers resemble piles, and therefore it was given as treatment for them. Culpeper advised that, made into an oil, ointment or plaster, it not only cured haemorrhoids, but also the king's evil with its tubercular tumours.

MADDER (*Rubia tinctorum*) has been cultivated in England from at least the Anglo-Saxon period. It is a climbing plant with evergreen leaves and small yellow flowers, followed by reddish black berries. Its long roots are the source of dyes known as rose madder and Turkey red, harvested after two years. Culpeper recommended that the root was also used to treat jaundice, sciatica and bruises, while the leaves could treat freckles and other discolorations of the skin.

MARIGOLD is the name given to two distinct plants. The first, an early introduction from western Asia, *Chrysanthemum segetum*, is the corn marigold, once prevalent and regarded as a nuisance in cornfields. With its lovely yellow flowers, it featured among the plants in celebrations for St John's Eve. The second, *Calendula officinalis*, is the pot marigold, probably a native of southern Europe (left). Gerard described it as 'something sweete, with a certain strong smell, of a light saffron colour, or like pure golde'. The petals were used in broths and soups, and Gerard thought they could comfort and strengthen the heart. Fresh or dried, they were used as a cheaper substitute for saffron in cooking.

MARSH MALLOW (*Althaea officinalis*) has velvety grey leaves and pink flowers. Culpeper described how the roots of this member of the mallow family were dug up from salt marshes and infused in water to produce a sweet-tasting jelly, which became the basis for the confectionery. For Culpeper, however, the roots and leaves were an ingredient of the all-important 'opening herbs' that provided relief for a long list of medical conditions, including the cure of wounds and 'to ease pains in any part of the body'.

MAIDENHAIR FERN (*Adiantum capillus-veneris*) has beautiful fan-shaped leaflets on black wiry stalks (opposite). Culpeper considered the plant a gentle diuretic, and therefore a remedy for jaundice and kidney complaints, while the Duchess of Lauderdale noted it as an ingredient in a herbal tea to treat consumption. Given its name, it is not surprising that it features in recipes to strengthen the hair.

MEADOWSWEET (*Filipendula ulmaria*) has white flowers which give off a sweet scent that some find over-powering. Its name comes from neither the meadow nor sweet, but rather from its use to flavour the honey drink mead. It was much used as a strewing herb because of its sweet scent, and an alternative name is 'bride wort', as it was traditionally strewn on the floor of churches for weddings.

MINT comes in a variety of species. Culpeper listed Water Mint (*Mentha aquatica*), Garden Mint (*M. viridis*), Peppermint (*M. piperita*) and Spearmint (*M. spiccata*), along with their medicinal purposes. The herb appears comparatively rarely in seventeenth-century culinary recipes: the green garden pea had yet to have its day. For Gerard the practical strength of mint was as a strewing herb: 'The savour or smell of the water Mint rejoiceth the hart of man, for which cause they strowe it in chambers and places of recreation, pleasure and repose, and where feasts and banquets are made.' Not least of mint's virtues was that mice disliked it.

MUGWORT (*Artemesia vulgaris*) is thought to have acquired its rather ugly name from 'midge' wort, as it was an effective repellent to midges, and to other nuisances such as fleas. Its rather more attractive name was *Mater Herbarum*, the 'Mother of Herbs', as it was traditionally used to remedy female disorders. Culpeper not surprisingly attributed mugwort to Venus, hastening delivery and a remedy against inflammation in childbirth. It is a tall plant, over 4 feet in height, with deeply cut leaves and little yellow flowers that Culpeper described as 'chaffy', like ears of wheat. All parts of the plant could be used medicinally. Along with

St John's wort (see p. 125), it was smoked and purified in bonfires on St John's Eve, 23 June, and garlands were hung on doors to keep off the powers of evil.

ORPINE (*Sedum telephium*) has as alternative names 'livelong', because of its lasting qualities, which made it a useful plant for flower arrangements, and 'midsummer men', as it was one of the plants used to decorate houses and streets on the eve of the festival of St John the Baptist (left). John Aubrey recounted how maidservants would place two sprigs of orpine into holes in joists, to divine the course of their courtships: whether the sprigs inclined to each other, moved apart, or withered and died.

PARSLEY (*Petroselinum sativum*) was in the seventeenth century, as it still is, one of the principal pot herbs for the kitchen. Its sweet taste went particularly well with 'white meats' such as rabbit and poultry. For Gerard it was an 'opening herb', with the leaves 'singular good to take away stoppings, and to provoke urine' while the roots 'do notably performe if they be boiled in broth; they be also delightfull to taste, and agreeable to the stomacke'. This was garden parsley, but both Gerard and Culpeper also mention Parsley Piert and Parsley Breakstone, which grew wild and bore a resemblance. These were brought to market by herb-women as a remedy for stones in the kidneys and bladder.

PELLITORY OF SPAIN (*Anacyclus pyrethrum*), as its name suggests, originated from the Mediterranean. It has a flower like a daisy, so an alternative name is 'Mount Atlas daisy'. Like its namesake 'of the wall' (see below), its pungent root was recommended by Culpeper for the relief of toothache by being chewed. He also advised that the root and leaves, if powdered, could be stuffed up the nostrils to cause sneezing and thus cure a headache and lethargy.

PELLITORY OF THE WALL (*Parietaria judaica*) particularly favours stone walls, and in fact the *Parietaria* part of its name is from the Latin for 'wall'. Because of this habitat, through the doctrine of signatures, it is traditionally associated with the treatment of stones in the kidneys and bladder, common ailments in the seventeenth century. In addition, Culpeper recommended it for a whole range of other problems, from sore throats to a skin cleanser and to relieve toothache.

PENNYROYAL (*Mentha pulegium*) is a small, creeping species of mint with pungent leaves and small purple flowers. Bullein selected it to illustrate in his medical book as it was considered one of the major healing plants, and herb-women brought large quantities to sell pennyroyal in London's markets. With its sedative qualities it was used to help in birth delivery, and as a syrup to ease whooping cough and sore throats. It was used to deter fleas, as suggested by its binominal name.

PLANTAIN (*Plantago major*). A ubiquitous plant, to be found in paths, lawns to the annoyance of gardeners, and grassland (left). In the seventeenth century, it was an important healing herb, used to cure ulcers, wounds and burns with its elastic and resilient leaves, and was added to baths. It was one of the group of plants featured in celebrations on the eve of St John's Day.

ROSEMARY (*Rosmarinus officinalis*), with its pointed aromatic leaves, was one of the principal pot herbs in the seventeenth century, used in dishes for every course of dinner. Distilled, the flowers of blue or white were the main ingredient of Hungary water, a predecessor of eau de cologne. Sprigs were picked for cleaning teeth, and it was used in 'bathings'. Traditionally it was associated with the Virgin Mary: one legend was that she hung her linen to dry on the bush, giving the herb its distinctive fragrance; another that her blue cloak turned the white flowers into blue.

RUE (*Ruta graveolens*), with its blue-green leaves, was described by Gerard as having 'a very strong and ranke smell, and a biting taste', enjoying sunny and open spaces and prospering in rough ground (opposite). An alternative name for rue was 'herb of grace', referring to its use in exorcisms, when a bunch was added to holy water. With its anti-spasmodic properties, it was recommended by both Gerard and Culpeper for a whole range of medical

problems. Despite its bitterness, it has
been used in cooking, added to eggs,
cheese and fish.

SAGE (*Salvia officinalis*) is a member
of the extensive salvia family. Its
very name indicates its importance
as a medicinal herb, from the Latin
salvere, to save. Originating from
the north Mediterranean, it was
introduced into English gardens in
the Middle Ages and used as one
of the principal culinary herbs.
Seventeenth-century recipes often
stipulate red sage, to which Gerard
attributed the Galenic qualities of
hot and dry, and thus 'stoppeth the
flux, expelleth winde, drieth the
dropsie, helpeth the palsie, strengtheneth the sinewes, and cleanseth
the blood'. He also strongly recommended sage ale.

ST JOHN'S WORT (*Hypericum perforatum*) is a perennial with golden yellow
flowers from June to September (see overleaf). The stems yield a blood-red
juice that was associated in medieval times with the beheading of St John
the Baptist, hence the plant's name. *Perforatum* comes from the translucent
dots that speckles the leaves: these resemble tiny holes when the leaves are
put to the light, so the plant was considered sympathetic for the treatment
of wounds. It was one of the key plants in the festivities at midsummer,
carried in torchlight processions and burnt to purify communities. This
was probably a pagan celebration that was adopted by the Church, for the

feast of St John takes place on 24 June. A traditional recipe was to take the flowers and stems and put them on a windowsill in water, until the sun turned the liquid red, and the so-called blood of St John could then be used to treat skin complaints.

SOAPWORT (*Saponaria officinalis*) is a relation of the pink, as can be seen in its pretty little flowers. The crushed leaves boiled in water will produce a lather, so have been used for centuries for washing delicate textiles. Although Gerard regarded it simply as an ornament to the garden, Culpeper advised that it cured French Pox, and in North America its leaves and roots were applied to the rash caused by poison ivy. With its fragrance, it was used as a strewing herb.

SWEET CICELY (*Myrrhis odorata*) is an umbelliferous perennial with creamy-white flowers that resemble cow parsley. Culpeper recommended candying the roots to prevent infection from the plague, while Gerard wrote that the leaves, with their aniseed taste, were good in salads. In the Lake District the seeds were used both in puddings and as a polish for furniture.

SWEET FLAG or CALAMUS AROMATICUS (*Acorus calamus*) was introduced from Turkey into Western Europe in 1567 and planted in water gardens. The root in particular gives a scent resembling orange peel, warm and pungent, so was used for strewing, scenting wall hangings and clothes and as an ingredient of sweet bags.

SWEET GALE (*Myrica gale*), also known as bog myrtle, is a shrub of wet, acid moorland that emits a balsamic fragrance, especially when it is in flower. It was used to make candles, with the wax constituents melted off the berries and leaves and added to aromatic resins, hence an alternative name of 'candleberry'. A versatile plant, it has also been used to scent linen, drive away moths and fleas, act as an insect repellent, provide a yellow dye and to flavour ale.

SWEET MARJORAM (*Origanum majorana*) is a native of the Mediterranean, but brought to England in the Middle Ages it could survive winter in gardens if given protection. Gerard described it as 'a lowe and shrubbie

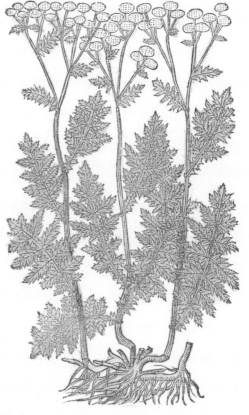

plant, of a whitish colour and marvellous sweete smell, a foote or somewhat more high … The flowers grow at the top in scalie or chaffie [wheat-like] spiked eares of a white colour'. Its sweet smell, combined with anaesthetic properties, made it a favourite for nosegays for officials to carry against infections and the general smell of crowds. Gerard went on to recommend sweet marjoram for 'odiferous ointments, waters, powders, broths and meates', and as an oil, for treating cramps and aches.

TANSY (*Tanacetum vulgare*) has bright yellow flowers (right). Its ferny, aromatic leaves are so bitter that they were traditionally eaten at Easter to kill 'phlegm and worms' acquired as the result of the Lenten diet of fish. The herb is particularly associated with eggs, and Pepys and his contemporaries referred to a dish like a herb omelette as a 'Tansie'.

THYME (*Thymus vulgaris*) has long been one of the principal pot herbs used in cooking, often being included in faggots of sweet herbs, the seventeenth-century equivalent of the bouquet garni. There are many species of thyme, all containing the volatile oil thymol, which can be used as an antiseptic, so along with sweet marjoram it has been a traditional element of nosegays carried by dignitaries to ward off infectious diseases. Culpeper recommended its use as a strengthener of the lungs, to help women in childbirth, and for those afflicted by gout. 'The herb taken inwardly, comforts the stomach much, and expels wind.'

TORMENTIL (*Potentilla erecta*) is a low-growing perennial with small, four-petalled flowers, found on moors and heaths. Its name is derived from the Latin, *tormina*, and explains its medicinal use. The woody, astringent roots were traditionally boiled in milk and given to calves and children as a remedy against the torments of colic.

WELD (*Reseda luteola*) has spires of feathery flowers of a yellowish green. Also known as dyer's rocket, it gives a brilliant and fast yellow colour. Geoffrey Chaucer mentions it in one of his poems alongside rose madder and woad as the three staple dyestuffs of the Middle Ages. In the seventeenth century it was cultivated as a crop in fields in eastern England from Kent, through Essex, Cambridgeshire and Lincolnshire, up to Yorkshire.

WOAD (*Isatis tinctoria*) is a member of the cabbage family, a tall plant with shiny blue-green leaves and clusters of delicate yellow flowers (opposite). The leaves, crushed to pulp in a mill and moulded into balls, were dried in the sun and allowed to ferment before being pulped again and formed into cakes to produce blue dye. Gerard described this process as 'profitable to some few, and hurtful to many', referring to the unpleasant side effects of the industry. Woad was also used medicinally, with Culpeper recommending it as an ointment to cool inflammation.

WOODRUFF (*Galium odoratum*), also known as sweet grass, has tiny, pin-like white flowers on upright stems adorned by ruff-like leaves. The sweetness comes when the plants are picked and dried, producing a scent like hay that has been freshly mown, which is retained for several months. In the seventeenth century bunches were placed in clothes presses to give scent and to deter moths, as well as being strewn on the floor and pressed between pages of books.

WORMWOOD (*Artemisia absinthium*) Gerard described wormwood as having 'leaves of grayish colour, very much cut or jagged'. The bitter, pungent taste made it an ideal deterrent of fleas and moths, so it was much used in the clothes press and in strewing herbs. As the name suggests, it was used to cure worms, as well as an antidote against the consumption of harmful fungi. It has traditionally been used in the preparation of aperitifs and wines, such as vermouth and absinthe.

An index of the booke of Simples.

Parcelie.   **Planten.**   **Peniroyall.**

Rose.   **Sage.**   **Chicorie.**

Houſleke.   **Alkakengi.**   **Tilia.**

Health & Beauty

It shall be good also for necessity sake (for it concerneth the Good
Huswife to know manie remedies for diseases …) to shape out certain
beds for Physick hearbes.

Gervase Markham, *The English Huswife*

I
N SEVENTEENTH-CENTURY HOUSEHOLD MANUALS, recipes for
succulent roasts, ingenious salads and luscious desserts appear alongside those for remedies for ailments of all kinds, major and minor.
These serve as a sharp reminder of the perils that afflicted people's health,
and occasionally reflect the troubled times. As Markham makes clear, it
was often the housewife who was responsible for maintaining the health
of her family, using physic herbs – those with medicinal properties – as
ingredients for her remedies and ointments.

There were, of course, men who had received some medical training:
physicians and surgeons, and apothecaries who supplied them with their
medicines and potions. The physicians were regulated by the Royal
College of Physicians that had been established in 1518 when Henry VIII
issued a charter at the instigation of his doctor, Thomas Linacre. Licences

Images of some of the most useful medicinal herbs from *A Bulwarke of Defence Againste all
Sicknes, Sornes and Woundes* by the physician William Bullein, published in 1562. On this
page are shown two 'opening roots', parsley and pennyroyal, along with plantain and
houseleek, used in poultices.

were given to physicians to administer medicine and oversee internal health.

Anyone applying for such a licence had to have studied at either Oxford or Cambridge, where the training was in the principles of Galen, a Greek physician from the second century BCE. Galen derived his theory from Aristotle, who believed that the universe was made up of four elements: fire, air, water and earth. Each element had two of four primary qualities, giving the possible combinations of hot and dry (fire), hot and moist (air), cold and moist (water), and cold and dry (earth). One quality dominated in each combination, giving the four cardinal humours associated with the principal fluids of the body: blood, phlegm, choler and melancholy.

Herbals, such as those by Gerard and Culpeper, listed the 'virtues' of the different plants that could restore the balance of these humours, and physicians were particularly concerned to purge the body through bleeding and the application of enemas and irritant plasters. Some physicians also embraced the ideas of a Swiss physician, who went by the splendid name of Philip Theophrastus Bombast von Hohenheim. He had rejected the pathology based on humours, and instead taught that ailments arose from the seeds of disease agents settling in a particular site in the body. If something went wrong with an organ, the fault lay with that organ, not humours. He applied chemistry to medical theory, asserting that no disease was beyond cure. By the time of his death in 1541, his theory had been given his nickname, Paracelsus. He also developed the ancient concept of the doctrine of signatures, the idea that the curative benefit of a plant might be deduced from its form or appearance. An example of this was eyebright, which through its appearance looked like eyes and therefore might be used to treat eye infections, while lungwort had the colour and shape of lungs and thus was a remedy for problems with breathing.

It is estimated that between twenty and forty physicians were granted licences in the sixteenth century. In addition, there were around a hundred men who were part of the London Company of Barber-Surgeons, looking after the tending of wounds, amputations and external operations. The herbalist John Gerard was a barber surgeon, serving as master, and supervising the garden attached to their hall in the City. Although the Annals kept by the Royal College of Physicians show that the number of doctors granted licences grew during the seventeenth century, it remained small. In 1700 there were only 136 doctors in London, serving a population of about 600,000, being supplied with medicines and ointments by about 400 apothecaries. Outside the capital the proportion of 'professional' medical practitioners compared to population was even more unbalanced.

It was probably this limited number that caused Henry VIII's government to pass an act in 1543 allowing those experienced in the nature of herbs, roots and waters to practise and use them as a gesture of Christian charity, the so-called Quack's Act. The people so permitted formed an eclectic group: lawyers and clergymen, opportunists, and of course women, who for centuries had adopted the unofficial role of healers. These were dubbed 'empiricks'. Deborah Harkness, in her study of Elizabethan London, gives us some examples: a midwife going to a Frenchman, Matthew Desilar, a silk weaver, to be treated for heart pain; Mrs Barker of Newgate Street seeking out treatment for a chronic cough from Alice Skeres, wife of a merchant; a clergyman, Henry Holland, tending to the medical problems of his family and of the poor of his parish.[1]

The ad hoc arrangement infuriated the medical establishment. William Clowes, an ambitious surgeon, summed this up in intemperate terms, listing a whole raft of tradesmen who had turned to healing: '[quacks] who doe forsake their honest trades, whereunto God hath called them, & do daily rush into Physicke & Chirurgerie. And some of them Painters, some Glasiers, some Tailors, some Wevers, some Joiners, some Cutlers, some Cookes, some Bakers & some Chandlers', and so the list continued. His ire was also turned on women, 'bawds and witches' in town and country, 'having no more perseverance, reason, or knowledge of this art then a goose'.[2]

The Royal College of Physicians summoned 'empiricks' before their court for administering medicine and giving advice. One interesting case was a poor woman, Margaret Kennix, who was accused of supplying her friends and neighbours with herbal remedies. Elizabeth I made a personal intervention, instructing her secretary of state, Sir Francis Walsingham, to order the College to leave the woman in peace, as God had given her 'especial knowledge'. The queen also noted that Margaret's husband was unable to work, and thus the family was dependent on the exercise of her skill. Although the College bowed to this authority, a note was added in their Annals that 'the woman's weakness and insufficiency is such as is rather to be pitied of all, then either envied of us or maintained of others'.[3] A fine example of having the last word.

A much more positive attitude was shown towards gentlemen and gentlewomen who made up their own medicines and dispensed them to the local community. Given the few doctors and apothecaries there were outside towns and cities, these services were often vital. Correspondence from the seventeenth century shows how fathers and husbands wrote about the health and ailments, and subsequent treatment, of their families, of dependants and of their neighbours. Medicinal manuscripts of recipes have survived, sometimes with abbreviated Latin as if compiled from notes of physicians and apothecaries. There are so many of these that one historian has, aptly, referred to a 'recipe fever'.[4]

A gentlewoman who provided medical care was Lady Margaret Hoby. Among reiterations of prayers and Bible readings in her diary are notes of this care provided to her neighbours. For example, for 17 September 1599 she records 'after private prayer, I saw a mans Legg dressd'. This suggests that somebody else was doing it, either for her instruction or that she was doing the instructing. Other diary references show that she helped women in childbirth and, unusually, performed operations.[5]

Another provider of healthcare was Lady Grace Mildmay. Born at Lacock Manor in Wiltshire around the year 1552, she married Anthony

Mildmay and set up home at Apethorpe Manor in Northamptonshire. In her autobiography she explained how her governess had 'good knowledge in physic and surgery' and 'set me to read Dr Turner's herbal and in Bartholomew Vigoe'. Turner's herbal, published in three parts from 1551 to 1568, was the first authoritative reference book of its kind in English, while John Vigoe's book on surgery was translated by Bartholomew Traheson in 1543. Once married, Grace described how 'Every day I spent some time in the herbal and books of physic and in ministering to one or other by the directions of the best physicians of mine acquaintance.'[6]

Her garden at Apethorpe provided her with a very wide range of herbs. Just as Turner, and later Gerard and Culpeper, noted the parts of the body that were to be treated with certain herbs and flowers, so too did Grace. For example, she noted for treatment of the heart and arteries seven herbs, including *Carduus benedictus*, the 'blessed thistle'. Shakespeare in *Much Ado About Nothing* has Hero's maid suggesting she lays a distillation of the herb against her heart to remedy a qualm, providing him with the opportunity to make a pun on Beatrice and Benedict.

Grace Mildmay's recipes, which are exclusively medicinal, were put not into a book, but on separate sheets, bequeathed to her daughter: 270 have survived, although there were more. She would appear to have received these recipes from a group of London physicians, maintaining correspondence with them, and collaborating with other healers in the course of treatments. The inventory of her still room gives an idea of the scale of her enterprise, with twenty-one large bottles of cordials, oils and waters, along with shelves of pills and powders. We also know the amounts of money that Grace expended: a cordial water would have cost over £2 to make, with all the requisite exotic ingredients. A bill for such expensive ingredients has survived in the archives of the Duchess of Lauderdale: a few ounces of musk, civet, bezoin, storax, cloves and amber cost her over £10.

Grace Mildmay and the Duchess were both women of means. Most housewives, whether in rural or urban communities, would have used recipes handed down to them orally by their mothers and other members of the family, or, if they could read, would have used printed herbals for reference to the plants that they might use from their gardens as ingredients for their medicines and ointments. As noted earlier, the two English herbals most widely used in a domestic context in the seventeenth century were those of John Gerard and Nicholas Culpeper. Gerard's *Herball or Generall Historie of Plantes* was first published in 1597, with an updated and emended edition produced in 1636 by a London apothecary, Thomas Johnson. With its many woodcuts, it was an expensive book, only affordable to the wealthy. Its value to the household is reflected by the fact that it was left by women in their wills to their daughters, a status comparable to that of the family Bible. Two women even chose to depict it in their portraits. Lady Anne Clifford's *The Great Picture*, attributed to Jan van Belcamp, where she shows the formative books of her youth, has her 'Epitome', her extract of the herbal, alongside such literary works as Sir Philip Sidney's *Arcadia* and the poems of Edmund Spenser. Susan, the second wife of the keen gardener Sir Thomas Hanmer, had her portrait painted with a copy of the herbal open on a stand in front of her.[7]

Culpeper's herbal presents a total contrast. First published in 1652 as *The English Physitian*, it carried a note on the original title page of a price of three pence, to prevent booksellers charging more. It was not illustrated, but in accessible language the apothecary Culpeper provided an invaluable resource, clearly laid out alphabetically, with location, cultivation and medicinal uses for housewives. In so doing, he was challenging the Royal College of Physicians, which for many years had been working on a pharmacopoeia or dispensary of prescriptions, to be dispensed by apothecaries in their shops. In order to keep this knowledge from the public, the physicians' committee decided to produce the list in Latin, which was strongly opposed by apothecaries partly because they were not always firmly grounded in the classics, but also because they felt they knew more about the ingredients of many medicines. Culpeper incurred

Portrait of Susan, second wife of the florist Sir Thomas Hanmer, by an unknown artist. She chose to be depicted reading a copy of Gerard's *Herball*.

the fury of the College when he produced his herbal, but as his biographer later pointed out: 'To the poor he prescribed cheap but wholesome Medicines; not removing, as many in our times do, the Consumption out of their Bodies into their Purses; not sending them to the *East Indies* for Drugs, when they may fetch better out of their own Gardens.'⁸ The medicine chest had been unlocked and its secrets revealed for lay people.

The range of plants used in this way in the seventeenth century was very wide, but some were considered to be particularly useful. We get an idea of these from the illustrations that were chosen for reproduction in a book by the Tudor physician William Bullein, *A Bulwarke of Defence Againste all Sicknes, Sornes and Woundes*, first published in 1562. The first part, a *Boke of Simples*, emphasizes the importance of the garden in the form of a dialogue between Mercellus, a gardener, and Hillarius, a physician. Hilarius gives the virtues of a long list of plants, from herbs and flowers, through to fruit, vegetables and trees, and even touching on minerals and animals. At the end of this section, Bullein's 'short list' of illustrated plants includes: the rose and lavender, the basis of oils; the houseleek and the plantain, used in poultices; the multi-purpose herbs, parsley, pennyroyal and hyssop; and the narcotic, 'great nightshade'.

Recipe books, both printed and in manuscript, often make mention of 'opening roots'. Ann Fanshawe picks out pennyroyal, rue, wormwood, red sage and lavender, while Mary Doggett refers to opium, fennel, asparagus and parsley. John Gerard ascribes to all of these the virtues of purgatives and cleansing, quoting the Galenic humour that was hot and dry. Of sage, he advises that it 'stoppeth the fluxe thereof incontinently, expelleth winde, drieth the dropsie, helpeth the palsie, strengtheneth the sinews, and cleanses the blood'. Fennel he describes as 'very good for the lungs, the liver, and the kidneis, for it openeth the obstructions or stoppings of the same, and comforteth the inward parts'. Parsley in all its forms, according to Culpeper, is under Mars and a strong decoction of the roots a powerful diuretic, assisting in removing obstructions of the bowels.[9]

Among the physic herbs picked out by Markham for the housewife's garden is *Nicotiana*, the tobacco plant In his herbal, Gerard provided an exceptionally long list of the medicinal applications, with the leaves as a remedy against migraine and for 'a cold stomach', especially in children. The juice, applied with a cloth, was recommended by both Gerard and Culpeper for the relief of toothache. Ralph Josselin, an Essex clergyman, farmer and schoolteacher, is particularly informative in his diary about the medical ailments that afflicted his family and the community. So painful was the toothache experienced by his wife that he recorded that she felt she had been brought, as it were, to death's door until she got relief from tobacco juice.

Tobacco was also taken internally as a purge, but Gerard issued a health warning, that those who inhaled the smoke from the dried leaves in a pipe might experience hard knots in their system. He felt that a syrup was better than 'this smokie medicine'. A recipe for such a syrup was included in Elinor Fettiplace's book of receipts, with the note that it had come from Sir Walter Raleigh, a distant relative who had set up a still room in the Tower of London during his long imprisonment there.

Take a quart of water & three ounces of tobaccho, put the tobaccho in the water, & let it lie a night & day close covered, then boile it from a quart to a pinte, then straine it, & put to everie pint a pound of sugar, then put in the whites of three or fowre eggs finelie beaten, then set it on the fire, & when it boiles, scum it, then cover it close, & let it boile, till it bee serop.[10]

The remedies quoted above are all 'simples', using one medicinal ingredient. The first part of Bullein's book consists of simples, while the last part looks at 'compounds', recipes with several ingredients. Some medicinal recipes can include over twenty plants from the garden and the hedgerow, and it is a tribute to the good housewife that she could muster these. Other products from the garden could also be brought into play. Earthworms would be roasted and ground to be applied to gums to counter scurvy, which suggests that they were thought to provide much-needed vitamins. With their viscous quality, they could also be added to lesser celandine, or pilewort, in the treatment of haemorrhoids, as one of its names suggests, and to relieve joint pains.

SARAH JINNER'S SNAIL WATER
Take a pottle of Snails and wash them well in 2 or 3 waters, and then in Small Beer, bruise them, shells and all, then put them into a gallon of Red-cows milk, Red rose leaves dryed, the whites cut off Rosemary, sweet Marjoram, of each one handful, and distil them in a cold still, and let it drop upon powder or white sugar-candy.

A combination of worms and snails appears in a recipe provided to the Duchess of Lauderdale. The worms were washed and then opened up with a sharp bodkin to clean them 'of all filth'. This process may strike the modern reader as unpleasant, but the duchess and her ladies were made of sterner stuff. They added the cleaned worms to snails that had had their shells removed, barberry bark, saffron and brandy, and the mixture was left to steep overnight. The following morning more brandy was added before distilling with the addition of angelica, wormwood and rue, ivy, hartshorn and sorrel roots, and lastly ground turmeric.

'Snail Water' appears in many recipe books, such as the one reproduced on the previous page.[11] The patient should drink this decoction first thing in the morning and last thing at night, and at four o'clock in the afternoon, a wine glass at a time. It was noted that this recipe was particularly good for 'weak children and old people', a reminder that housewives had the care of their family from cradle to the grave.

Beginning even before the cradle, the failure to conceive came under scrutiny. The first entry in Samuel Pepys's diary, for 1 January 1660, recorded not only the arrival of General Monck and his troops in London as a prelude to Charles II's restoration, but also the arrival of Elizabeth Pepys's menstrual period. The hope that they might have children was dashed yet again. Pepys also records consulting 'gossips' about remedies. Ten suggestions were provided, from wearing drawers of Holland linen, thought to be cooling, to drinking sage juice. William Bullein recommended just such a drink for conception, but in the case of Pepys it did not prove effective, for he had undergone an operation to remove a stone from his bladder, which had probably rendered him infertile.

Although Elizabeth and Samuel missed out on the joys of children, they also avoided the attendant perils, as reflected in the diary of Ralph Josselin. He and his wife Jane had ten children in all, but with each pregnancy he expresses both his own fears for his wife and hers that she would not survive the birth. They had good reason to fear, for it is estimated that in the first half of the seventeenth century, deaths in childbirth lay between 125 and 158 per 1,000, dropping very slightly in the second half, to between 118 and 147 per 1,000. Wealth for once did not favour, for aristocratic and gentlewomen usually put their babies out to wet nurses, resulting in shorter periods between pregnancies, and constant childbearing often caused debilitation. Ann Fanshawe, for instance, had a child every year from 1645 to 1656, then a break of four years, with miscarriages, followed by two more children, making a total of thirteen births and three miscarriages. Ann lived to fifty-five, but it is thought that around a

Mugwort was one of the important plants for helping in childbirth and for female disorders. Gerard suggested the mother should sit in a bath of boiled leaves, or drink a concoction of the tender tops.

quarter of aristocratic women died before fifty from complications of childbirth.

Mugwort and betony were considered key herbs for helping with childbirth. Mugwort is an *Artemisia*, a relation of wormwood and sharing its strongly aromatic qualities. Culpeper, unsurprisingly, attributed it to Venus, recommending mugwort for hastening delivery and as a remedy against inflammation in childbirth. Sarah Jinner in her almanacs provided recipes for helping women in childbirth, remarkable in itself, for this kind of advice was excised from many herbals and medicinal books of the period. One of her recipes 'to provoke the terms', speeding up labour, recommends a syrup of mugwort and betony, to which a decoction of betony and hyssop had been added.[12] Mugwort is not a very attractive plant, growing up to 4 feet in height, with a fondness for spreading along the sides of paths or roads so that it can look dusty and bedraggled. However, women have long recognized its efficacy, keeping a bed of it in the garden, and there are references to the issuing of strict instructions that the plants should not be pulled up by a tidy-minded gardener. The other 'heal all' for female disorders, betony, is a member of the dead-nettle family, with elegant rose lavender flowers which are attractive to bees.

Flowers and herbs traditionally associated with the Virgin Mary – lilies, roses, columbines, marjoram and rosemary – were often included in recipes to help in childbirth. Once the child was born, a reviving water might be offered, such as this highly complex recipe: 'Take 4 gallons Strong Ale, 5oz of Anniseeds, Liquorish scraped half a pound; of sweet Mints, Angelica, Betony, Cowslip Flowers, Sage and Rosemary flowers, sweet Marjoram of each three handfuls, Pellitory of the Wall one handful.' This mixture was distilled and added to cinnamon, fennel seeds, juniper berries, buds of red roses, roasted apples and dates, and distilled again. Precious ingredients, such as ambergris, pearl, and even gold leaf, were put in a linen bag, and hung in the water.[13]

The mother, and her child, might survive the rigours of the actual birth, but there were plenty of perils ahead for young children. A theme in Josselin's diary is concern for the survival of his children, who seemed constantly to fall into the fire, only to be rescued by vigilant siblings. Salves for scalds and burns were made up from animal fat, often combined with animal dung. A typical example of this combination is a recipe 'For a burning or scalding, or any green wound'. This takes mutton suet and sheep's dung boiled with the inward bark of the elder tree, strained and then placed in the wound or burn, when, according to the recipe, it would heal without fear.[14] Recipes have dung from a variety of animals, including deer, pigs and geese. The theory behind this ingredient would seem to be that the putrefaction brought new life, and thus healing.

The garden would be raided for the herbs for these salves. The greater plantain, selected by Bullein for an illustration, has elastic, resilient leaves that herbalists, with their concept of 'sympathetic remedies', identified as good for the treatment of wounds and ulcers. In fact, the leaves contain tannins and astringent chemicals, which, when they are crushed, can be applied to small cuts and to give relief from nettle stings in the absence of dock leaves.

With their strong herbal content, these salves were sometimes known as green ointments. One example from a later seventeenth-century manuscript book claims it was good 'for all Bruises, paines in the limbs, Blasts, red swellings either in the face or other partes, for cold got in the breast or limbe'. It contains no fewer than thirty-three herbs and flowers, which the author recommended should be gathered in the heat of the day, in full sunshine or before four o'clock in the afternoon. One of the herbs was self-heal, a form of bugle, described by Culpeper as under Venus, used for syrups for 'inward' wounds, and in unguents and plasters for wounds that were 'outward'.[15]

A rather less elaborate recipe, using bay, wormwood, red sage and rue, specifies it should be made up in May. Again, the herbs should be picked in the heat of the day and cleaned but not washed. Once the herb mixture was ground in a mortar to make a green sauce it was added to finely shredded suet of a freshly killed sheep, and olive oil. The mixture should be worked by hand until it became soft and even in colour, and then put into an earthen-ware vessel and kept in a cold place for eight days. A day should be spent boiling it on a low fire, with the 'best oile of Spike [Lavender]' added halfway through. To tell whether it was sufficiently boiled, a drop should be put on a clean saucer, and if it looked 'duskish' it should then be boiled longer. If the colour was a good green, then it was strained and kept in a gallipot. After all this work, it is noted that the ointment would last for seven years.[16]

Houseleek was used for wounds and for burns from gunpowder, a reminder that a Civil War was being waged in the mid-seventeenth cen-tury. Although wounds on the battlefield were tended by barber surgeons, housewives were often called upon to deal with such problems. One domestic recipe took two heads of houseleek, also known as sempervivum, groundsel and boar's grease. These were ground together and added to the fresh dung of sheep and geese, fried and strained into an earthenware pot.[17]

Confusingly, there are two other herbs called houseleek, both from the sedum family. One, known as wall pepper, flourishes on walls and the roofs of low buildings, as the name indicates. Culpeper noted that this was 'commended for king's evil'. As a radical nonconformist who served in the parliamentary army during the Civil War, it was unlikely that he believed the monarch could cure an illness merely by touching the patient, although many people did. King's evil was the swelling of the lymph nodes, a tubercular condition. The custom of touching began in the Middle Ages, but was stopped during the Interregnum. When Charles II was restored to the throne in 1660, a revival took place, with the king touching more than 100,000 people during his reign.

Many herbs and flowers from the garden, and from the hedgerow, are recommended in a recipe for a drink for the king's evil given to Ann Fanshawe by her brother. It begins by telling the reader to gather bramble, hawthorn and oak buds in April. In May, twenty-two herbs, leaves and flowers, from avens to wormwood, should be collected and boiled in white wine and spring water, until the liquid was reduced by half. Removing the herbs, the liquor was added to honey, set over a fire, boiled and scummed before cooling and put into stone bottles. It was to be drunk every morning first thing, and then every two hours until four in the afternoon.[18]

Charles II touched a remarkably large number of people for the king's evil, but the condition was a comparatively unusual one. Much more common were the everyday illnesses and conditions that are still with us. Both Pepys and Josselin in their diaries refer to suffering from colds, coughs and 'rheums'. One remedy taken by Ralph Josselin for a bad cold was to smoke a mixture of aniseed and coltsfoot leaves in a pipe. Culpeper in his herbal gives coltsfoot the alternative name of cough-wort, explaining how good it was for those who had 'thin rheums and distillations upon the lungs'. He concurred with Josselin that the dry leaves, smoked like tobacco, would help.[19]

Hyssop was another herb that Mary Josselin made into a syrup to relieve her husband's colds. The shrubby plant, with dark green leaves and flowers of royal blue, was widely recommended in medical works and herbals. Gerard, for instance, mixed hyssop with figs, honey and rue to make a gargle for a persistent cough, while a domestic recipe recommended boiling

Gerard particularly commended the beauty of the blue-flowered hyssop. He also provided a series of medicinal uses, including a hyssop syrup for easing coughs and helping colds.

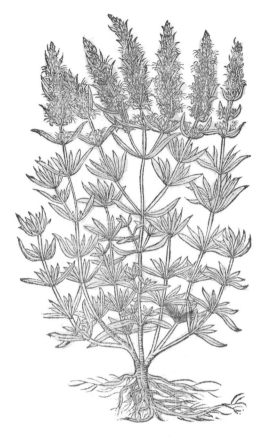

hyssop water with liquorice and then setting the syrup in the sun for three weeks before being made into lozenges. Hyssop water also formed the basis for recipes for wormwood conserve, which could be used as an antidote to seasickness. It was one of a list of supplies recommended by John Josselyn to be taken on the transatlantic voyages undertaken by early settlers in New England.[20]

Alehoof was not only a herb used in brewing, as noted in the previous, but could prove efficacious in problems with ringing in the ears, which we now refer to as tinnitus. Culpeper wrote how 'the juice dropped into the ear doth wonderfully help the noise and singing of them, and helpeth the hearing which is decayed'. It was also used in treating problems with eyes. Culpeper added the herb to greater celandine and field daisies with a little to sugar to make a juice that could be dropped into the eyes as 'a sovereign remedy for all pains, redness and watering of them'. When the apothecary Thomas Johnson emended Gerard, he also recommended this mixture, applied with a feather to the affected eye. He goes on to suggest it could also relieve 'pin or web' in the eyes of horses and cows, a reminder that the housewife might also have charge of the welfare of household animals. However, he adds 'But I list not to over eloquent amongst Gentlewomen, to whom especially my Works are necessarie', implying that in wealthier establishments such matters were taken care of by the farm manager.[21] The very name 'daisy' comes from 'day's eye', when the flower opened with the dawn, while another herb distilled with water to be dropped into the eyes to improve clarity was eyebright.

Problems with teeth abound in seventeenth-century diaries. In one entry, Ralph Josselin recorded scrubbing his teeth so briskly with a sprig of rosemary to relieve his toothache that he made his mouth sore. Rosemary appears in many recipes for keeping teeth both clean and sound. Sometimes it is combined with root of pellitory. In fact, there are two herbs so called: the first is 'pellitory of Spain' or common, which was cultivated in gardens, while the second, 'pellitory of the wall', as the name suggests, grew wild by the sides of walls. The following recipe used the 'of Spain' alternative:

> Take one handful of woodbinds flowers & leaves, as much of rosemarie flowers, as much of the leaves of ivie that grows on the north side of the tree, brown sage as much, the leaves of pellitorie of spaine half a handful, cloves one pennieworth, long pepper as much, bruse the cloves and the pepper, & chop the herbs, then laie tham all night in white wine, the next daie still them in a still, & with a root of pellitory of Spaine dried & scraped cleane, rub your teeth every morning being dipped in some of these waters first.[22]

This recipe specifies one pennyworth of cloves. Such a reference, relating to the price charged by the grocer or apothecary, quite often appears, alongside handfuls of herbs for around a halfpenny from a herb-woman at the market. In February 1660 Pepys recorded how his mother sent her maid, Besse, to the market in Cheapside to buy a handful of herbs to make up a water to ease a canker, ulcer, in his mouth. Pepys does not specify what these herbs might be, but a recipe for a mouth canker from an early-eighteenth-century herbal has rue, red sage, brambles and the leaves of ivy and honeysuckle, added to vinegar and honey.[23]

Alehoof or ground ivy. Gerard mentioned its use not only in the brewing of ale, but also 'against the humming noise and ringing sounds of the ears' and, mixed with daisies and celandine, to ease itching and inflammation in the eye.

Far more serious for the Pepys family were the recurring problems that they endured with the stone. Suffering from stones in the gall bladder and in the kidneys would appear to have been a frequent complaint of the period, and surprisingly common in children. One theory is that this frequency was exacerbated by a high intake of protein combined with the adulteration of flour by the addition of chalk as a whitening agent.[24] The early-seventeenth-century records of St Thomas' Hospital in London show not only how physicians and an apothecary were employed - along with the herb-woman – but also a man to cut out bladder stones.

Margaret Pepys suffered from stones all her life, which must have given her enduring pain and may explain why she comes over in her son's diary as a difficult woman. Samuel inherited the problem, but so severely that he had to undergo a terrifying operation to remove a stone from his bladder, which he recorded was the size of a tennis ball. Miraculously he survived and lived to a surprisingly old age. One of Ralph Josselin's neighbours also was cut for the stone, casting his fate upon God. He too survived, and like Pepys held a celebration feast every year as a commemoration.[25]

Samuel's was a severe case, but even after his operation he had problems with stones. In his diary he talks of drinking horse radish in ale, and even

Castile soap in a posset to relieve his condition. A physician provided Elinor Fettiplace with a recipe for a water. With a wine base, it took spices such as ginger, cinnamon, nutmegs and cloves, along with seeds such as fennel and caraway. To these were added herbs both from the garden and wild, such as pellitory of the wall, and all put in a limbeck and distilled for twelve hours before being ready to drink.[26]

The two most terrifying diseases afflicting seventeenth-century Britain were the plague and smallpox. Throughout his long diary, Ralph Josselin charts the arrival of both in his locality, describing the plague as the 'arrow of death'. There were two strains of plague, pneumonic and bubonic. Plague was brought by black rats on ships, affecting ports, and particularly London, spreading to country villages when the fleas were transferred to their brown British cousins. Recently, it has been suggested that the offending fleas were in fact carried by people. Whether rodents or humans are to blame, plague alarmingly recurred in the seventeenth century. The churchwardens' accounts for the Nottinghamshire village of Upton-by-Southwell near Newark provide a glimpse of the effect of its arrival in March of 1609. Out of Upton's population of 300, 83 died in eight months. To keep the sick separate from the rest of the community, cabins were built out in the common fields. The devastation wrought is reflected in the fate of one family. William Beacocke was a landless labourer, employed as scourer of dykes and drains. He lived in a two-roomed cottage with his wife and four children. The plague not only killed him, but also all the children, leaving Mrs Beacocke grieving the loss of her family and in fear of how to survive financially.[27]

Although outbreaks of plague continued intermittently through the seventeenth century, the best-known example took place in London in 1665–6, known now as the Great Plague. Out of a population of approximately half a million, the official death toll was 68,576, but in reality around 100,000 perished. Pepys reported how the clerk of his parish, St Olave's, had noted that in one week nine had died, though he had only returned six, 'which is a very ill practice, and makes me think it is so in other places, and

Garden rue in Gerard's herbal comes with a long list of medicinal properties, from treating shingles to running ulcers, earache and nose bleeds. But for apothecaries and physicians, its importance was that it could serve as a counterpoint to poisons, and, mixed with walnuts and figs, it hopefully offered an antidote to the plague.

therefore the plague much greater than people take it to be'.[28] This disparity was probably due to the fact that the 'searchers of the dead' were usually old women employed by parishes to examine corpses to ascertain the cause of death with little or no medical knowledge. Plague was made more terrifying because it was such an unknown factor. Theories ranged from miasma, or bad air, to divine wrath fetched on to a sinful population.

The precaution that Pepys took against the plague was to chew tobacco, as it had been observed that no deaths were recorded among tobacconists. In his diary for 7 June 1665, having seen the doors of infected houses marked with a red cross, he noted: 'I was forced to buy some roll=tobacco to smell and chaw [chew] – which took away the apprehension.' The following month Elizabeth Carteret, the wife of one of his naval colleagues, gave him a bottle of plague water, a distillation of herbs thought to be efficacious against the threat. Elizabeth was a friend of Pepys's fellow diarist John Evelyn; at the end of 1665, when the number of cases had dropped, he felt able to write a playful letter in which he teased her about holding a bunch of rue under her nose when a pair of slippers arrived from

London. Rue, also known as the herb of grace, was used in England before the Reformation in exorcisms, when a bunch was added to holy water. The blue-green herb was described by John Gerard as having 'a very strong and ranke smell and a biting taste'. It served as a counterpoint to deadly plant poisons such as aconite and the bite of snakes and the sting of scorpions. As an antidote to the plague he recommended mashing the leaves with the kernels of walnuts and figs.[29]

In her book published in 1672, Hannah Wolley included a recipe advertised as 'most esteemed of in the last great Visitation', the Plague of 1665:

> Take three pints of Muskadine [wine], boil therein one handful of Sage, and one handful of Rue until a Pint be wasted, then strain it out, and set it over the Fire again.
> Put therein a Penniworth of Long Pepper, half an Ounce of Ginger, and a quarter of an Ounce of Nutmegs, all beaten together, boil them together a little while close covered, then put to it one pennyworth of Mithridate, two pennyworth of Venice Treacle, one quart of a Pint of hot Angelica Water.
> Take one Spoonful at a time, morning and evening always warm, if you be already diseased, if not once a day is sufficient all Plague Time.
> It is a most excellent Medicine, and never faileth, if taken before the heart be utterly mortified with the Disease.'[30]

Mithridate is a reference to a remedy said to have been taken daily by Mithridates, ruler of Pontus in the first century BC. Consisting of fifty-five herbs and spices, it was thought to counter any poisons. From the Middle Ages onwards, a modified mixture was sold by apothecaries as a remedy against plague, often being marketed as Venice Treacle. The Duchess of Lauderdale had a recipe for treacle water, which boiled spring water with hartshorn until the liquid was reduced to a quart. To this was added a range of roots – elecampane, gentian, cypress, angelica – along with the flowers of borage, bugloss and rosemary – and citrus rinds. Next, a pound of 'old treacle' was added, and the whole mixture distilled with red rose water until 'well infusd'. Other recipes against the plague were noted as 'imperial water'. Elinor Fettiplace had one that included many herbs from her garden steeped in white wine, to which she added Mithridate, turmeric root, sugar candy, aniseed and liquorice. She noted that it was good against not only the plague, but any infectious diseases.[31]

While remedies for the plague are offered with determined optimism, those for another devastating disease are marked by their rarity: for small-pox. Until vaccination with the relatively benign cowpox was developed by Edward Jenner at the end of the eighteenth century, there was no cure for smallpox, which killed around a fifth of those who contracted it. It was a disease with no respect for status: several members of the royal family perished from smallpox in the 1660s, and in 1694 Queen Mary II died from it at the age of thirty-two. John Evelyn caught smallpox while on his travels in Europe in 1646, but recovered, thus securing himself immunity, but two of his daughters succumbed to it in their early twenties within weeks of each other, as recorded with terrible grief in their father's diary. When spots appeared on Ralph Josselin's children, he nervously awaited to see whether these were a sign of an infantile rash or the relatively less dangerous disease of measles, rather than the dread smallpox.

Ann Fanshawe included in her book of receipts 'The Lady Allen's Water for the Stomacke Small pox or Surfett', with a range of herbs and flowers from the garden. Among these were powerful medicinal plants such as henbane, with painkilling properties, and herbs for wounds such as scabious and tormentil. The roots of the herbs were thinly sliced, put into a glazed earthenware pot with liquorice and white wine. The pot was then sealed and kept in the cellar for two days, after which the mixture was distilled in a cold still.[32]

Despite marking this recipe with a cross to indicate that the remedy had proven successful, Ann was unable to save her eldest daughter, Nan, from dying from smallpox at the age of eight in the summer of 1654, one of many losses endured by the Fanshawes. Most books of recipes simply do not have any remedies; as Sir Kenelm Digby wisely noted, 'in this Disease the less you meddle, the better it is commonly for the Patient'. This advice is reflected in Elinor Fettiplace's recommendation just to keep the patient warm, but not too hot, and giving them saffron to drink in milk.

However, those who did survive often bore the scars or pockmarks, especially on their faces, and recipes for dealing with these, perhaps the most serious of beauty treatments, do frequently appear. One recipe advised that when the scabs began to dry out, they should be anointed with a pomatum or salve made of 'hogs licor', and, as soon as the carer dared, the face should be washed with malmsey and melted butter, before trying to remove the scabs 'for feare they fasten on againe'. A second salve could then be applied, of roasted bacon fat in rose water.[33]

The after-effects of smallpox were particularly cruel in an age when one of the most important signs of beauty in women was to have fair, smooth faces. This is shown by the frequency of recipes in printed books and household manuscripts for remedies for faces that were red, sunburnt or freckled. While John Gerard recommended oil of fig for 'pockets on the face', he also advised that cucumbers should be cut up and cooked in oatmeal to make an ointment for the cure of 'copper faces, red and shining firie noses (as red as red Roses) and pimples, pumples, rubies and such-like precious faces'. Samuel Pepys in his diary noted how his wife Elizabeth got up before dawn to set out to Woolwich to gather May dew to wash her face. It was thought that dew collected in the month of May at daybreak not only made the face fair, but also had medicinal properties. It was even purportedly offered for sale by apothecaries. A fellow of the Royal Society, Thomas Henshaw, conducted a series of experiments with the dew, writing a paper in 1665. Sadly, he could find no medicinal value, only putrefaction and outbreaks of gnats and flies if it was left for a time. Hannah Wolley, however, had no doubt of its qualities, adding it with marsh mallow roots to boar's grease or lard as an ointment to clear the skin.[34]

Although Sarah Jinner's first almanacs provided recipes to help with reproduction, or 'generation' as she put it, her edition published in 1660 moved on to 'preservation'. 'For heat or pimples in the Face' she recommended 'Take the Liverwort that groweth in the Well. Stamp and strain it, and put the juice into cream to anoint your Face so long as you will.' A water to counter sunburn used a whole series of flowers: white thorn, bean, water-lily, garden lily, elderflower, tansy and marsh mallow. These were added to the whites of eggs and French barley. To make the face fair, she recommended a water made by distilling French bean blossom in a limbeck.

The concept of beauty in seventeenth-century England that came to be considered the ideal is encapsulated in John Aubrey's description of Venetia, the wife of Kenelm Digby: 'She had a most lovely and sweet turn'd face, delicate darke brown hair. She had a perfect healthy constitution; strong; good skin; well proportioned... The colour of her cheeks was just that of the Damaske rose, which is neither too hot nor too pale.'[35] For those who did not have the requisite colouring, paint and powder were on hand.

The custom of painting the face was more widespread in mainland Europe. Pepys in his diary for May 1662 noted how the Portuguese princess Catherine of Braganza, who had just married Charles II, was 'a very agreeable lady and paints still', suggesting that this was rather out of the ordinary following the years of the Interregnum. Unsurprisingly, the Puritans were not in favour of cosmetics, which they felt served as an interference with God's handiwork. But earlier in the century the poet John Donne had posed the question, why should we mend houses and clothes when they fall into disrepair, but not allow this in our women? Ben Jonson in his play *The Epicene*, written in 1609, has Truewit advising that women should make the best of themselves, and 'practise any art to mend breath, clean teeth, repair eyebrows, paint and profess it'. But danger lurked in the cosmetics available. One of the most common was ceruse, white lead, produced from exposing lead plates to vinegar and then mixed into paint and powder. Rouge, to achieve the effect of Damask rose, was known as vermilion, made by adding dyes such as madder and brazil to ceruse.[36]

In 1660 a book was published in London focusing on cosmetics. In fact, there were two books, produced by different printers, and with different titles, although based on the same text. One was *Arts Masterpiece*, the second *Cosmeticks: or, The Beautifying Part of Physick*, with the author for both recorded as Johann Jacob Wecker, an eminent sixteenth-century Swiss physician with an interest in alchemy. On the title page of *Cosmeticks* it was noted that the text, 'never yet extant in the English Tongue before', was 'promised to the world by Mr Nic. Culpeper'. The recipes do include some from Continental sources, and reflect sixteenth-century fashion, but whether Wecker was really responsible for them, or that the Puritan Culpeper was the advocate for an English edition, remains a mystery. One man who owned a copy of *Cosmeticks*, as noted in his library catalogue, was John Evelyn. He disapproved of Culpeper's astrological beliefs, so it may have been acquired by Mary Evelyn, who was skilled in distilling. Whatever the origin of the book, it is interesting in reflecting the recipes that were considered both fashionable and necessary for beauty treatments.

Chemical ingredients, such as ceruse and sublimate – a concentrated product, often of mercury – appear in these recipes, which, for clarity's sake, will be ascribed to Wecker. Subsequent published books that include cosmetic recipes, such as Hannah Wolley's *Queene-like Closet*, also contain these ingredients. However, such dangerous ingredients rarely feature in manuscript recipe books of the time. One exception is a recipe from Elinor Fettiplace, 'a most excellent water to purifie & clense the skin'. In this she added white rosewater to ceruse, sublimate and oil of tartar.[37] The desire to attain perfect beauty was very much driven by the royal court. Ironically, when Venetia Digby died suddenly, aged just thirty-three, reports circulated that her husband had concocted viper wine to enable her to retain her looks.

Most women, if they used cosmetics at all, would have turned to plants for their ingredients. Even for those who did not have a still room, or the equipment for distilling, salves could be made in little pots on the edge of the fire, with beeswax grated into oil or animal fat. To these could be added flowers, especially rose petals.

It is often said that our ancestors did not wash much, and that personal hygiene was not an important factor. This is not borne out in contemporary accounts. Samuel Pepys obviously does not mention every time he washed or took a bath, but an entry in his diary notes him rushing to the office and not having time to eat breakfast or to wash, so we can assume that was his normal daily routine. He also notes, with a certain note of scepticism, how his wife Elizabeth in February 1665 went off with one of her servants to a hothouse 'to bath herself, after her long being within doors in the dirt, so that she now pretends to a resolution of being hereafter very clean – how long it will hold, I can guess'. This was a public steam bath, or *hammam*, an institution that was to become very popular in the eighteenth century, with many established in the area of Covent Garden. Elizabeth seems to have got her revenge for this scepticism, for Pepys notes the following day: 'lay last night alone, my wife after her bathing lying alone in another bed – so cold all night'.[38] Washing would normally have taken place in the bedchamber, with warmed water brought up in a basin, or, in less wealthy households, in the kitchen.

Bathrooms as such were a great rarity. Pepys recorded going to the house of Thomas Povey, treasurer for the king's brother, James, Duke of York, and secretary of the Committee for Foreign Plantations. His home was in Lincoln's Inn Fields and Pepys was shown not only his well-appointed wine cellar but also a bathroom at the top of the house. A 'Bathing Room' was created for the Duchess of Lauderdale within her apartment at Ham House. An inventory made in 1677 describes how she had a bathing tub installed in a small room paved in black and white marble. A canopy was arranged around the tub, enabling it to be like a Turkish bath, with a steamy atmosphere.

The sensual delight of such a bath is evoked by Ben Jonson in *Volpone*. In an attempt to seduce the merchant's wife, Celia, Volpone offered:

Thy baths shall be the juice of July-flowers,
Spirit of rose, and of violets,
The milk of unicorns and panthers' breath
Gathered in bags, and mixed with Cretan wines[39]

After bathing, Elizabeth Lauderdale could rest on an Indian bedstead hung with Indian printed striped satin, anointed in perfumed oils and wrapped in towels. At Ham there was also a bathhouse in the yard, presumably for household use.

A luxurious floral and herbal recipe, echoing Jonson's poetic fancy, was given in John Shirley's appropriately titled *Accomplished Ladies Rich Closet of Rarities*, published in 1687:

> To make a Sweet Bath: Take the flowers or peels of Cittrons, the flowers of Oranges and Gessamine [jasmine], Lavender, Hyssop, Bay-leaves; the flowers of Rosemary, Comfry, and the seeds of Coriander, Endive, and sweet Marjorum; the berries of Myrtle and Juniper: boil them in Spring-water, after they are bruised, till a third part of the liquid matter is consumed, and enter it in a Bathing-tub, or wash yourself with it warm, as you see occasion, and it will indifferently serve for Beauty and Health.[40]

Recipes often suggest that the bather should not eat meat for a couple of hours after emerging from their tub.

Thomas Povey and the Duchess of Lauderdale were both wealthy. Most households could not afford such luxuries, but, if possible, would have washed daily and tried to change their linen on a regular basis. There are many recipes for 'washing balls'. These were usually based on Castile soap made from olive oil imported from Spain and sold by apothecaries. One such recipe took orris, the root of the Florentine iris, cypress, sweet flag, and the petals of roses and lavender. These were ground in a mortar and then put through a sieve. Scrapings of Castile soap were dissolved in rose water, and incorporated with the aromatic powder, again using the mortar. The resulting mixture would be rolled into balls for use.[41] For those who could not afford the fine Castile soap, or did not have access to an apothecary, it was possible to make a soap based on lye. Wood ash percolated through water several times would be boiled up with animal fat, and salt added to solidify the cake. Oils such as spike, musk and flower waters could be added to give a scent.

As Aubrey indicated in his biographical portrait of Venetia Digby, dark hair was desirable in the seventeenth century, and many recipes were on offer to make hair black. Wecker provided a variety: one using privet leaves, crushed date stones, and water made from boiled bean rinds and oak galls; another with cypress, red wine and vinegar; a third with caper roots. According to a book published in 1694, black hair could be achieved with husks of green walnuts, oak bark, red wine and myrtle oil.[42]

A century earlier, the fashion had been quite different: blonde was the colour most sought after. An Italian book had recommended making a dye from celandine roots, saffron, cumin seeds and the bark of the box tree, mixed with the lees of white wine and honey. Rather as hairdressers today apply colouring, leave it for a time and then wash it out, so the sixteenth-century source advised leaving the dye for twenty-four hours, and then washing it out with lye made from cabbage stalks, ashes and rye straw. Wecker also recommended a lye, but this time of barley straw, with 'shavings of box', French lavender, citron and liquorice. He also had a recipe for making hair white, using the plant centaury with alum, arabic and tragocanth gums, and clean white soap. This should be applied to the head, and then the hair dried in the sun before being rinsed with lye.[43]

Recipes also abound for encouraging hair to grow. Maidenhair fern, appropriately, is an ingredient in many. Wecker offered a singular recipe that took the flesh of snails, wasps, bees and horse leeches, which were put with salt into a glazed earthenware vessel and left for several days, so that the liquid produced could drip out. This was rubbed onto the head. It must have been with relief that the reader moved on to a 'more effectual water against the shedding of hair' which used the herbs of hyssop, calamint and southernwood, added to wine, urine, honey, milk and mustard seed, and then ground to a powder and distilled. This recipe, it was claimed, would 'suddenly bring forth a beard' as well as restoring hair to bald patches. Elizabeth Birkett in her commonplace book noted bathing such patches with a water made from boiled marsh mallow roots, and an alternative of southernwood burnt to ashes and added to an oil made of radishes or dill. To get rid of unwanted hair, Wecker returned to the singular, taking the blood of frogs, sumach, roses and the juice of houseleek, and distilling them.[44]

John Evelyn claimed only to wash his hair once a year. He kept it fresh by combing it through with Hungary water, which he distilled from the flowers of rosemary. The decoction, known also as Queen of Hungary's water, had long been considered effective against the plague and putrefaction. Evelyn mourned the loss of his rosemary bushes when a particularly severe winter hit London in 1683–4. In a report to the fellows of the Royal Society, he explained: 'Among our shrubs, rosemary is entirely lost, and to my great sorrow; because I had not only beautiful hedges of it, but sufficient to afford me flowers for making a considerable quantity of hungary water.'[45] Hungary water can be regarded as a predecessor of eau de cologne.

Truewit's advice 'to practise any art to mend breath, clean teeth', was also well catered for in recipe books, printed and in manuscript. Toothbrushes with animal bristle began to appear in England towards the end of the seventeenth century, imported from China via Paris. Before this, 'plant toothbrushes' could be used, such as sprigs of rosemary. Ralph Josselin used his so vigorously that he made his gums sore, as noted on p. 146. Alternatives were sticks from the gum mastic tree and dentifrice pencils made from gum tragacanth, which could be purchased from apothecaries. Wecker provided a series of recipes for powders to whiten teeth. One, 'an excellent dentifrice', advised a mixture of the herbs, hyssop, oregano and mint, with alum, hartshorn and salt, all burnt in a pot over coals. Pepper, pumice stone, pellitory of spain, gum mastic, myrrh and cinnamon were added to make a fine, abrasive powder which could then be rubbed on the teeth.[46]

For 'a stinking breath', Hannah Wolley recommended woodbine and plantain bruised and added to honey and a little alum. Not only would it

Garden rosemary in Gerard's herbal. This was one of the most versatile herbs available in the seventeenth century: the distinctive smell of its leaves made it an important herb for cooking and for strewing. John Evelyn distilled the flowers to make a water that he applied to his hair, and rosemary sprigs were used as toothbrushes.

overcome halitosis, but would heal mouth ulcers and preserve the teeth. For a less extreme problem of oral hygiene, to sweeten breath, she gave a recipe involving butter, honey and the juice of the herb feverfew. An alternative was to suck 'kissing comfits', such as the violet cachous that Elinor Fettiplace made up in her still room (p. 79).[47]

By the end of the seventeenth century the number of medical practitioners was growing, albeit slowly, and, despite opposition from physicians, apothecaries were increasingly using their own authority to supply medicines and ointments. But the expense of summoning a physician and paying for medicaments was substantial, and treatments could be drastic, given the theories based on purgative drugs and bloodletting. One seventeenth-century woman summed up this situation in trenchant terms: 'Kitchen physic I believe is more proper than the Doctor's filthy physic.'[48] For many, especially in rural areas, herbs and other products from their gardens continued to provide the basis for remedies against every kind of disease or condition affecting men and women throughout their lives, as well as promoting their well-being.

Hempe   Howis

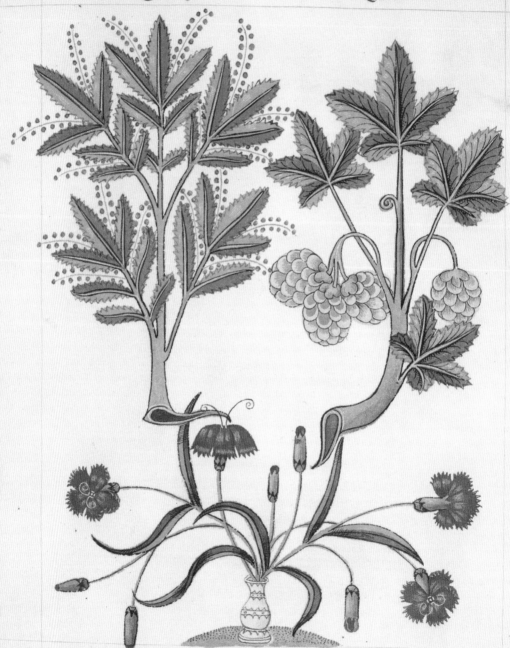

Care of Clothes

[The housewife] ought to cloath [her family] outwardly & inwardly; outwardly for defence from the cold and comelinesse to the person; and inwardly, for cleanlinesse and neatnesse of the skinne.

Gervase Markham, *The English Huswife*, 1623

THE SEVENTEENTH-CENTURY GARDEN and small plots of land could provide two important materials for clothing: hemp and flax. Hemp is a variety of the *Cannabis sativa* plant, a native of central and western Asia that was brought to Europe by the Goths in the early Middle Ages. They apparently valued the plant's narcotic properties, but these became weakened when grown in western Europe, so that rather than the leaves being smoked, the seeds and roots were used for medicines. Culpeper attributed hemp to Saturn, giving a list of various applications, including as a remedy against jaundice, gout and burns. Its principal use, however, was for clothing, together or separately with flax, a member of the genus *Linum*. Flax is first recorded being cultivated in the lands of the Fertile Crescent, but the boost for the crop came in the eighth century, when Charlemagne promoted its qualities both for hygiene as the material linen, and for health with linseed oil.

Hemp and hops from the *Tudor Pattern Book*, accompanied by a vase of pinks. The production of hemp, along with flax, for clothing was an important industry in the seventeenth century.

In the seventeenth century, seeds of both flax and hemp were sown in spring for harvesting in July or August, which was done by hand with the plants pulled from the earth to ensure maximum length of fibres. Hemp was particularly suited to small-scale cultivation, for it required little attention during the summer months when men might be busy looking after livestock, and it could also be grown in the same plot year on year without deterioration through lack of manuring. The processing of flax and hemp was similar: once harvested, the stems were retted or soaked in water, dried and crushed in a brake to separate out the fibres. This not only got rid of the woody parts but also started to soften and straighten the long fibres.

The flax and hemp would then be dressed, or 'heckled', by being pulled through iron spikes set on a wooden board, getting rid of waste matter and refining the fibres. All this work was usually undertaken by men, delivering the fibres to their womenfolk for spinning. The churchwardens' accounts for Upton in 1609 recorded that in one of the two rooms of the cottage of the landless labourer William Beacocke (p. 148) there were trestles for the dressing of the hemp, along with a loom and spinning wheel.

After describing the considerable tasks involved in preparation, Markham noted 'our English Hous-wife must be skilful in the making of all sorts of linenn cloth, whether it bee of hemp or flaxe, for from those two only is the most principall cloth derived.'[1] A wide range of household linen and clothes was produced. For example, the coarsest fibres from hemp, known as hards, were used for window cloths when glass could not be afforded or was unavailable. The early-seventeenth-century yeoman's house of Pendean at Singleton originally had such cloths in frames to be fitted into the windows.

The yeoman farmer Henry Best, of Elmswell in the East Riding of Yorkshire, kept a farming book from the 1620s to his death in 1645 in which were noted the costs and uses of varying grades of hemp and flax for clothes. The coarsest, costing 14–15d per yard, was for holiday aprons for maidservants and cross and neck cloths. This fabric was also known as Scotch cloth and was carried around by pedlars. Sometimes fabric woven from stinging nettles was passed off by these pedlars as Scotch cloth, much to the consternation of mercers concerned about the reputation of their trade. Medium quality linen at 12s 17d, Best noted, was suitable for table cloths. The dearest, at 24s 28d, was made into 'gentle folk shirts'. He also recorded that the finest linen available to him was Holland, said to be spun by nuns in the Low Countries and 'brought over by our Merchants, and solde to oure Linnen Drapers, att whose shopps our Country-pedlers furnish themselves. It is a stronge cloath and much used for men's bands, gentlewomans handkerchers, and cross-cloathes and half shirtes, etc.'[2]

The quotation from Markham at the beginning of this chapter makes the important distinction between outer and inner clothing. Linen, which was easier to launder, was the principal fabric for inner clothing. In addition there were cotton fabrics from India, usually referred to as calicoes, which were introduced into Europe in the early sixteenth century by Portuguese merchants. The first reference to their arrival in England comes in 1541, with a Portuguese pedlar bringing them to Southampton. Inventories for that city in the following decades list calico bed linen. With the establishment of the East India Company in 1600, cotton goods began to be imported in significant quantities.

Wool was most frequently used for outer garments, and the hairier the better for those obliged to work out of doors in harsh weather. While most linen got its hue from the length of time of bleaching in the sun, wool would usually be dyed. Some fleeces were degreased by first being scoured with urine or fuller's earth and then being 'dyed in the wool' before spinning to achieve a better quality of colour, but most were left undyed until after weaving. Spinning of thread was a cottage industry for poorer households, supplementing their income by selling to merchants. Homespun yarn might also be produced by more prosperous wives of farmers and their servants in occasional slack periods, though it is remarkable that such

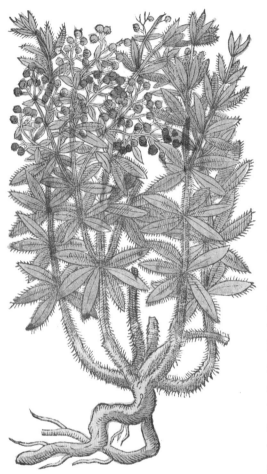

Rose madder in Gerard's *Herball*.
Although as a herbalist Gerard concerned
himself with the medicinal properties
of the plant, he acknowledged that the
roots when boiled with a fixative of
alum produced a red dye that would not
quickly fade.

busy women could possibly ever have
had times of slackness.

Many dyestuffs were derived from
native plants and could be cultivated
in the garden or acquired by forag-
ing. For dyeing wool black, Gervase
Markham advised the use of galls,
excrescences produced by a gall wasp
on oak trees, which were also used
to make ink. To these was added 'the
best green copperas' sulphate as a
fixing agent. For red, Markham gave
a recipe using wheat bran and madder
with alum as the fixative. Gerard
defined madder as a garden plant,
with 'long stalkes or trailing branches
dispersed farre abrode upon the
grounde, square, rough and full of joints, at every joint set rounde with
greene rough leaves in the manner of a starre … the flowers growe at the
top of the branches, of a faint yellow colour.'[3] The pigment was extracted
from the roots by boiling. As red was a popular colour for clothing, madder
was grown commercially in the Low Countries and exported to England,
although it was also cultivated in the southern counties.

For blue, Markham recommended an unidentifiable ingredient, 'neale',
mixed with 'old Chamberlie'. Chamberlie, or Chamberlye as it appears in

some recipes, was a mixture of urine from chamber pots with lye, or wood ash, and features frequently in laundry instructions. More arcane terms follow in Markham, including 'puke', a bluish black made from combining galls and copperas, and 'sinder' from putting red wool into puke liquor. His reference to 'Woodward' to produce yellow or green may be golden rod from its alternative names of 'wound-herb' or 'woundwort'. Gerard explained how in the sixteenth century dried golden rod was imported and sold for high prices, as the dressing of wounds was all too common a necessity. Then the plant was found 'even as it were at our townes end' in Hampstead Wood, 'neere unto the gate that leadeth out of the wood, unto a village called Kentish Towne', and in Essex and Kent, so that the price collapsed. Now it was used not only medicinally, but widely as a yellow dye.[4]

Once the woollen fleece was dyed, Markham advised a combination of dark and light colours for spinning, but warned not to mix too many colours together. Nevertheless even he, the advocate of self-sufficiency, recommended that the wives of yeomen farmers, after taking the fleeces from their sheep and spinning the yarn, should go to a professional weaver and then send the cloth to a dyer 'to bee dyed after her fancy'.[5]

There is a huge range of dye plants that can be grown easily in the garden, some indicated by their names, such as dyer's broom, dyer's rocket and dyer's greenweed, which all produce a yellow dye. Yellow can also be extracted from the stamens of the saffron crocus, *Crocus sativa*. As noted in the first chapter, saffron was grown as a commercial plant, requiring skilled pickers and a large number of stamens to get sufficient quantities for dyeing. It thus tended to be used on expensive fabrics such as silk and lace. The crocus could be grown in gardens, providing a lovely purple colour in autumn, but was much more likely to be used in a domestic context for cooking, the colouring of pastry for example, and for medicinal recipes.

Many dye plants are to be seen in 'Culpeper's Garden' in the Geffrye Museum in Hoxton, East London, and at the Weald and Downland

Museum in Singleton. It is, however, difficult to know how much home dyeing did take place on a regular basis in the seventeenth century. On a large scale, dyeing could be both skilled and antisocial. Despite the plant *Isatis tinctoria* producing a cloud of yellow flowers, it was an important source of the blue dye woad. The leaves were put through a process of pulping, moulding into balls, drying, powdering and then wetting again before being fermented to produce the blue colour. Not only was this difficult to do at home, but the noxious smell emanating from woad mills was notorious, while the poor workers were permanently stained, rather like their Ancient British warrior forebears if Julius Caesar is to be believed. Added to this, cultivation of the plants on a large scale exhausted the ground, making it unfit for other crops. Legislation was passed in 1587 restricting the size of fields of woad to 20 acres for individual growers, and 40 to 60 acres for parishes. This was repealed two years later, but another clause, forbidding any milling within 3 miles of royal residences, cities or market towns was retained: Elizabeth I had taken a particular dislike to the manufacture of woad.

A knowledge of what colours could be derived from these plants was certainly useful to the housewife, if not for actually carrying out the dyeing, for checking with the professional dyer, and for reviving colours in clothes that had faded. This may explain why Elizabeth Birkett, in her late-seventeenth-century commonplace book, carefully listed information on dyeing 'by the Instructions of a Scotch Woman'. Just as Markham noted oak galls, so Birkett recorded them with the addition of 'soure docks' or sorrel roots for black, and with madder for brown. Madder, she noted, was used for red, and for orange with addition of the bark of the crab-apple tree. Bark, this time of the blackthorn, could produce a brown, 'the Irish way', when added to pounded galls, copperas and logwood, an exotic dye imported from South America. For yellow, she had tansy, a versatile herb used in cooking, especially with eggs, and in medicinal recipes. It is a tall plant, 2 to 3 feet high, with ferny foliage and golden, button-like flowers.

For her dye, Birkett stipulated using the whole plant, including the roots. To produce green, she noted indigo, an exotic dye imported from India, combined with native ling, or heather.

All these recipes were for dyeing wool, but she also has one for producing orange linen. This combined wood ashes with 'arnotto' or anatta, an orange-red dye from *Bixa orellana*, native of South and Central America. As noted in the introduction, Elizabeth Birkett may have lived in the comparatively remote village of Troutbeck in the Lake District, but she had access to grocers locally, possibly in Kendal, as well as to London tradesmen by carrier. The inventories of late-seventeenth-century grocers in Lancashire include exotic dyes: logwood and sumac, a red dye from North America, are listed in the stock of James Berry from Ormskirk; indigo, verdigris and copperas in that of William Blackledge of Preston.[6]

Elizabeth's recipe for dyeing linen is a rare one. Given that clothes made from both flax and hemp were usually undyed, some housewives may have undertaken dyeing on a small scale, to provide them with, say, a kerchief in red or orange as a colourful contrast to the rest of their clothing. If so, the dyeing would take place in the kitchen, or in a back kitchen, using a cauldron or kettle set over a fire. The yarn would be lifted out of the dye liquor with sticks, and surplus water removed with twisting poles before being dried on a frame.

The kitchen was the place where laundry was undertaken, in both rural and urban homes. In larger establishments, a special service area would be set aside. At Ham House there were two laundries, one in the basement of the main house, the second in the yard, probably for the washing of servants' linen. The task of keeping the household linen and clothing clean was a formidable one. Mud and dirt abounded in both towns and the countryside, while seventeenth-century commentators noted how smoke from fires, especially from the sea coal brought down to London from Northumberland and Durham and used with growing frequency, hung over towns and cities on the eastern side of England like a louring cloud in winter. John Evelyn published a book, *Fumifugium*, on the threats posed by the polluted atmosphere, describing the 'Hellish and dismall Cloud of SEA-COALE, which was *Avernus* [infernal] to *Fowl* and kills our *Bees* and *Flowers* abroad, suffering nothing in our Gardens to bud, display themselves, or ripen'.[7]

Although laundry was considered a feminine task entirely, vigorous physical force was required to get clothes and household linen clean and fresh. The simplest method was to take the dirty linen to a nearby source of water and pound it, and, if a washing block was on hand, use an implement like a bat, known as a beetle or battledore. In 1682 a traveller on his way from London to Wales recorded in poetic terms how he saw 'she-Vulcans … hammering out with Battle-door the filth of the linen, whose unctuous distillations were the Nile that water'd the little Egypt of the adjacent garden'.[8] In running water, the laundry could be laid on stones and beetled or trampled underfoot.

When judged sufficiently clean, the laundry would be laid out on the grass or a convenient hedge to dry and bleach in the sun. The pedlar Autolycus in Shakespeare's *The Winter's Tale*, in his famous lines about snapping up unconsidered trifles, talks of 'the white sheet bleaching on the hedge', for his illicit 'traffic' in sheets. In a garden, rosemary bushes were particularly favoured as botanical clothes horses, for the aromatic leaves would also scent the linen. Thomas Tusser offered as alternatives 'box and bay / Haithorne [hawthorn] and prim [privet] for clothes trim'.[9]

An alternative washing method was to wash the linen in a solution containing a cleansing agent. This was usually stale urine, with its ammonia content, a method particularly convenient for town dwellers, who could share the barrels where urine was stored. Dung was also used. Another

Paul Sandby's watercolour of washing day dates from the mid-eighteenth century, but shows how laundry would have been carried out in earlier kitchens. The woman on the left is washing linen in a tub. Her companion is heating water in a cauldron over the fire – hot work, so she has dispensed with her outer gown.

traveller, this time visiting Edinburgh from London, in 1705 observed how the Scots 'put their cloaths with a little cow dung into a large tubb of water, and then plucking their pettycoats up to their bellyes, get into the Tubb, and dance about it to tread the cloaths'.[10]

Lye from wood ash, being an alkali, was used as a cleaning agent. Opinions varied as to which wood should be chosen for this purpose. Beech and fir were said to be the best, while oak was considered the strongest, and apple was thought to produce the whitest wash. Where wood was not in plentiful supply, ferns could be collected, half-dried and then burnt in pots to produce a reddish-grey ash. Staffordshire was apparently overrun by ferns in the seventeenth century, and commentators described how the cottagers made up balls from the 'potash' and took them down to London to sell on the streets at a penny a half-dozen. As with dyeing, the lye was often combined with urine, with instructions referring to 'Chamberlie'.

For washing with lye, the dirty linen would be arranged in a barrel-shaped vessel known as a buck basket or tub, with the dirtiest clothes placed on buck sticks at the bottom, and the less dirty at the top. Water was heated up in a cauldron over the kitchen fire, or in a built-in copper in the laundry of larger establishments, and lye added. This was then poured into the buck basket and the linen left to soak. A spigot at the foot of the basket would enable the lye to run off into a shallower tub, and could then be poured in again, or a new supply of lye added. Once judged clean, the linen was rinsed in cold water, with much beating and stirring. Linen is stronger when wet, so had to be wrung out forcefully. Sometimes a hook fixed to the wall would be used to give purchase. In wet weather, the laundry would have to dry in the kitchen, an inconvenience for the cook, as well as incurring the peril of smuts from the fire. Garrets could provide the space for hanging, but then the laundry had to be hauled upstairs. At Ham House, with the luxury of space, 'horses for drying Clothes' were provided for both laundries.

References in Pepys's diary show only too clearly the labour involved in washing day. It was anticipated with apprehension by Samuel himself, even though all the hard work fell upon his wife Elizabeth and their servant maids. Washing did not always take place on a Monday, and his diary mentions both Tuesday and Wednesday: the important thing was to get it done and all the subsequent tasks over by the Sabbath day. It would seem that the Pepys household did their washing every two or three weeks, indicating that they had enough clothes and table and bed linen to last this long. The poorest families had to undertake their washing every week, while very grand houses could defer theirs even for months. The records of Ham House describe in the basement 'one Deale Chest for faule Linnen'.

Washing day for the Pepys household began at an early hour, when the servants were roused from their beds by the ringing of a bell. On one day in October 1663, Elizabeth arose from her bed at 4 a.m. to wake their maids, but the bell proved not loud enough and they were late in starting their task of lighting the fire to heat the water in the kitchen. As a result, when Pepys brought guests back to the house for dinner at midday, he was 'vexed that it being washing-day, we had no meat dressed'. The equivalent of a takeaway was secured from the local cookhouse, but 'my people had so little wit to send in our meat from abroad in the cook's dishes, which were marked with the name of the Cooke upon them; by which, if they observed anything, they might know it was not my own dinner'. Social mortification followed for the diarist. Eventually, having had too many mishaps and cold meat dinners, Pepys was prevailed upon in 1667 to allow Elizabeth and her maids to take their laundry to professional whitsters or bleachers on the other side of the Thames, probably to the open spaces of Southwark or Lambeth Marsh.[11]

Unfortunately Pepys's diary, so full of information on the domestic scene, ended in 1669, so we do not know what he thought about the idea of a mechanical washing machine. This was made by a fellow of the Royal Society, Sir John Hoskins. In October 1677 Robert Hooke, the

Society's Curator of Experiments, recorded in his diary how he met up with Hoskins at Garaway's Coffee House and there discussed a device for washing clothes: 'Sir John Hoskins' way of rinsing fine linnen in a whip cord bag, fastened at one end and straind by a wheel and cylinder at the other. N.B. whereby the finest linnen is washt wrung and not Hurt.' Hooke appended a little sketch of how this worked, showing that the principle was on the same lines as that governing the operation of modern electric washing machines.[12] There is no record that Hoskins demonstrated this at a meeting of the Royal Society, and nothing seems to have come of the idea, although many housewives of the time would surely have supported the development of such a machine. It must, however, be remembered that the Royal Society was exclusively a male institution.

Much kinder on linen than lye was soap. The best soap, as noted in the previous chapter, was Castile soap from Spain and Italy, made from olive oil; but an already expensive commodity was made even more so by the imposition of tax in 1643. To make the Castile soap go further, tallow from animal fat was mixed in, although this too could be expensive as it was also in demand for candle-making, for cooking and for making up ointments. For those who could not afford or obtain Castile soap, lye could be boiled up with fat and the mixture precipitated into a form of curd by adding salt. This would be kept in a bowl to be scooped out when needed, or rolled into balls. Bristol was particularly known for its soapmaking; in her book on domestic arrangements in historic houses, Christina Hardyment describes a competition held in 1633 between the laundresses of the West Country city and soapmakers from London to test out the efficacy of their respective products. Two Bristol laundresses 'washed their linen napkins in public and proved that Bristol soap washed as white and sweet – "in good faith rather sweeter" than those washed with the London brand'.[13]

Most households economized by combining lye and soap for their laundry, so that one early-eighteenth-century housewife, Elizabeth Purefoy, divided her washing, 'one day soap and another day ye Buck'.

Others washed their favourite clothes in soap and left the rest of the laundry for bucking. Any stains that persisted after the general wash could be removed with a wash ball of soap. A recipe 'to take stains out of Lineen, which many times happens by Cooking or Preserving', consisted of hard white soap pounded in a mortar with sliced lemons and a little rock alum. Lemon was also recommended for dealing with iron mould, by putting the garment in a chaffing dish over a fire, and rubbing it with the juice until the stain had gone.[14]

Soapwort might be used for more delicate materials. The plant was given its name by the Tudor herbalist William Turner, who also described it as the fuller's herb, because in the Middle Ages fullers soaped their wool with it before the cloth went under the stamps of the mill. Taken by the settlers to New England, its laundering qualities were supplemented by its leaves and roots being used as a remedy against poison ivy. A relation of the carnation and the sweet william, it has small clusters of pink or purple flowers, and exudes a strong scent at night. It is used today by the National Trust to wash precious old textiles and tapestries.

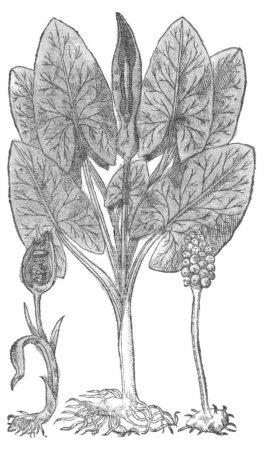

The roots of cuckoo pint could provide the starch essential for the stiffening of the ruffs that were so fashionable in the late sixteenth and early seventeenth centuries. But Gerard warned that laundreses could suffer from blistering when they used the decoction.

The need for starch became important during the reign of Elizabeth I, with the fashion for ruffs, large and stiff. Isinglass, a gelatine obtained from fish bladders, was often used, but plants could also provide stiffening properties. One such was cuckoo pint, also known as starchwort, and as dragons because of its reputation as a mystic plant, used in concoctions by witches. John Gerard was more prosaic about it, noting that 'the most pure and white starch' was made from the root, but warning 'it is most hurtfull to the hands of the Laundresse that hath the handling of it; for it chappeth, blistereth, and maketh the hands rough and rugged and withall smarting'.[15] Tradition has it that a Dutch woman, Dinghen van den Plasse, who came to London in 1564 as a religious refugee, first taught English laundresses the use of the plant.

For the knife-like pleats so desired in early-seventeenth-century ruffs, the roots of bluebells could be used during laundry. In earlier times the viscous substance had been scraped off the roots for attaching feathers to arrow shafts, as noted by John Gerard in his description of the 'blew Harebel or English Jacinth'. He explained how 'the roote is Bulbus, ful of slimy glewish juice', which was not only effective with feathers but also 'to paste bookes'.[16]

Once laundered, clothes and linen would be stored in chests or presses, usually placed at the end of the bed: the hanging wardrobe was an early-nineteenth-century innovation. A very unusual image from the title page of a sixteenth-century German herbal shows a woman in an apothecary's shop putting plants into such a chest (overleaf). One of the plants might have been *Acorus calamus*, sweet flag, also known as sweet rush. When Gerard wrote his *Herball* in 1597, he recorded how the sweet flag that he grew in his garden had only arrived thirty years earlier from the Levant. He called it the 'Aromaticall Reede … of a darke dun colour, full of joints and knees easie to be broken into small splinters, hollow and full of a certain white pith, cobweb wise'.[17]

This aquatic plant in time made the journey across the Atlantic with some of the early settlers. One of the first books to be published about the plants of New England was John Josselyn's *New-Englands Rarities Discovered*, which he published in London after returning from an eight-year sojourn in America. He noted of sweet flag how 'There is a little Beast called a Muskquash, that liveth in small Houses in the Ponds, like Mole Hills, that feed upon these Plants.' He then described the 'Cods' as sweet like musk that 'will last a long time handsomely wrap'd up in Cotton wool; they are very good to lay amongst the Cloaths'.[18] He advised using the cods in May when their fragrance was strongest.

To protect clothes from the unwelcome attention of fleas, housewives could call upon a whole range of herbs that went under the name of fleabane. The strong, bitter-tasting rue and wormwood and its close relation southernwood were used to deter moths. Indeed, southernwood was known by the French as *garde-robe*. Another herb brought into the battle against both pests was bog myrtle, or sweet gale, a deciduous, suckering shrub with aromatic foliage. One of its local names from Northumberland is flea-wood. John Partridge in his *Treasurie of Hidden Secrets*, realizing that

The title page of a sixteenth-century German herbal, reproduced from Agnes Arber's *Herbals*, published in 1912. The woodcut illustration depicts the garden and shop of an apothecary. In the right-hand foreground, a woman is shown putting fragrant herbs into a clothes press.

moth eggs may have got into the very fabric of a clothes press, provided a recipe for fumigation. He suggested making a powder out of cypress or juniper wood, dried rosemary, benjamin and cloves, mixed with a substantial amount of dried wormwood leaves. These would then be placed in a chafing dish of coals, put in the press and the lid closed shut – a proposal that must surely also have constituted a fire hazard.[19]

Housewives would have also added to their linen what were described as 'sweet bags'. From her garden at Appleton Manor in Berkshire, Elinor Fettiplace gathered her flowers and herbs to be dried, powdered and distilled, while from London she purchased her exotic spices and gums. Her task for December was to make up 'sweet powders' and to refresh ones that had been made as much as a year or so earlier. Elinor ground the gums, spices and roots of herbs into a fine powder. Rose petals that had been gathered in the summer and stored in lead-lined earthen pots sealed with corks were then dried along with sweet marjoram, and added to the mixture.[20]

The elaborate mixture, with some of its ingredients expensively acquired from the apothecary or the grocer, had to be long lasting. So it was kept in bags tightly sealed to retain the scent.

One of the herbs mentioned in the recipe is sweet marjoram, a native of the Mediterranean that can be cultivated in English gardens as a half-hardy annual if protected over winter. In his recipe for a

SWEET POWDERS

Take Negeloromano [Nigella romana], Calamus [root of sweet flag], Ciprus [root of sweet cyprus], origanum, orris roots, storax, Beniamyn [gum bezoin], Cloves, lignu rhodium [sweet-scented candlewood], oringe pilles, damask roses, sweet marioram, beat all the woods & gums and roots by themselves into small powder, and dry your roses and marioram verie drie, & beat them into powder, then mingle them all together, to such a quantitie, as the smell may best like you.

sweet bag, John Partridge also gave information about how sweet marjoram should be harvested to ensure its continued growth in the garden. 'Take of sweet Mariorum when it hath in him Seedes ripe, cut the braunch so the Roote maye springe agayne, when this Mariorum is dried, then rubbe out the sedes and keepe them to soake until Easter, and the Huskes or leves that grow about the Seeds take for your purpose.'[21] Its strong perfume made it a good candidate not only for bags, but also for nosegays, literally ornaments for the nose. Marjoram has anaesthetic properties, so civic dignitaries, such as judges and aldermen, would carry nosegays to mask the smells of unwashed crowds and the threat of plague.

Another important constituent of sweet bags was orris powder. Orris comes from the rhizome of the Florentine iris, dried and ground to produce a powder with a scent like violets. Clothworkers and drapers had long used the powder to sweeten their cloths. In the seventeenth century, for domestic use, the sweet powder was kept in little terracotta containers, galley pots. In a recipe entitled 'To Dry Roses for sweet powder', orris powder was added to rose petals that had been dried for a couple of days on a table, then dried further by heating over charcoal. For another recipe, 'A Sweet Powder for Linnen', musk and ambergris, the strongly scented substance from the intestines of the spermaceti whale, were mixed with lemon juice and orange flower water. Cloves were soaked in this liquid before being tied into the buds of Damask roses. After the buds were dry, they were ground up and mixed with the orris powder.[22]

Wecker's book of cosmetics, referred to in the previous chapter, also included recipes for 'sweet waters' to freshen clothes and household linen. This is the recipe for an Italian sweet water, 'which they call Damask-Water':

> Take of cynamon one ounce, cloves half an ounce, sweet marjoram, rosemary, lavender, bay leaves, penny-royal, green province roses, each a handful, mallego [Malaga] wine, rose-water, each a pint and a half. Cut the green things, powder the dry ones, and set them in the Sun six days, then distill them in a double vessel. Some add to them citron pill, storax calamine, orrice, each one dram, and flowers of jasmine. They sprinkle this water on their garments, linen, hands and nostril.[23]

Leather gloves could be freshened by steeping them in a perfumed mixture. A printed recipe for 'divers excellent sents for Gloves' instructed the reader to lay some ambergris on hot coals until it began to crack. Once this was cooled, it was ground with yellow ochre to get the required colour for the gloves. A smooth stone was then poked into each glove, and a hair brush used to rub on the ambergris mixture, ensuring that the colour was applied all over, including seams. They were then hung to dry on a line, before the perfume was applied. This was made up of gum tragacanth dissolved in rose water and oil of benjamin or of sweet almonds.[24] This recipe was for lambskin gloves, with an accompanying note that those made from the skin of goats or kids had a powerful natural scent, so the

The Florentine iris, whose roots can be ground to produce a sweet-scented powder, orris. Gerard noted its use by clothworkers to sweeten their textiles, and housewives for their linen, as well as its medicinal applications such as countering bad breath.

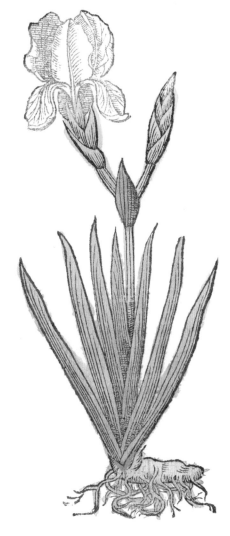

perfume needed to be stronger and the process repeated.

The care of clothes in the seventeenth century was an exhausting business, a telling example of how 'a woman's work is never done'. Pepys in his diary mentioned how after washing day Elizabeth was worn out and the 'house foul'. Domestic peace might not have been restored by a suggestion made by Elinor Fettiplace for looking after leather gloves. She noted how, after perfuming the leather, she wrapped the perfumed gloves in silk and laid them 'betweene the blanket & the bed' and dried them by lying on top of them.[25] Care of clothes even extended to sleeping on them.

In this chapter we have seen how plants have provided basic textiles for clothing and household linen, and the importance of herbs in colouring them and keeping them clean and sweet. Now, in the last part of our tour, we shall also see how, through herbs and flowers, cleanliness and sweetness might be maintained in the home.

Fragrant Chambers

'Where's the cook? Is supper ready, the house trimmed, rushes strewed, cobwebs swept…?'

William Shakespeare, *The Taming of the Shrew*, IV.1

I N THESE LINES from *The Taming of the Shrew*, Shakespeare is evoking a household busily getting prepared for the return of the master, in this case Petruchio. His servant, Grumio, checks that one of the important tasks of keeping a house clean and pleasant, 'strewing' or scattering the floors with rushes, has been completed.[1]

At this period, the turn of the seventeenth century, the ground floor of homes was flagged with stone or tiles, or in more modest houses with stamped earth or a kind of composition of lime ash. Upper floors were boarded with oak timber. Rushes and sedge, and fragrant herbs if available, could be strewn over these surfaces to release their scents when walked upon. Sedge and rushes were cut from reed beds and would be supplied to urban housewives by itinerant sellers, whose traditional cry was 'Green rushes O'. For Londoners the rushes were brought along the Thames: fifteenth-century legislation ordered that they should be sold

Henry, Prince of Wales, the elder son of James I, in a portrait by Marcus Gheeraerts painted in 1603. The prince is shown standing on woven straw matting, which represented the acme of floor coverings at this period.

by the cartload, made up in bundles on the barges themselves, and not on the wharves.

The English were celebrated for their delight in using plants in their houses, as noted by the Dutch scholar and physician Levinus Lemnius on a visit to England in 1560. He wrote in his diary: 'the better to qualifie and mitigate the heate, it shalbe very good to sprinckle on the pavements and coole the floores of our houses or chambers with the springing water, and then strew them over with sedge.' He also described how 'their chambers & parlours strewed over with sweete herbes, refreshed mee'. Lemnius suggests that it was the 'living rooms' on the ground floor and upper storeys that were so furnished: the parlour, study, closet, bedchamber and, in larger establishments, the long gallery. The physician William Bullein likewise specifies that 'rushes that growe upon drie groundes bee good to strewe in Halles, Chambers and Galleries', protecting clothes from dust.[2]

The aim of protecting clothes from dust and dirt was combined with a quest to keep the house fragrant. The smell of the farmyard could offend rural households, although, as earlier chapters have shown, urine and dung from animals were used for all kinds of purposes, and for the poorest having animals close by was a source of warmth. The stench of cities and towns could be intolerable, especially during the summer months. John Evelyn wrote of how urban life was 'inviron'd with rotten Dung, loathsome and common Lay Stalls' (see p. 73), forbearing to add the lack of fragrance of some citizens. But perhaps more important was the smells within a household, from rotting food and the presence of privies. Although Lemnius waxed lyrical about the English practice of strewing, a fellow Dutchman sounded a note of caution about maintaining fragrance. In a letter to an English physician in 1530, Erasmus wrote of the houses of the less well off:

> As to the floors, they are usually made of clay, covered with rushes
> that grow in the fens, which are so slightly removed now and then that
> the lower part remains sometimes for twenty years together, and in it

Meadowsweet, also called Queen of the Meadow, from Gerard's *Herball*. With its strong scent it was the favourite strewing herb of Queen Elizabeth I.

a collection of filthiness not to be named. Hence, upon a change of weather, a vapour is exhaled, very pernicious, in my opinion, to the human body. I am persuaded it would be far more healthful if the use of these rushes were quite laid aside.[3]

Among the herbs providing fragrance to rooms was meadowsweet. With its clusters of delicate creamy-white flowers, meadowsweet emits such a strong smell that some find it overpowering. Gerard, however, was having none of this, writing:

the leaves and flowers far excel all other stroowing herbes, for to decke up houses, to strowe in chambers, hals, and banketting houses in the summer time; for the smell thereof maketh the hart merrie, delighteth the senses: neither doth it cause headach, or lothsomnesse to meate, as some other sweete smelling herbes do.[4]

John Parkinson, writing in 1640, recalled that meadowsweet was Elizabeth I's strewing herb of choice, noting that she 'did more desire it than any other herb to strew her chambers withal'.[5]

Despite its name, Elizabeth I's favourite strewing herb, meadowsweet, was a plant of the garden as well as the meadow, grown to flavour the drink mead, and sometimes called meadsweet. The appellation 'sweet' was particularly applied to herbs that could be used for strewing. One such was sweet grass or woodruff. Gerard described how the little pin-like white flowers and shiny green leaves were woven into garlands or gathered in bundles to bring into the house. Not only was woodruff strewn on floors, but also was added to the stuffing for beds.

Another 'sweet' plant was *Calamus aromaticus*, known as sweet flag or sweet rush. This aquatic plant, with its scent like orange peel, was introduced into English gardens from Turkey in the mid-sixteenth century. The physician Sir Thomas Browne, who made a special record of the plants growing in his native, watery Norfolk, described how the cathedral in Norwich and one of the churches in the suburbs were carpeted with sweet flag. John Josselyn in his book *New-Englands Rarities Discovered* tells of how sweet flag kept feet warm as well as scenting rooms, indicating that the custom of strewing floors had travelled to North America along with the rushes.

Just as scented herbs could be used to deter insects in clothes presses, as noted in the previous chapter, so they could be scattered in rooms. Mint was considered inimical to mice, tansy a deterrent to flies, while housewives could call upon wormwood and rue, with their strong bitter taste, against the unwelcome attention of fleas. In his verses for July in *Five Hundred Pointes of Good Husbandrie*, Thomas Tusser advises:

> While Wormwood hath seed, get a handful or twain
>   to save against March, to make flea to refraine:
> Where chamber is sweeped, and wormwood is stroone,
>   no flea, for his life dare abide to be known.[6]

From Tusser we also get a long list of plants for strewing, including the aromatic herbs camomile, lemon balm and marjoram, and flowers like daisies, lavender, roses and violets. These would have added colour as well as scent, and indeed the mixture at times must have looked rather like modern bowls of pot pourri on a large scale.

Shakespeare's depiction of the preparations for a homecoming reflects the association between rushes and hospitality. It was a token of respect to strew floors when guests were expected, and if this was not done the host was said not to care a rush for them. But, like Erasmus, the Tudor physician William Bullein warned against leaving them down too long, comparing used rushes to old courtiers, 'when thei be nothyng worthe: then thei be caste out of the doores; so many that doe tread upon them'.[7]

During the seventeenth century, the widespread custom of strewing diminished. Although we know that Elizabeth I had her palaces strewn, evidence for the practice during the reigns of her successors is almost non-existent, apart from a reference in 1660. When Charles II was restored to the throne, Bridget Rumney petitioned him to confirm her in the 'office of providing Flowers and Sweet Herbs for the Court' that had been granted to her and her mother by Charles I. Two of her sons had been killed at the Battle of Naseby in 1645, and in recognition of this the king appointed her as Royal Strewer. Bridget held the post until 1671, at an annual salary of £24, half paid by Charles II, the other half by his consort, Catherine of Braganza. This was a generous amount for a woman at this time, compared to the meagre £4 paid annually to the herb-woman employed by St Thomas' Hospital at the beginning of the century (p. 51). Both women undoubtedly had to grow the herbs themselves on a market-garden scale. It may be that Bridget was called upon to provide the flowers and herbs for special occasions rather than to keep the apartments strewn, a theory reinforced by the fact that her successors to the post over many decades were paid exactly the same salary.[8]

Samuel Pepys, so informative in the minutiae of daily life, makes only one reference to strewing. In February 1667, just six months after the Great Fire, he had a conversation with the manager of the King's Company, Thomas Killligrew, about the latest developments in the theatre, reporting 'That the stage is now by his pains a thousand times better and more glorious then ever heretofore.' Wax candles had replaced tallow, there were three times more musicians, and 'then, nothing but rushes upon the ground and everything else mean, and now, all otherwise'. Instead of the rushes strewn on the stage in Elizabethan playhouses, a green cloth was now spread to protect the costumes of the actors. Post-fire private houses in London likewise seem to have dispensed with rushes on the floors. Strewing, however, continued in modest rural homes for many decades. When Alfred Burton wrote a book on the subject of rushes in the late nineteenth century, he recalled a visit to a farmhouse in Cheshire where the flagged floor of the parlour was traditionally strewn on 1 May with green rushes and sprigs of lavender and rosemary.[9]

From Tudor times the wealthiest could afford rushes woven into braided strips, sewn together to fit a room, as depicted in portraits, and reproduced in marble under reclining monumental figures. Exchequer rolls show how these were used in the royal residences. In 1614/15 for James I's house at Newmarket, Nathaniel Swain was paid for 'laying with new bulrush mats the King's bedchamber' along with the privy lodgings of some of his courtiers. Well-preserved pieces of rush matting have been found at Hampton Court Palace, nailed to a plaster floor. They are made up of two and a half strips of braided bulrushes, each composed of nine strands, seamed together with rush.

Not only the floors but also walls were sometimes covered by this rush matting. An entry in the exchequer rolls note how James I's favourite, the Duke of Buckingham, had new matting in two of his chambers extended up the walls under the tapestry hangings.[10] To keep the rushes fresh and fragrant, and damp down dust, they would be sprinkled with water. A ceramic watering pot with its sprinkler, dating from around 1600 and probably made in London, can be seen at the Geffrye Museum in Hoxton. At the chateau of Azay-le Rideau in the Loire Valley, the rush matting both on the floor and up the walls is still freshened with water.

If a household could not stretch to a 'fitted carpet' of rush matting, a mat might be bought to place by the bed, as shown in contemporary prints. These sometimes were described as Cornish mats. Richard Carew in his survey of the Duchy, published in 1602, wrote how

The women and children in the West part of Cornwall, doe use to make Mats of a small and fine kinde of bents [grass-like rushes] there growing, which for their warme and well wearing, are carried by sea to London and other parts of the Realme, and serve to cover floores and wals. These bents grow in sandy fields, and are knit from over the head in narrow bredths after a strange fashion.[11]

Seventeenth-century prints of itinerant sellers show men offering circular mats for the door and strips of matting for the bedroom.

With the development of international trade, these home-grown mats were joined by more exotic decorative grass floor coverings variously described as Portugal, Tangier, Barbary, Africa and Dutch. Samuel Pepys, with his naval connections, was well placed to receive one of these fashionable objects. On 15 June 1666 he mentions in his diary how a neighbour who specialized in the Mediterranean trade 'presented me yesterday with a very fine African matt (to lay upon the ground under a bed of state) being the first fruits of our peace with Guyland [a treaty with the leader of the Berbers]'.[12]

One of the Cries of London drawn by Marcellus Laroon and published in 1687. The pedlar is shown offering door mats and strips of matting for the bedroom. Another seller is shown in the image on pp. 62–3.

In the mid-seventeenth century the traditional timbering for floors, oak, was joined by deal or fir imported from Scandinavia and Russia. Towards the end of the century, for the very wealthy and privileged, exotic woods were available from further afield, such as mahogany from the Americas. At Dyrham Park in Gloucestershire, for example, William Blathwayt, who was auditor general for the colony of Virginia, installed one staircase of walnut and another of cedar.

Timber floors at this period were seldom polished, but instead they could be regularly washed and sometimes scrubbed with small beer and vinegar. Another method of keeping them clean was 'dry rubbing' with materials such as fuller's earth and sand to preserve the colour of the boards. In a book published in 1760 it was recommended to

> Take tanzy, mint and Balm; first sweep the Room, then strew the Herbs on the Floor, and with a long hard Brush rub them well all over the Boards, till you have scrubb'd the Floor clean. When the Boards are quite dry, sweep off the greens, and with a dry Rubbing brush dry-rub them well, and they will look like mahogany, of a fine brown, and never want any other washing, and give a sweet smell to the Room.[13]

There is no earlier record of this practice in England, but this suggests that dry rubbing was the natural successor to strewing.

Above floor level, sweet herbs were again used to impart fragrance. Wooden furniture could be polished with sweet cicely, *Myrrhis odorata*, producing a scent reminiscent of anise and liquorice. For the polish, the seeds from the umbelliferous flower heads were crushed to make a paste or oil, either used alone or added to beeswax. A nineteenth-century source from the Lake District recommended 'rubbing upon oaken panels, which, when dry, being rubbed again with a cloth, receive a fine polish and agreeable scent'.[14]

The versatile herb alecost was not only used in brewing and in the battle against moths, but also in looking after books. Among the herb's several names was bible leaf, reflecting its use to scent the pages of Bibles, and no doubt any book. At a time when many people could neither read nor write, and books were very expensive, a shelf of books would be regarded as a library. Samuel Pepys is credited with having the first bookcases enclosed by glass, inspired by the cupboards on-board ship and made up for him by a naval joiner. Until his innovation, books were kept in coffers or chests, or on open shelves, where they might suffer from mildew in damp houses, so alecost could scent the pages and reduce the problem of mustiness.

Sweet flag was used to scent wall hangings. John Evelyn in his diary noted how his friend Flower Hyde, Lady Clarendon, not only grew sweet flag on the banks of her water garden at Swallowfield in Berkshire, but also hung the rushes in her 'Closset, that retaines the smell very perfectly'.[15] Closets, sometimes described as cabinets, were little private rooms leading off bedchambers, where men and women could withdraw for privacy, prayer or study and where they might have a collection of curiosities, kept, rather confusingly, in a cabinet. Both Evelyn and Pepys describe in their diaries how these rooms might be furnished with cloth hangings of cotton or wool, so the orange scent of sweet flag would have infused the room.

The sweet powders described in the previous chapter for scenting clothes could also be used to scent rooms. The term 'pot pourri', to mean a mixture of scented flowers, herbs and spices, did not come into common usage until the eighteenth century. The idea of an open bowl containing the scented mixture would have seemed profligate to seventeenth-century housewives, for the costly oils and gums soon dried up and lost their potency. So, the sweet powders noted in domestic manuals could be stored in jars set by the hearth and, when warm, the stopper removed to release the fragrance into the room. Bowls with perforated lids began to be manufactured at the end of the seventeenth century. A rare example of a Delft lid can be seen at Dyrham Park. In her classic work *Food in England*, Dorothy Hartley even suggested that a different fragrance might suit a certain room, with Damask rose for a parlour, dried walnut leaves with bay

Mary Doggett's recipe for Rose Beads

Take a quarter of an ounce of Musk, half a quarter of an ounce of Civitt, a quarter and half quarter of an ounce of Ambergreece, not half a quarter of an ounce of spirit of roses, 7 ounces of Benjamin, almost a pound of Damask Rose Budds, cut Gumdragon [Gum Tragacanth] in rose water. And with it make up your Pomander into beads as big as nutmegs and colour them with Lamb black when you make them up with your hands with oile of Jasamy to smooth them. Then make them have a gloss. This quantity will make seven bracelets.

leaves and tonquin beans for a library, verbena and lemon balm for a bedchamber, although she does not specify whether this was a seventeenth-century practice.[16]

Occupants of rooms could also help to make them fragrant by wearing pomanders. 'Pomander' is derived from the French for apple, referring to its shape. Some were the size of a modern tennis ball, carried in pierced metal cases worn at the waist. Others were much smaller, sometimes known as rose beads. Soft resinous substances such as benjamin and gum tragacanth, imported from the Orient, were mixed together with clay or wax. A recipe for beads, reproduced here, took the scented gums and distilled rose water, and mixed them with the buds of Damask roses. These were coloured with lamp black, the soot collected from oil lamps, rolled in the hand with jasmine oil and given a gloss. They were then made into bracelets.[17]

Wecker's book on cosmetics has a series of pomander recipes, including some intended to keep away the plague: an optimistic hope, no doubt dashed by the major outbreak that devastated the population of London in 1665, just five years after the book was published. One such recipe took the flowers of water lilies, bugloss, violets and roses and mixed them with

An early-seventeenth-century silver pomander, which could be worn around the waist.

citrus rind, mace, sandalwood, white poppy seed, camphor, labdanum (the resin of rock rose) and ambergris. Ground to a powder, the mixture was made into sweet balls with distilled lettuce water and liquid styrax, another exotic ingredient imported from the East.[18]

The most effective way of scenting a chamber was with 'fumitories' that were heated in pans over coals. One of the simplest suggestions was to steep leaves of rosemary and bay in small beer and then put them in a hot fire shovel. The leaves could readily be bought from sellers, such as the one depicted in the series of the Cries of London reproduced on pp. 62–3. A more complex recipe took a piece of a pomander the size of a hazel nut, bruising it, and putting it into a fuming dish with some sweet water. Leaves of bay, basil and a little rosemary, with cloves and some grains of musk, could then be added. It was explained that this could 'purge all pestiferous and corrupt ayre out of your house'.[19] At this time it was thought that a possible cause of plague was bad air, hence the importance of such fumigation.

In the household accounts of Edward Sackville, 4th Earl of Dorset, are instructions on how to prepare for a banquet at his great house of Knole in Kent, to be held on 3 July 1636. The room, he stipulated, should throughout the meal be scented with orange flowers on a hot pan.[20] The 'flowers' were probably in the form of pastilles or tablets, made up in the still room from orange peel mixed with aromatic gums and, given the wealth of the Sackvilles, orange flower water.

The banquet was the special course that ended some dinners. In the sixteenth and seventeenth centuries, dinner was the main meal of the day, served in the hall for the household, but in the great chamber for wealthier families and their honoured guests. Towards the end of the seventeenth century, references begin appearing in inventories and records to dining or eating rooms, but even then the room would not be set up permanently for meals: the tables, which were usually gate-legged with folding tops, were kept against the walls or in corridors, to be brought in when needed.

At the beginning of the century, dinner started before midday, but got later as the decades passed. While in modest homes it was a simple meal of one or two dishes, for wealthier households it would be presented in the style now described as *à la française*. Two courses were served, with all the dishes for a course put on the table at the same time, in the style of a modern Chinese meal. Printed cookery books that provided plans suggesting how the various dishes should be laid out show how crowded the table could be. It comes, therefore, as rather a surprise that John Aubrey in his biographical sketches of his seventeenth-century contemporaries, *Brief Lives*, recorded how Sir Francis Bacon 'at every meale, according to the season of the yeare, ... had his Table strewed with Sweet Herbes and Flowers, which he sayd did refresh his spirits and memorie'.[21] Bacon was especially fond of flowers, so having them present at every meal may have been unusual, and that is why Aubrey makes particular mention of them.

Flowers, however, represented an important component of banquets, the additional third course where fresh fruit was on offer, and in grand establishments sweetmeats accompanied by sweet wines. By the end of the seventeenth century this course was more usually known as dessert, often taken in a separate room, or even in a separate building. To entertain the French ambassador at Greenwich in 1560 Elizabeth I had a temporary banqueting house erected in the park, 'made with fir poles and decked with birch branches and all manner of flowers both of the field and of the garden, as roses, julyflowers, lavender, marygolds and all manner of strewing herbs and rushes'.[22]

The connection between the garden and banqueting was close. When Edward Phelips built his fine house at Montacute in Somerset around the year 1600, he included little banqueting houses at the corners of one of the garden compartments. William Lawson in his ideal layout for a garden included a similar notion, with little houses set on mounts at the four corners (see p. 19). Bess of Hardwick even had a banqueting house set in one of the roof turrets at Hardwick Hall in Derbyshire. Honoured guests would have to cross the leads of the roof to enjoy their banquet, looking down upon the elaborate garden parterre three storeys below.

After the Restoration, the fashion for table decorations at banquets was to pile fruit up in pyramids, reflecting the formal, clipped pyramids of box and yew that ornamented gardens. From the diaries of Samuel Pepys and John Evelyn we know that flowers could be inserted among the fruit, because they both mention allergic reactions. Pepys wrote in July 1666 how, dining with George Monck, Duke of Albemarle, when the dessert arrived with roses upon it, the Duchess bid one of the guests to try to make the flowers cause pimples by rubbing them on his skin, 'but they rubbed and rubbed, but nothing would do in the world'. Four years later Evelyn wrote

A scheme for decorating the dinner table, with a large vase of flowers as the central focus and single flowers adorning pyramids of fruit. This design comes from François Massialot's *Des Garnitures et Enjolivement des Services*, published in 1698.

of a dinner where 'My Lord Viscount Stafford rose from Table in some Disorder, because there were roses stuck about the fruite, when the Discert was set on the Table: such an Antipathie it seems he had to them.'[23]

For dining, including the banquet course, artificial light would not have been required, as this meal took place in the middle of the day. It would, however, have been necessary for supper and for evening entertainments. In the seventeenth century, the kind of lighting available after sundown was dependent on what the household could afford. For the majority of the population, this would have been firelight from the hearth, and rushlights: mature rush stalks that had been gathered in summer or autumn, dried and steeped in household fat, preferably mutton or grease from bacon. Tallow candles made from animal fat, either manufactured at home or bought from chandlers, provided a better light, although the wick had to be frequently trimmed, and the smell was not very pleasant. Beeswax candles gave a steady white light, and a more fragrant smell, but were very expensive.

Recipes for making scented candles are given in contemporary books. One, using neither beeswax nor tallow, brought into play a whole range of gums and resins, along with flowers, spices, berries and rose water, with the claim that they were effective against 'Poyson and Pestilence':

Take of Labdanum three ounce, Styrax-calamita ten drams, sweet Asa [Asafoetida plant] six drams, Frankincense one ounce and a half, French Lavender two ounces, red Roses, Cloves, each three ounces, Pomecitron-pills, yellow Saunders, each two drams, Juniper berries half an ounce, Ambergreece, Musk, each half a scruple, Coals of Lime-Tree one pound and a half, mix them all with Gum-tragacanth and Rose-water warm, and bring them into a Masse, then make small Candles out of it, and dry them gently.[24]

This is a complex recipe, with many expensive ingredients. But early settlers in North America could produce perfumed candles much more easily. Although honey bees were introduced into Virginia in the early seventeenth century, beeswax candles would have been beyond the means of most colonists. It was soon discovered that the berries of the bayberry shrub, if boiled for several hours, would yield a wax that floated to the surface of the water and could then be used for tapers. An account written in 1698 rejoiced that instead of the stink of tallow, they were perfumed like incense, providing a clear, consistent light. It took a lot of bayberries to make such candles: the proportions were estimated to be 15 lb for 1 lb of wax, so they were much prized and often saved for Christmas and the New Year, with the adage 'a bayberry candle burnt to the socket brings food to the larder and gold to the pocket'.[25]

Levinus Lemnius was struck by how the English delighted in flowers, noting 'their nosegays finelye entermingled with sondry sortes of fragraunte flowers in their bedchambers and privie rooms'. Even city streets and the exteriors of houses were decorated with flowers at certain festivals. One of the most important of these festivals was that of St John the Baptist, which took place on 24 June. In fact, the festivities began the previous evening when various flowers and plants were carried in torchlight processions. St John's wort was especially connected with the saint, and burnt to purify communities, probably a pagan practice adopted by the Church. John Stow in his chronicles of London described how every door was garlanded with birch, fennel, orpine and lilies, while John Parkinson recorded that the leaves of orpine were intertwined with corn marigold flowers on strings and hung up in houses, on bushes and on maypoles.[26]

In wet, low-lying areas of the country, willow would be brought into the house in the summer. Gerard wrote that 'the greene boughes with the leaves may very well be brought into chambers, and set about the beds of those that be sicke of agues: for they do mightily coole the heat of the aire, which thing is a wonderfull refreshing to the sicke patients.'[27] We now know willow, *Salix*, contains salicylic acid, an essential ingredient of aspirin, so this practice may well have been effective.

At the other end of the year, evergreen shrubs and branches were brought in from the garden to deck or decorate houses to celebrate Christmas. Songs such as 'The Holly and the Ivy', and the Gloucestershire Wassail, dating back centuries, are reminders of this practice, but Robert Herrick in a poem, 'Candlemas', shows that decking the house in this manner in fact occurred throughout the seasons. Candlemas was celebrated on 2 February when lighted candles were carried in church processions in memory of Simeon's words, 'to be a light to lighten the Gentiles', at the presentation of the infant Christ in the Temple, and Christmas decorations were taken down. Herrick begins:

> Down with rosemary and bayes,
> Down with mistleto,
> Instead of holly, now up-raise
> The greener box, for show

As the year proceeds:

> When yew is out, then birch comes in,
> And many flowers beside,
> Both of a fresh and fragrant kinne
> To honour Whitsuntide

> Green rushes then, and sweetest bents [grass-like rushes],
> With colour oken boughs,
> Come in for comely ornaments,
> To re-adorn the house.

In his instructions for the summer banquet at Knole in 1636, Lord Dorset also stipulated the decoration of the chamber. There should be 'fresh bowls in every corner and flowers tied upon them, and sweet briar, stock, gilly-flowers, pinks, wall-flowers and any other sweet flowers in glasses and pots in every window and chimney'.[28]

Having commented on the English delight in decorating houses with flowers and plants, Lemnius, rather surprisingly given the horticultural enthusiasms of the Dutch, compared his compatriots unfavourably in the use of greenery in the home: 'Altho' we do trimme up our parlours with green boughes, fresh herbes or vine leaves; which thing although in the Low Country it will be usually frequented, yet no nation does it more decently, more trimmely, nor more sightly than they do in England.'[29]

Hugh Platt went into considerable detail about flower decorations for the house. In *Floraes Paradise*, a little octavo volume published in 1608, he covered every activity of cultivation from orchards to flower gardens, but also included a section entitled 'A garden within doors'. 'I hold it for a most delicat & pleasing thing to have a faire gallery, great chamber or other lodging that openeth fully upon the East or West sun, to be inwardly garnished with sweet herbs and flowers, yea & fruit if it were possible.' With his fertile brain, Platt dreamt up all kinds of ideas. For example, he suggested pots of marjoram and basil, carnations or rosemary be kept on shelves. By rigging up a pulley system, these pots could be lowered through the windows and into the garden to be refreshed by the sunshine and temperate rain. Square frames of wood or lead could be installed in each window, filled with earth and planted with herbs and flowers. For shady parts of the room, he proposed plants such as sweet briar, bay and germander, although warned that they should be put in front of open windows at certain times of the day to revive them. He even described how the Italians hung up cucumbers and pumpkins 'pricked full of Barlie' to keep away flies.

Platt also proposed a kind of container with 'ranks of sloping holes'.

Set in the midst of the pot a Carnation or a Lily, and in every of the holes, a plant of Thyme or hyssop, keep the Thyme or Hysop as it groweth, even with clipping ... Also you may make piramides, losings [lozenges], circles, pentagons, or any form of beast or fowl, in wood or burnt clay, full of slop holes (as before) ... these being planted with hearbs will very speedily grow green, according to the form they are planted in: And in this manner may you in two years space make a high pirimad of Thyme, or Rosemary.

An early-eighteenth-century chimneyboard, painted in *trompe l'oeil* with an English Delftware vase containing an arrangement of roses, lilies, irises and tulips. Flower arrangements were often installed in empty fireplaces during the summer months.

These ingenious shapes of greenery could then be added to 'the Garden within Doors to grace it in winter' or be set upon 'fair pillars in your Garden, to make a beautiful shew'.[30]

Many busy housewives would have found his recommendations time-consuming to undertake, but certainly could follow his advice to take advantage of the fireplaces not in use during the summer months to display plants. Platt wrote of filling the empty spaces 'with a fine banke of moss', and planting them with columbine, or with branches of orpine, *Sedum telephium*, which was popularly known as 'livelong' because of its lasting qualities. Hannah Wolley expanded on this idea:

> To dress a chimney very fine for the summertime, as I have done many, and they have been liked very well. First take a pack thread and fasten it to the inner part of the chimney, so high as you can see no higher as you walk up and down the house ... Then get a good store of old green moss from trees and melt an equal proportion of Beeswax and Rosin together and while it is hot, dip in the wrong ends of the moss in it and press it down hard with your hand ... then several other kinds of moss ... then any kind of fine snail shells, in which the snails are dead, and little toad stools that look like velvet, or any other thing that is old and pretty, and place it here or there as your fancy serves ... then for the hearth orpen sprigs (it will grow as it lies), according to season what flowers you can, and a few springs of sweetbriar. The flowers you must renew each week, the moss will last all summer till it will be time to make a fire. The orpen will last near two months. A chimney doth grace a room exceedingly.[31]

Also included is a section entitled 'The Lady's Diversion in her Garden'. This was written by Thomas Harris, billing himself as a gardener based in Stockwell in south London. He would appear to be related to the printer of the work, who was providing him with publicity, and it is highly probable that it was included without Wolley's permission, if indeed she was still alive, for this edition appeared in the year of her death, 1675. The lists of plants and how to care for them are neither very original nor indeed very informative. However, this section also contains 'Brief Directions for the Nice Adorning Balconies, Turrets, and Windows, with Flowers and Greens every Month of the Year', which complements Wolley's directions for the dressing of fireplaces. For balconies and window boxes Harris suggests shrubs such as juniper and laurel in gilded pots, and even trees, including clipped *Phillyrea*, then very fashionable. For fragrance wafting through the windows in the summer he proposed roses and gillyflowers.

Much more informative is John Evelyn's advice on plants for the house in his various horticultural publications. When he wrote *Directions for the Gardener* in 1687 for his apprentice gardener, Jonathan Mosse, he instructed him to set aside a part of the nursery specially for growing flowers for cutting for the house: 'you should raise in their distinct beds; all sorts of Flowers, which spring & are increased from Seedes, Bulbs or other Rootes … that they may be ready to … be gathered for Bough-pots & adorning the house'.[32] His list included anemones, auriculas, carnations, crown imperials, irises, hyacinths, narcissus, peonies and tulips. Exotic plants could be grown alongside lemons, myrtles and oranges in hotbeds with the heat generated by dung, sometimes topped up with tan bark.

One of the last of Evelyn's horticultural books was his translation of the work of Jean Baptiste de la Quintinie, supervisor of Louis XIV's famous kitchen garden at Versailles. It was published as *The Compleat Gard'ner and Right Ordering of Fruits and Kitchen Gardens* and published in London in 1693. Among its contents were suggestions for the use of plants from the kitchen garden, arranged month by month. For some of these months, suggestions for flowers to be used for decoration are also given. There was, of course, a dearth of flowers for January, but it was suggested that laurel rose leaves might be used as a garnish for dishes on the dining table. In June came an abundance of flowers, not only to garnish dishes, but 'to set out our Flower-Pots', such as poppies, carnations, pansies and roses of all kinds.

From the garden hotbed, Evelyn recommended bringing in tuberoses, one of the most exotic and sought-after flowers of the seventeenth century, introduced from Mexico where the Aztecs had used them for garlanded wreaths. Evelyn considered that the tuberoses could be brought into the house right through to November. They would be arranged in bough pots and placed in the empty fireplaces to fill the rooms with their powerful scent. The inventory taken at Ham House in 1679 recorded that in the long gallery the Duchess of Lauderdale had 'seaven boxes carv'd and gilt for tuby roses'. Tuberoses were available only to a fortunate few, but Evelyn also put on his list for June flowers of the modest cottage garden, such as valerian, foxglove, featherfew and golden rod.[33]

One fashion for displaying flowers in houses was to make garlands, twining foliage and flowers together, and draping them around a room, or on furniture, such as the buffet, where the household's plate was displayed. John Gerard singled out columbine, writing that they were cultivated in gardens for the beauty and variable colours of the flowers, listing blue, red, purple and white, and referred to a mixture of colours, so that they were particularly suited to be made up into garlands.[34] Not only could garlands provide colour, but also fragrance, from flowers such as roses, honeysuckle and lavender, and foliage such as rosemary, myrtle and bay. Plasterwork swags and garlands that adorn grand seventeenth-century houses serve as a reminder of these flower decorations, albeit without their vibrant colours.

Another fashion in flower arranging in the seventeenth century was to have a mixture of flowers, colours and sizes, forming an upright shape displayed in a vase. Dramatic flowers such as the iris or lily were known as coronary or crowning, providing the climax of the arrangement. Dutch still-life paintings of the period show this kind of arrangement, although the artist would often bring together flowers from different seasons, so that they could provide a calendar of blooms to hang in the home. Hugh Platt recommended that long galleries were particularly suitable for displaying flower arrangements and for plants in pots. Knole, the palatial home of

Still Life with Flowers, painted by the Dutch artist Ambrosius Bosschaert in 1619. He has chosen to display the flowers in the fashionable upright shape, in an oriental vase. Crowning the arrangement is a flamed tulip, highly prized by the Dutch in the early seventeenth century.

A flower pyramid in Delftware, made in the Netherlands in the last decade of the seventeenth century. Flower pyramids are sometimes known as tulip vases, but they were used to display all kinds of individual blooms.

the Sackville family, had three long galleries. In one of these, the Cartoon Gallery, a frieze was created when the room was remodelled in the first decade of the seventeenth century, and decorated with paintings of various flower arrangements, some with simple mixtures, such as red roses with white lilies, or lilies with summer snowflakes, while others are of little lemon trees. In the summer, real flower arrangements and potted plants would be set on the floor of the gallery to mirror the paintings above.

In the late seventeenth century, blue and white Delft pots became very fashionable, with Queen Mary having a particularly spectacular collection of them at Hampton Court Palace. Some are tiered like pyramids: each layer can be removed and filled with water for cut flowers. These are often described as tulip vases, but contemporary illustrations indicate that all kinds of individual blooms, such as roses and lilies, borage and nasturtium could also be displayed in the different spouts. These flower arrangements represented the acme of luxury and lavish display. But at the other end of the social scale, humble households could decorate and scent their rooms with flowers picked from their garden and displayed in earthenware galley pots.

Our tour of the seventeenth-century house, great and small, is now complete. From the testimony in this and earlier chapters, we can but admire housewives and their servants at this period for their hard work and ingenuity. Households were fed and watered, their health cared for, their clothes cleaned and preserved. Houses were kept clean, and where possible rooms were imbued with fragrance and decorated.

The recipes for all of these activities inevitably come down to us from the more affluent members of society, and often contain expensive ingredients, available only from apothecaries and grocers. It is clear, however, that gardens played a vital role, whatever the circumstances of the seventeenth-century household.

Notes

INTRODUCTION

1. John Worlidge, *Systema Horti-culturae or The Art of Gardening*, London, 1677, pp. 4–5.
2. In his classic work *The Making of the English Landscape*, first published in 1955 (Hodder & Stoughton, London), W.G. Hoskins argued that the period from 1570 to 1640 saw a development in vernacular architecture, which he described as 'the Great Rebuilding'. This was made possible by the rise in the levels of wealth among 'the middling sorts'. The Tudor chronicler William Harrison, in his description of England in 1577, divided the population into four parts: gentlemen, citizens or burgesses, yeomen, and artificers or labourers. The 'middling sorts' would have been the second and third categories. With their new-found prosperity, such people wanted more privacy, and this could be achieved architecturally by the insertion of chimney stacks into existing houses, while new houses were given two storeys built around a central stack.
3. Daniel Defoe, *A Plan of the English Commerce*, Charles Rivington, London, 1728, pp. 304–5.
4. John Gerard's *The Herball or Generall Historie of Plantes* (London, 1597) was amended in 1636 by the apothecary Thomas Johnson, but the references throughout this book are to the 1597 edition unless specifically stated.
5. Nicholas Culpeper, *The English Physitian or An Astrological-physical Discourse of the Vulgar Herbs of this Nation*, London, 1652. I have used the title *Culpeper's Complete Herbal* throughout for clarity.
6. Letter to Samuel Hartlib, 11 November 1659, Hartlib Papers, Sheffield, Ref. 62/25/1A-4B.
7. Thomas Hardy, *The Mayor of Casterbridge*, ch. 10.
8. *The Diary of Samuel Pepys*, ed. Robert Latham and William Matthews, 11 vols, Bell & Hyman, London, 1970–83, 11 August 1663, vol. 4, pp. 272–3.
9. *Martha Washington's Booke of Cookery*, Columbia University Press, New York, 1995; Katharine A. Harbury, *Colonial Virginia's Cooking Dynasty*, University of South Carolina Press, Columbia, 2004. Work is in progress on a database of historical cookery books, both printed and in manuscript, in US institutions: www.manuscriptcookbookssurvey/org. All the seventeenth-century manuscript recipe books are English in origin.
10. Her commonplace books are in the Kendal Record Office, WD/TE/

Box16/1. The recipes are on the National Trust Transcriptions Master, www.nationaltrust.org.uk/townend/documents/elizabeth-birketts-recipe-book.pdf.

11. Add MS 27466. It can be accessed online in *Defining Gender, 1450–1910*, published by Adam Matthew.

12. *Lady Fanshawe's Receipt Book: The Life and Times of a Civil War Heroine*, Atlantic Books, London, 2017. The household book, MS. 7113, is available on the Wellcome Library website.

13. Vol. 1 was published in 1994, vols 2 and 3 in 1999, by Stuart Press, Bristol. Hilary Spurling, *Elinor Fettiplace's Receipt Book: Elizabethan Country House Cooking*, Viking Salamander, London, 1986.

THE PRODUCTIVE GARDEN

1. John Gerard, *The Herball or Generall Historie of Plantes*, London, 1597, pp. 1327, 1260.

2. Ibid., p. 780.

3. John Frampton, *Joyfull newes out of the newe-found world*, 1576, title page. The original Spanish text was written by the physician Nicolas Monardes, *Primera y segunda tercara partes de la historia medcinal*, Seville, 1569.

4. Gerard, *Herball*, p. 286.

5. James I, *Counterblaste to Tobacco*, 1605, pp. 1–8.

6. John Goodyer in R.T. Gunther, *Early British Botanists and Their Gardens*, Oxford University Press, Oxford, 1922, p. 34.

7. Magdalen College, Oxford, Archives, Goodyer MS 11, fol. 117.

8. Gervase Markham, *The Countrie Farme*, London, 1616, ch. III, p. 158.

9. Thomas Tusser, *Five Hundred Pointes of Good Husbandrie*, 1580 edn collated with 1573 and 1577 edns, and unique 1557 edn of *A Hundreth Good Pointes of Husbandrie*, ed. with notes and glossary by W. Payne and S.I. Herrtage for the English Dialect Society, London, 1878, pp. 41, 40, 129.

10. Sarah Jinner, *An almanac or prognostication for the year 1658. Calculated for London and may indifferently serve for England, Scotland and Ireland*, London, 1658, n.pag.

11. W. Ryves, *The Life of the Admired Physician and astrologer of our times, Mr Nicholas Culpeper…*, London, 1659, sig. C3r.

12. Nicholas Culpeper, *The English Physitian or An Astrological-physical Discourse of the Vulgar Herbs of this Nation*, London, 1652, pp. 186–7.

13. *Elysium Britannicum*, insertion p. 55, British Library, Add MS. 78342

14. Elinor Fettiplace, *The Complete Receipt Book of Ladie Elynor Fettiplace*, vol. 2, Stuart Press, Bristol, 1999, p. 12.

15. John Parkinson, *Paradisi in Sole*, London, 1629, epistle to the reader.

16. Margaret Hoby, *The Private Life of an Elizabethan Lady: The Diary of Lady Margaret Hoby 1599–1605*, ed. Joanna Moody, Sutton Publishing, Stroud, 1998, p. 130.

17. Thomas Hanmer, *The Garden Book of Sir Thomas Hanmer*, Gerald Howe, London, 1933, pp. 144ff.

18. Finch Hatton papers in the Northamptonshire Record Office, 2455.

19. Gerard, *Herball*, p. 1079.

20. Fettiplace, *The Complete Receipt Book*, vol. 2, p. 11.

21. See John Evelyn, *Directions for the Gardiner and other Horticultural Advice*, ed. Maggie Campbell-Culver, Oxford University Press, Oxford, 2009, p. 123.

22. John Evelyn, *Kalendarium Hortense*, London, 1691, p. 153.

23. Hans Sloane, British Library, Sloane MS 1906; in *The Correspondence of John Ray*, ed. Edwin Lankester, The Ray Society, 1848, p. 158.

24. John Evelyn, *The Diary of John Evelyn*, ed. E.S. de Beer, 6 vols, Clarendon Press,

Oxford, 1955; rev. edn 2000, 6 August 1685, vol. 4, p. 462.

25. British Library, Add MS. 78300, f. 40, 14 August 1691.

26. Evelyn, *The Diary of John Evelyn*, 19 August 1668, vol. 3, p. 513.

27. Jon Stobart, *Sugar and Spice: Grocers and Groceries in Provincial England, 1650–1830*, Oxford University Press, Oxford, 2012, ch. 1.

28. Lancashire Record Office, WCW 1649.

29. Lichfield Record Office, B/M, 1614.

30. Cornwall Record Office, B1531, 1606; Stobart, *Sugar and Spice*, p. 28.

31. William Shakespeare, *The Winter's Tale*, IV.3.36–37, 44; IV.4.219–228, *The Oxford Shakespeare*, 2nd edn, Clarendon Press, Oxford, 2005.

32. See Margaret Spufford, *The Great Reclothing of Rural England: Petty Chapmen and Their Wares in the Seventeenth Century*, Hambledon Press, London, 1984.

33. Quoted in W.B. Rye, *England as Seen by Foreigners in the Days of Elizabeth and James the First*, J.R. Smith, London, 1865, p. 104.

34. Quoted in J.A. Rees, *The Grocery Trade: Its History and Romance*, 2 vols, Duckworth, London, 1932, vol. I, p. 222.

35. Report of the Rev. Dr Hamilton, quoted in Sue Minter, *The Apothecaries' Garden: A History of Chelsea Physic Garden*, Sutton Publishing, Stroud, 2000, p. 7.

36. Francis Higginson, *New England's Plantation, or a Short and True Description of the Commodities and Discommodities of that Countrye*, London, 1631, quoted in Ann Leighton, *Early American Gardens in New England: 'For Meate or Medicine'*, Cassell, London, 1970, pp. 25–6.

37. Ibid., p. 190.

38. The National Archives PL6/66/19.

39. See C. Paul Christianson, 'Herbwomen in London, 1660–1836', *London Gardener 6*, 2000–2001, pp. 22–31.

40. Stationers' Company Archives, TSC/1/F/05/03/01.

41. Ann Robey, 'The Village of Stock, Essex, 1550–1610: A Social and Economic Survey', PhD thesis, LSE, 1991.

42. Cheshire Archives and Local Studies, DLT/B51: see Stobart, *Sugar and Spice*, p. 192.

43. Gerard, *Herball*, pp. 599, 604, 1120.

44. Hugh Platt, *Delightes for Ladies*, London, 1609, Part II, section 14, p. 63; reprinted by Crosby Lockwood, London, 1948.

45. William Harrison, *The Description of England*, ed. Georges Edelen, Dover, New York, 1994, pp. 350–51.

46. *The Countrie Farme*, London, 1600, p. 4.

FOR THE TABLE

1. Thomas Tusser, *Five Hundred Pointes of Good Husbandrie*, 1580 edn collated with 1573 and 1577 edns, and unique 1557 edn of *A Hundreth Good Pointes of Husbandrie*, ed. with notes and glossary by W. Payne and S.I. Herrtage for the English Dialect Society, London, 1878, p. 229.

2. Kenelm Digby, *The Closet of Sir Kenelm Digby Opened* (1669), ed. from the 1st edn with notes by Jane Stevenson and Peter Davidson, Prospect Books, Totnes, 1997, p. 102.

3. These are all in the Pepys Library, Magdalene College, Cambridge: *The Gentlewoman's Delight in Cookery*, Penny Merriments II (32); *The Gentlewoman's Cabinet Unlocked*, Penny Merriments II (5); *The Complete Cookmaid*, Penny Merriments II (11); *The Compleat Cook/ Accomplished Servant-Maids Necessary Companion*, Penny Merriments I (39); and *The Queens Royal Closet Newly Opened*, Penny Merriments I (12).

4. Gervase Markham, *Countrey Contentments, or The English Huswife*, London, 1623, Booke I, p. 4.

5. William Shakespeare, *The Taming of the Shrew*, IV.5.25–27, *The Oxford Shakespeare*,

2nd edn, Clarendon Press, Oxford, 2005; Thomas Dawson, *The Good Housewife's Jewel* of 1596, with an intro. by Maggie Black, Southover Press, Lewes, 1996, p. 9.

6. Elinor Fettiplace, *The Complete Receipt Book of Ladie Elynor Fetiplace*, 3 vols, Stuart Press, Bristol, 1999, vol. 3, p. 34.

7. Mary Doggett, 'booke of receits', 1684, British Library Add. MS 27466; online in *Defining Gender, 1450–1910*, published by Adam Matthew, p. 262; Pepys, *The Compleat Cook*, fol. A2.

8. Samuel Pepys, *The Diary of Samuel Pepys*, ed. Robert Latham and William Matthews, 11 vols, Bell & Hyman, London, 1970–83, 4 April 1663, vol. 4, p. 95. This dinner was a celebration for Pepys's survival from the terrifying operation of having a stone removed from his bladder in 1658.

9. The recipe book of Grace Carteret, Lady Granville, Wellcome MS 8903, f. 48a.

10. Elizabeth Birkett, www.nationaltrust. org.uk/townend/documents/elizabeth-birketts-recipe-book.pdf, 11.

11. François Misson, *Memoires et Observations Faites par un Voyageur en Angleterre*, La Haye, 1698, p. 395.

12. Fettiplace, *The Complete Receipt Book of Ladie Elynor Fetiplace*, vol. 3, p. 29.

13. Birkett, www.nationaltrust.org.uk/townend/documents/elizabeth-birketts-recipe-book.pdf, 39.

14. Hannah Wolley, *The Queene-like Closet or Rich Cabinet*, London, 1672, p. 292.

15. John Gerard, *The Herball or Generall Historie of Plantes*, London, 1597, pp. 275–6; Juan Altamiras, *New Art of Cookery: A Spanish Friar's Kitchen Notebook, by Juan Altamiras*, ed. Vicky Hayward, Rowman & Littlefield, Lanham MD, 2017, p. 129.

16. Gerard, *Herball*, p. 781.

17. Hugh Platt, *Delightes for Ladies*, London, 1609, Part I, section 69, p. 52; reprinted by Crosby Lockwood, London, 1948.

18. Fettiplace, *The Complete Receipt Book of Ladie Elynor Fetiplace*, vol. 2, p. 45.

19. Ann Fanshawe's 'book of receipts', Wellcome MS. 7113, p. 284.

20. Robert May, quoted in Sara Paston-Williams, *The Art of Dining: The History of Cooking and Eating*, National Trust, London, 1993, p. 176.

21. Pepys, *The Gentlewoman's Delight in Cookery*, n.pag; Pepys, *The Gentlewoman's Cabinet Unlocked*, f. A2r.

22. John Evelyn, *Acetaria*, in *Directions for the Gardiner and Other Horticultural Advice*, ed. Maggie Campbell-Culver, Oxford University Press, Oxford, 2009, pp. 187–9, 164, 210–12.

23. See Paston-Williams, *The Art of Dining*, p. 121.

24. Birkett, www.nationaltrust.org.uk/townend/documents/elizabeth-birketts-recipe-book.pdf, 11.

25. Ralph Josselin, *The Diary of Ralph Josselin, 1616–1683*, ed. Alan Macfarlane, Oxford University Press for the British Academy, Oxford, 1976, p. 61; Margaret Hoby, *The Private Life of an Elizabethan Lady: The Diary of Lady Margaret Hoby 1599–1605*, 22 July 1600, ed. Joanna Moody, Sutton Publishing, Stroud, 1998, 1998, p. 100; Fettiplace, *The Complete Receipt Book of Ladie Elynor Fetiplace*, vol. 2, p. 11.

26. Hilary Spurling, *Elinor Fettiplace's Receipt Book: Elizabethan Country House Cooking*, Viking Salamander, London, 1986, p. 148.

27. John Partridge, *The Treasurie of Hidden Secrets*, London, 1573, ch. 56, in *Making Gardens of their Own: Advice for Women, 1550–1750*, ed. Jennifer Monroe, Aldershot, Ashgate 2007; Ann Fanshawe's 'book of receipts', p. 264.

28. Fettiplace, *The Complete Receipt Book of Ladie Elynor Fetiplace*, vol. 2, pp. 22, 38.

29. Hugh Platt, *Floraes Paradise*, London, 1608, pp. 28–30.

30. Partridge, *The Treasurie of Hidden Secrets*,

ch. 14; Wolley, *The Queene-like Closet or Rich Cabinet*, p. 89.

31. Fettiplace, *The Complete Receipt Book of Ladie Elynor Fetiplace*, vol. 1, p. 6.

32. Birkett, www.nationaltrust.org.uk/townend/documents/elizabeth-birketts-recipe-book.pdf, 32.

33. Ibid., 15, 16.

34. Ben Jonson, *The Staple of News*, IV.2.

35. Pepys, *The Complete Cookmaid*, p. 8.

SMALL BEER & STRONG LIQUORS

1. Gervase Markham, *Countrey Contentments, or The English Huswife*, London, 1623, p. 190.

2. John Gerard, *The Herball or Generall Historie of Plantes*, London, 1597, pp. 624, 524.

3. Andrew Boorde, *Introduction of Knowledge and Dyetary of Health*, ed. F.J. Furnivall, Early English Text Society, London, 1893, ch. 10, p. 256; John Taylor, *Ale-vated into the Ale-titude, A learned Oration before a Civill Assembly of Ale Drinkers*, London, 1653, p. 11.

4. Francis Bamford, ed., *A Royalist's Handbook*, Constable, London, 1936, p. 207.

5. John Aubrey, *Aubrey's Brief Lives*, ed. Oliver Lawson Dick, Secker & Warburg, London, 1949, p. 12.

6. Mary Doggett, 'booke of receits', 1684, British Library Add. MS 27466; online in *Defining Gender, 1450–1910*, published by Adam Matthew, p. 94.

7. William Shakespeare, *Love's Labour's Lost*, V.2.897–898, 909, 910, *The Oxford Shakespeare*, 2nd edn, Clarendon Press, Oxford, 2005.

8. Recipe book of Hannah Hickes, 1709, Wellcome Library, London, MS. 2834

9. Samuel Pepys, *The Diary of Samuel Pepys*, ed. Robert Latham and William Matthews, 11 vols, Bell & Hyman, London, 1970–83, 6 January 1668, vol. 1, p. 13; 3 December 1662, vol. 3, p. 274.

10. William Shakespeare, *The Merry Wives of Windsor*, V.5.139–140, 156–157, *The Oxford Shakespeare*, 2nd edn.

11. Kenelm Digby, *The Closet of Sir Kenelm Digby Opened* (1669), ed. Jane Stevenson and Peter Davidson, Prospect Books, London, 2010, p. 3.

12. Ibid., p. 4.

13. Ibid., p. 13.

14. Elinor Fettiplace, *The Complete Receipt Book of Ladie Elynor Fettiplace*, 3 vols, Stuart Press, Bristol, 1999, vol. 3, p. 37.

15. For an account of Leonard Wheatcroft, see Margaret Willes, *The Gardens of the British Working Class*, Yale University Press, New Haven CT, 2015, pp. 75–7.

16. William Shakespeare, *Twelfth Night*, I.5.151–153, *The Oxford Shakespeare*, 2nd edn.

17. Digby, *The Closet of Sir Kenelm Digby Opened*, p. 81.

18. John Evelyn, *Sylva*, annex *Pomona, Or An Appendix concerning Fruit-Trees in relation to Cider; the Making and several ways of Ordering it*, London, 1664, pp. 3–4.

19. Ibid., pp. 15, 29.

20. Pepys, *The Diary of Samuel Pepys*, 10 January 1661, vol. 2, p. 9; vol. 4, pp 25, 58.

21. Pepys, *The Diary of Samuel Pepys*, 12 November 1661, vol. 2, p. 12.

22. Fettiplace, *The Complete Receipt Book of Ladie Elynor Fetiplace*, vol. 3, pp. 29–30.

23. Pepys, *The Diary of Samuel Pepys*, 22 June 1660, vol. 1, p. 181.

36. Markham, *The English Huswife*, pp. 97–8; Fettiplace, *The Complete Receipt Book of Ladie Elynor Fetiplace*, vol. 2, pp. 45–6.

37. Pepys, *The Diary of Samuel Pepys*, 24 July 1663, vol. 4, p. 243; 9–10 June 1668, vol. 9, p. 227.

38. Pepys, *The Diary of Samuel Pepys*, 1 February 1660, vol. 1, p. 36; 8 April 1664, vol. 5, p. 117.

24. Fettiplace, *The Complete Receipt Book of Ladie Elynor Fetiplace*, vol. 3, p. 12.
25. Doggett, 'booke of receits', p. 37.
26. Fettiplace, *The Complete Receipt Book of Ladie Elynor Fetiplace*, vol. 3, pp. 36, 35, 38. She does not specify whether the celandine was the greater or the lesser
27. The duchess's recipe appears in the receipt book of Katherine Palmer, Wellcome MS. 7976, p. 134.
28. John Evelyn, *Acetaria*, in *Directions for the Gardiner and Other Horticultural Advice*, ed. Maggie Campbell-Culver, Oxford University Press, Oxford, 2009, p. 216.
29. John Evelyn, *The Diary of John Evelyn*, ed. E.S. de Beer, 6 vols, Clarendon Press, Oxford, rev. edn 2000 (1955), 29 May to 2 July 1637, vol. 2, p. 18.
30. Pepys, *The Diary of Samuel Pepys*, 25 September 1660, vol. 1, p. 253; 28 June 1667, vol. 8, p. 302.
31. Transcribed from a paper of Thomas Povey, 20 October 1686, British Library MS. Sloane 1039, f. 139.
32. Digby, *The Closet of Sir Kenelm Digby Opened*, p. 109.
33. Pepys, *The Diary of Samuel Pepys*, 24 April 1661, vol. 2, p. 88.
34. Ann Fanshawe's 'book of receipts', Wellcome MS. 7113, p. 332; Doggett, 'booke of receits', p. 60.

HEALTH & BEAUTY

1. Deborah Harkness, *The Jewel House: Elizabethan London and the Scientific Revolution*, Yale University Press, New Haven CT, 2007, ch. 2, 'The Contest over Medical Authority'.
2. William Clowes, 'Of Blind Buzzards and Cracking Combatters', in *A briefe and necessary Treatise* (London, 1585), in *Selected Writings of William Clowes*, ed. F.N.L. Poynter, Harvey & Blythe, London, 1948, p. 77.
3. Annals of the Royal College of Physicians, 2: 7a–8a.
4. Elaine Leong, *Recipes and Everyday Knowledge: Medicine, Science, and the Household in Early Modern England*, University of Chicago Press, Chicago IL, 2018, p. 2.
5. Joanna Moody, ed., *The Private Life of an Elizabethan Lady: The Diary of Lady Margaret Hoby, 1599–1605*, Sutton Publishing, Stroud, 1998, p. 18.
6. Grace Mildmay, Autobiography, fols 11 and 46. See Linda A. Pollock, *With Faith and Physic*, Collins & Brown, London, 1993, pp. 26, 35.
7. *The Great Picture* is in Abbot Hall Art Gallery, Kendal, Cumbria. Lady Hanmer's portrait is reproduced in Margaret Willes, *The Making of the English Gardener: Plants, Books and Inspiration, 1560–1660*, Yale University Press, New Haven CT, 2015, p. 236.
8. *Culpeper's School of Physick*, London, 1696, C6r.
9. John Gerard, *The Herball or Generall Historie of Plantes*, London, 1597, pp. 624, 878; Nicholas Culpeper, *The English Physitian or An Astrological-physical Discourse of the Vulgar Herbs of this Nation*, London, 1652 p. 260.
10. Ralph Josselin, *The Diary of Ralph Josselin, 1616–1683*, ed. Alan Macfarlane. Oxford University Press for the British Academy, Oxford, 1976, 17 July 1646, p. 64; Gerard, *Herball*, p. 288; Elinor Fettiplace, *The Complete Receipt Book of Ladie Elynor Fetiplace*, 3 vols, Stuart Press, Bristol, 1999, vol. 1, p. 29.
11. The duchess's recipe is in a book attributed to Katherine Palmer, Wellcome Library MS. 7976, p. 80; Sarah Jinner, *An almanac or prognostications for the year 1658[–60]*, London, 1660, B3.
12. Jinner, *An almanac*, 1660, B3.
13. Ibid.

14. *The Queens Royal Closet Newly Opened and the Art of Physic discovered by that most famous physician, Dr R. Boules,* 1682.
15. Receipt book of Mrs Mary Chantrell, Wellcome MS. 1584, pp. 30–32; Culpeper, *The English Physitian,* pp. 328–9.
16. Elizabeth Birkett, www.nationaltrust. org.uk/townend/documents/elizabeth-birketts-recipe-book.pdf, 29.
17. Ann Fanshawe's 'book of receipts', Wellcome MS. 7113, p. 60.
18. Ibid., p. 8.
19. Josselin, *The Diary of Ralph Josselin,* 25 February 1648, p. 115. Culpeper, *The English Physitian,* p. 97.
20. Josselin, *The Diary of Ralph Josselin,* 13 October 1650, p. 218; Gerard, *Herball,* p. 465; Birkett, www.nationaltrust.org.uk/townend/documents/elizabeth-birketts-recipe-book.pdf, 30; John Josselyn, *An Account of Two Voyages to New-England,* London, 1674, p. 13.
21. Culpeper, *The English Physitian,* p. 21; Gerard, *Herball,* Johnson emendation, 1636, p. 856.
22. Josselin, *The Diary of Ralph Josselin,* 29 January 1651, p. 234; Elinor Fettiplace, *The Complete Receipt Book of Ladie Elynor Fetiplace,* 3 vols, Stuart Press, Bristol, 1999, vol. 1, p. 20.
23. Samuel Pepys, *The Diary of Samuel Pepys,* ed. Robert Latham and William Matthews, 11 vols, Bell & Hyman, London, 1970–83, 13 February 1660, vol. 1, p. 54; Hannah Hickes, Wellcome MS. 2834, p. 8.
24. See Liza Picard, *Restoration London,* Weidenfeld & Nicolson, London, 1997, p. 89 and n37.
25. Josselin, *The Diary of Ralph Josselin,* 9 February 1665, 27 March 1665, pp. 515–16.
26. Pepys, *The Diary of Samuel Pepys,* 16 September 1664, vol. 5, p. 272; 12 February 1663, vol. 4, p. 41; Fettiplace, *The Complete Receipt Book of Ladie Elynor Fetiplace,* vol. 1, p. 20.
27. See F.H. West, *Rude Forefathers: The Story of an English Village,* Bannisdale Press, London, 1949.
28. Pepys, *The Diary of Samuel Pepys,* 30 August 1665, vol. 6, pp. 206–7.
29. Pepys, *The Diary of Samuel Pepys,* 7 June 1665, vol. 4, p. 120; 20 July 1665, p. 163; John Evelyn, *Letterbooks,* letter 268, 14 December 1665, vol. 1, p. 403; Gerard, *Herball,* p. 1071.
30. Hannah Wolley, *The Queene-like Closet or Rich Cabinet,* London, 1672, pp. 2–3.
31. Duchess of Lauderdale, in the receipt book of Katherine Palmer, Wellcome MS. 7976, p. 85; Fettiplace, *The Complete Receipt Book of Ladie Elynor Fetiplace,* vol. 1, p. 50.
32. Ann Fanshawe's 'book of receipts', Wellcome MS. 7113, p. 179.
33. Kenelm Digby, *Choice and Experimented Receipts,* London, 1668, p. 30; Fettiplace, *The Complete Receipt Book of Ladie Elynor Fetiplace,* vol. 1, pp. 41–2.
34. Gerard, *Herball,* pp. 1327, 765; Pepys, *The Diary of Samuel Pepys,* 28 May 1667, vol. 8, p. 240; 10 and 11 May 1669, vol. 9, p. 549; Hannah Wolley, *The Accomplisht lady's delight in preserving, physick and cookery,* London, 1675, p. 85.
35. *Aubrey's Brief Lives,* ed. Oliver Lawson Dick, Nonpareil Books, Boston MA, 1999, p. 101.
36. Pepys, *The Diary of Samuel Pepys,* 23 May 1662, vol. 3, p. 89; Ben Jonson, *The Epicene,* I.1.
37. Fettiplace, *The Complete Receipt Book of Ladie Elynor Fetiplace,* vol. 1, p. 9.
38. Pepys, *The Diary of Samuel Pepys,* 21–22 February 1665, vol. 6, pp. 40–41.
39. Ben Jonson, *Volpone,* III.7.
40. John Shirley, *The Accomplished Ladies Rich Closet of Rarities: or the Ingenious Gentlewoman and Servant Maids Delightfull Companion,* London, 1687, p. 69.
41. Hugh Platt, *Delights for Ladies,* London, 1609, section 8, reprinted by Crosby Lockwood, London, 1948, p. 90.

42. Johann Jacob Wecker, *Cosmeticks: or, The Beautifying Part of Physick*, London, 1660, p. 6; *Ladies Dictionary*, London, 1694, p. 212.

43. Giambattista della Porta, *Natural Magick*, London, 1669, p. 233; Wecker, *Cosmeticks*, p. 8.

44. Wecker, *Cosmeticks*, p. 9; Birkett, www.nationaltrust.org.uk/townend/

CARE OF CLOTHES

1. Gervase Markham, *Countrey Contentments, or The English Huswife*, London, 1623, p. 162.

2. Henry Best, *The Farming and Memorandum Books of Henry Best of Elmswell, 1642*, ed. Donald Woodward, Clarendon Press for the British Academy, Oxford, 1984, pp. 110ff.

3. John Gerard, *The Herball or Generall Historie of Plantes*, London, 1597, p. 957.

4. Ibid., p. 349.

5. Markham, *The English Huswife*, pp. 154–9.

6. Birkett, www.nationaltrust.org.uk/townend/documents/elizabeth-birketts-recipe-book.pdf, 4–6; Lancashire Archives: James Berry of Ormskirk, WCW, 1686; William Blackledge of Preston, WCW 1685.

7. John Evelyn, *Fumifugium*, London, 1661, p. 5.

8. William Richard, *Wallography; or the Britton describ'd...*, O. Blagrave, London, 1682, p. 52.

9. William Shakespeare, *The Winter's Tale*, IV.3.5, 23, *The Oxford Shakespeare*, 2nd edn, Clarendon Press, Oxford, 2005; Thomas Tusser, *Five Hundred Pointes of Good Husbandrie*, 1580, January's abstract, p. 76.

10. Joseph Taylor, *A Journey to Edenborough in Scotland*, W. Brown, Edinburgh, 1903, p. 136.

11. Samuel Pepys, *The Diary of Samuel Pepys*, ed. Robert Latham and William Matthews, 11 vols, Bell & Hyman, London, 1970–83, 6 October 1663, vol. 4, pp. 325–6; 12 August 1667, vol. 8, p. 383.

12. Robert Hooke, *Diary of Robert Hooke,*

documents/elizabeth-birketts-recipe-book.pdf, 28, 29.

45. *Philosophical Transactions* 158, 1684, p. 559.

46. Wecker, *Cosmeticks*, p. 123.

47. Wolley, *The Accomplisht lady's delight in preserving, physick and cookery*, p. 88.

48. Ann Windsor, Nottingham RO, Saville MS 221/97/7.

F.R.S., 1672–1680, ed. Henry Robinson and Walter Adams, Taylor & Francis, London, 1935, 6 October 1677, p. 318.

13. Christina Hardyment, *Behind the Scenes: Domestic Arrangements in Historic Houses*, National Trust, London, 1997, p. 225.

14. Elizabeth Purefoy in *The Purefoy Letters 1735–1753*, 2 vols, ed. G. Eland, Sidgwick & Jackson, London, 1931, vol. 1, p. 153; Hannah Wolley, *The Queene-like Closet or Rich Cabinet*, London, 1672, p. 223; Birkett, www.nationaltrust.org.uk/townend/documents/elizabeth-birketts-recipe-book.pdf, 7.

15. Gerard, *Herball*, p. 686.

16. Ibid., p. 99.

17. Ibid., p. 56.

18. John Josselyn, *New-Englands Rarities Discovered*, London, 1672, p. 53.

19. John Partridge, *The Treasurie of Hidden Secrets*, 1627, ch. 48, in *Making Gardens of their Own: Advice for Women, 1550–1750*, ed. Jennifer Monroe, Ashgate, Aldershot, 2007.

20. Elinor Fettiplace, *The Complete Receipt Book of Ladie Elynor Fettiplace*, 3 vols, Stuart Press, Bristol, 1999, vol. 2, p. 17.

21. Partridge, *The Treasurie of Hidden Secrets*, ch. 43.

22. Mary Doggett, 'booke of receits', 1684, British Library Add. MS 27466; online in 'Defining Gender, 1450–1910', published by Adam Matthew, p. 18.

23. Johann Jacob Wecker, *Cosmeticks: or, The Beautifying Part of Physick*, London, 1660, p. 3.

24. Hugh Platt, *Delightes for Ladies*, London, 1609, section 34, reprinted by Crosby Lockwood, London, 1948.

25. Fettiplace, *The Complete Receipt Book of Ladie Elynor Fetiplace*, vol. 2, p. 26.

FRAGRANT CHAMBERS

1. *The Oxford Shakespeare*, 2nd edn, Clarendon Press, Oxford, 2005.
2. Lemnius, quoted in W.B. Rye, *England as Seen by Foreigners in the Days of Elizabeth and James the First*, John Russell Smith, London, 1865, pp. 80, 77; William Bullein, *Bulwarke of Defence Againste All Sicknes, Sornes, and Wounds*, London, 1579, fol. xxi.
3. Erasmus letter, translated from Latin in Alfred Burton, *Rush Bearing*, Brook & Crystal, Manchester, 1891, p. 8.
4. John Gerard, *The Herball or Generall Historie of Plantes*, London, 1597, p. 887.
5. John Parkinson, *Theatrum Botanicum*, London, 1640, p. 593.
6. Thomas Tusser, *Five Hundred Pointes of Good Husbandrie*, 1580, p. 123.
7. Bullein, *Bulwarke of Defence*, fol. xxi.
8. See Audrey Le Lievre, 'Herb Strewer to the King', *Country Life*, 12 February 1987, pp. 72–3. Remarkably, the office of Royal Herb Strewer continued through to the reign of William IV, although their duties must increasingly have been confined to special occasions.
9. Samuel Pepys, *The Diary of Samuel Pepys*, ed. Robert Latham and William Matthews, 11 vols, Bell & Hyman, London, 1970–83, 12 February 1667, vol. 8, p. 55; Burton, *Rush Bearing*, p. 11.
10. Exchequer rolls E351/3249 and E351/3257 Mews, 1623–4.
11. Richard Carew, *Survey of Cornwall 1602*, facsimile edn, Theatrum Orbis Terrarum and Da Capo Press, New York, 1969, p. 18.
12. Pepys, *The Diary of Samuel Pepys*, 15 June 1666, vol. 7, p. 167.
13. Hannah Glasse, *The Servants Directory*, quoted in the *National Trust Manual of Housekeeping*, Viking Penguin, London, 1984, p. 91.
14. Troutbeck, by a member of the Scandinavian Society, quoted in Geoffrey Grigson, *The Englishman's Flora*, Paladin, 1958, p. 228.
15. John Evelyn, *The Diary of John Evelyn*, ed. E.S. de Beer, 6 vols, Clarendon Press, Oxford, 2000 (1955), 23 October 1685, vol. 4, p. 482.
16. Dorothy Hartley, *Food in England*, Little Brown, Boston MA, 1996, p. 649.
17. Mary Doggett, 'booke of receits', 1684, British Library Add. MS 27466; online in 'Defining Gender, 1450–1910', published by Adam Matthew, p. 40.
18. Johann Jacob Wecker, *Cosmeticks: or, The Beautifying Part of Physick*, London, 1660, p. 134.
19. John Partridge, *The Treasurie of Hidden Secrets*, 1627, ch. 47, in *Making Gardens of their Own: Advice for Women, 1550–1750*, ed. Jennifer Monroe, Ashgate, Aldershot, 2007.
20. Quoted in Robert Sackville-West, *Inheritance: The Story of Knole and the Sackvilles*, Bloomsbury, London, 2010, p. 57.
21. John Aubrey, *Aubrey's Brief Lives*, ed. Oliver Lawson Dick, Nonpareil Books, Boston MA, 1999, p. 9.
22. Quoted in Sara Paston-Williams, *The Art of Dining: The History of Cooking and Eating*, National Trust, London, 1993, p. 138.
23. Pepys, *The Diary of Samuel Pepys*, 12 July 1666, vol. 7, p. 204; Evelyn, *The Diary of John Evelyn*, 18 June 1670, vol. 3, p. 550.
24. Wecker, *Cosmeticks*, pp. 139–40.
25. Bog myrtle, also known as candleberry and sweet gale, is the northern European

relation of the bayberry, and has been used to make candles in the same way, but I have not found any recipes or references to its use in seventeenth-century England.

26. Lemnius, quoted in W.B. Rye, *England as Seen by Foreigners*, p. 77; John Stow, *Survey of London*, repr. from the 1603 text, ed. Charles Lethbridge Kingsford, 2 vols, Clarendon Press, Oxford, 1971, vol. 1, p. 101; Parkinson, *Theatrum Botanicum*, p. 729.

27. Gerard, *Herball*, p. 1206.

28. Quoted in Sackville-West, *Inheritance*, p. 57.

29. Lemnius, quoted in Rye, *England as Seen by Foreigners*, p. 80.

30. Hugh Platt, *Floraes Paradise*, London, 1608, pp. 30–39.

31. Hannah Wolley, *The Queene-like Closet or Rich Cabinet*, London, 1675 edn, pp. 127–9.

32. John Evelyn, *Directions for the Gardiner and other Horticultural Advice*, ed. Maggie Campbell-Culver, Oxford University Press, Oxford, 2009, pp. 97–8.

33. John Evelyn, *The Compleat Gard'ner and Right Ordering of Fruits and Kitchen Gardens*, Part VI, vol. 2, London, 1693, pp. 173–7.

34. Gerard, *Herball*, pp. 935–6.

Select Bibliography

PRIMARY MANUSCRIPT SOURCES

Elizabeth Birkett's commonplace books, Kendal Record Office, WD/TE/Box16/1. The recipes are on the National Trust Transcriptions Master, www.nation-altrust.org.uk/townend/documents/elizabeth-birketts-recipe-book.pdf.

Mary Doggett's 'booke of receits', British Library Add. MS 27466; online at 'Defining Gender, 1450–1910', published by Adam Matthew.

John Evelyn's *Elysium Britannicum*, British Library Add. MS 78342; available in John E. Ingram, ed., *Elysium Britannicum or The Royal Gardens by John Evelyn*, University of Pennsylvania Press, Philadelphia, 2000.

Ann Fanshawe's household book, Wellcome Library, MS. 7113; available online in the Wellcome Library Catalogue.

PRIMARY PRINTED SOURCES

Aubrey, John, *Aubrey's Brief Lives*, ed. Oliver Lawson Dick, Nonpareil Books, Boston MA, 1999.

Boorde, Andrew, *Introduction of Knowledge and Dyetary of Health*, ed. F.J. Furnivall, Early English Text Society, London 1893.

Bullein, William, *Bulwarke of Defence Against All Sicknes, Sornes, and Wounds*, London, 1562.

Culpeper, Nicholas, *The English Physitian or An Astrological-physical Discourse of the Vulgar Herbs of this Nation* [known as *Culpeper's Complete Herbal*], London, 1652.

Dawson, Thomas, *The Good Housewife's Jewel*, ed. Maggie Black, Southover Press, Lewes, 1996.

Digby, Kenelm, *The Closet of Sir Kenelm Digby Opened* (1669), ed. Jane Stevenson and Peter Davidson, Prospect Books, Totnes, 1997.

——— *Choice and Experimented Recipes*, London, 1668.

Evelyn, John, *The Diary of John Evelyn*, ed. E.S. de Beer, 6 vols, Clarendon Press, Oxford, 1955; rev. edn, 2000.

——— *The French Gardiner*, London, 1658.

——— *Directions for the Gardiner and other Horticultural Advice*, ed. Maggie Campbell-Culver, Oxford University Press, Oxford, 2009.

——— *Sylva*, annex *Pomona, Or An Appendix concerning Fruit-Trees in relation to Cider; the Making and several ways of Ordering it*, London, 1664.

——— *The Compleat Gard'ner and Right*

Ordering of Fruits and Kitchen Gardens, London, 1693.

Fettiplace, Elinor, *The Complete Receipt Book of Ladie Elynor Fetiplace*, Stuart Press, Bristol, vol. 1, 1994; vols 2 and 3, 1999.

Forster, John, *England's Happiness Increased*, London, 1664.

Gerard, John, *The Herball or Generall Historie of Plantes*, London, 1597.

Hanmer, Thomas, *The Garden Book*, facsimile edn, Gerald Howe, London, 1933.

Hoby, Margaret, *The Private Life of an Elizabethan Lady: The Diary of Lady Margaret Hoby 1599–1605*, ed. Joanna Moody, Sutton Publishing, Stroud, 1998.

Jinner, Sarah, *An almanac or prognostications for the year 1658 [-60], etc*, London, 1658, 1659, 1660, 1664.

Josselin, Ralph, *The Diary of Ralph Josselin, 1616–1683*, ed. Alan Macfarlane, Oxford University Press for The British Academy, Oxford, 1976.

Josselyn, John, *New-Englands Rarities Discovered*, London, 1672.

———— *An Account of Two Voyages to New-England*, London, 1673.

Lawson, William, *A New Orchard and Garden*, London, 1618.

Markham, Gervase, *Countrey Contentments, or The English Huswife*, London, 1623.

———— *The Countrie Farme*, London, 1616.

Parkinson, John, *Paradisi in Sole*, London, 1629.

———— *Theatrum Botanicum*, London, 1640.

Partridge, John, *The Treasurie of Hidden Secrets* (1627), in *Making Gardens of their Own: Advice for Women, 1550–1750*, ed. Jennifer Monroe, Ashgate, Aldershot, 2007.

Pepys, Samuel, *The Diary of Samuel Pepys*, ed. Robert Latham and William Matthews (eds), 11 vols, Bell & Hyman, London, 1970–83.

———— *Penny Merriments: The Gentlewoman's Delight in Cookery* (n.d.); *The Gentlewoman's Cabinet Unlocked* (n..d); *The Complete Cookmaid* (1684); *The Compleat Cook / Accomplished Servant-Maids Necessary Companion* (n.d.); *The Queens Royal Closet Newly Opened* (1682), Magdalene College, Cambridge.

Mildmay, Grace, in Linda Pollock, *With Faith and Physic*, Collins & Brown, London, 1993.

Platt, Hugh, *Floraes Paradise*, London, 1608.

———— *Delightes for Ladies*, London, 1609; reprinted by Crosby Lockwood, London, 1948.

Tusser, Thomas, *Five Hundred Pointes of Good Husbandrie* (1580 edn collated with 1573 and 1577 edns, and unique 1557 edn of *A Hundreth Good Pointes of Husbandrie*), ed. W. Payne and S.J. Herrtage, English Dialect Society, London, 1878.

Wecker, Johann Jacob, *Cosmeticks: or, The Beautifying Part of Physick*, London, 1660.

Wolley, Hannah, *The Queene-like Closet or Rich Cabinet*, London, 1672, 1675.

Secondary Sources

Blacker, Mary Rose, *Flora Domestica: A History of Flower Arranging, 1500–1930*, National Trust, London, 2000.

Burton, Alfred, *Rush Bearing*, Brook & Crystal, Manchester, 1891.

Davidson, Caroline, *A Woman's Work is Never Done: A History of Housework in the British Isles, 1650–1950*, Chatto & Windus, London, 1982.

Gilbert, Christopher, James Lomax and Anthony Wells-Cole, *Country House Floors, 1660–1850*, Temple Newsam Country House Studies 3, Leeds City Art Galleries, Leeds, 1987.

Grigson, Geoffrey, *The Englishman's Flora*, Paladin, London, 1975.

Harbury, Katherine E., *Colonial Virginia's Cooking Dynasty*, University of South Carolina Press, Columbia, 2004.

Hardyment, Christina, *Behind the Scenes:*

Domestic Arrangements in Historic Houses, National Trust, London, 1997.

Harkness, Deborah, *The Jewel House: Elizabethan London and the Scientific Revolution*, Yale University Press, New Haven CT, 2007.

Laroche, Rebecca, *Medical Authority and Englishwomen's Herbal Texts, 1550–1650*, Ashgate, Aldersot, 2009.

Leighton, Ann, *Early English Gardens in New England, 'For Meate or Medicine'*, Cassell, London, 1970.

Leong, Elaine, *Recipes and Everyday Knowledge: Medicine, Science, and the Household in Early Modern England*, University of Chicago Press, Chicago, 2018.

Mabey, Richard, *Flora Britannica: The Definitive New Guide to Wild Flowers, Plants and Trees*, Sinclair-Stevenson, London, 1996.

Moore, Lucy, *Lady Fanshawe's Receipt Book: The Life and Times of a Civil War Heroine*, Atlantic London, London, 2017.

Mortimer, Ian, *The Dying and the Doctors: The Medical Revolution in Seventeenth-century England*, Studies in History, Royal Historical Society and the Boydell Press, Woodbridge and New York, 2009.

Paston-Williams, Sara, *The Art of Dining: A History of Cooking and Eating*, National Trust, London, 1993.

Pennell, Sara, *The Birth of the English Kitchen, 1600–1850*, Bloomsbury, London, 2016.

Picard, Liza, *Restoration London*, Weidenfeld & Nicolson, London, 1997.

Pollock, Linda A., *With Faith and Physic*, Collins & Brown, London, 1993.

Ribeiro, Aileen, *Facing Beauty: Painted Women in Cosmetic Art*, Yale University Press, New Haven CT, 2011.

Robey, Ann, 'The Village of Stock, Essex, 1550–1610: A Social and Economic Survey', PhD thesis, London School of Economics, 1991.

Spufford, Margaret, *The Great Reclothing of Rural England: Petty Chapmen and Their Wares in the Seventeenth Century*, Hambledon Press, London, 1984.

Spurling, Hilary, *Elinor Fettiplace's Receipt Book: Elizabethan Country House Cooking*, Viking Salamander, London, 1986.

Stobart, Jon, *Sugar and Spice: Grocers and Groceries in Provincial England, 1650–1830*, Oxford University Press, Oxford, 2012.

Tankard, Danae, *Houses of the Weald and Downland: People and Houses of South-east England, c. 1300–1900*, Carnegie, Lancaster, 2012.

Thornton, Peter, *Authentic Décor: The Domestic Interior, 1620–1920*, Weidenfeld & Nicolson, London, 1984.

West, F.H., *Rude Forefathers: The Story of an English Village*, Bannisdale Press, London, 1949.

White, Eileen, ed., *The English Cookery Book: Historical Essays*, Prospect Books, Totnes, 2004.

Willes, Margaret, *The Making of the English Gardener: Plants, Books and Inspiration, 1560–1660*, Yale University Press, New Haven CT, 2011.

———— *The Gardens of the British Working Class*, Yale University Press, New Haven CT, 2015.

———— *A Shakespearean Botanical*, Bodleian Library, Oxford, 2015.

Picture Credits

© Bodleian Library, University of Oxford
1911 d.31, p. 225: **p. 176**
Antiq.e.E.1657.3 (1), title page: **p. 99**
Douce G 526 (1): **p. 42**
G.A. Lond. c.81, plate 6: **p. 187**
Lawn e.8, title page: **p. 21**
Lawn f.250, frontispiece: **p. 75**
MS. Ashmole 1461, fol. 139r: **p. 83**;
fol. 127r: **p. 101**; fol. 133r: **p. 102**;
fol. 25r: **p. 105**
MS. Ashmole 1504, fol. 10v: **p. 84**;
fol. 3v: **p. 90**; fol. 10r: **p. 160**; fol.
7v: **p. 115**
MS. C17:48 (9): **p. 13**
(OC) 70 c.64: **p. 56**
L 1.5 Med., Gerard, *Herball*: (p. 545)
p. vi; (title page): **p. viii**;
(p. 1327): **p. 22**; (p. 285): **p. 24**;
(p. 991): **p. 32**; (p. 153): **p. 37**;
(p. 844): **p. 40**; (p. 1119): **p. 53**;
(p. 861): **p. 61**; (p. 781): **p. 67**;
(p. 1079): **p. 76**; (p. 66): **p. 79**;
(p. 523): **p. 91**; (p. 866): **p. 113**;
(p. 577): **p. 114**; (p. 526): **p. 116**;
(p. 259): **p. 117**; (p. 467): **p. 119**;
(p. 600): **p. 120**; (p. 985): **p. 121**;
(p. 416): **p. 122**; (p. 338): **p. 124**;
(p. 1070): **p. 125**; (p. 432): **p. 126**;
(p. 525): **p. 127**; (p. 394): **p. 129**;
(p. 945): **p. 141**; (p. 464): **p. 145**;
(p. 705): **p. 147**; (p. 1070): **p. 149**;
(p. 1109): **p. 159**; (p. 957): **p. 164**;
(p. 360): **p. 173**; (p. 685): **p. 174**;
(p. 47): **p. 179**; (p. 886): **p. 183**

A.C. Cooper: **p. 137**

Bibliothèque nationale de France,
Paris: **p. 194**

Bridgeman Images/British Library,
BL2962610: **p. 16**

Photo © Christie's Images/Bridgeman
Images, CH8149: **pp. 2–3**

Library and Information Centre of the
Hungarian Academy of Sciences,
Department of Manuscripts and Rare
Books, Ráth 32, title page: **p. 47**

Reproduced by permission of the
Pepys Library, Magdalene College,
Cambridge, PL 2973 pp 422–3:
pp. 62–3

© National Portrait Gallery, London,
NPG 2562: **p. 180**

Private Collection/Johnny Van
  Haeften Ltd., London/Bridgeman
  Images: **pp. 30–31**

Rijksmuseum, Amsterdam: **pp. 70–71**;
  p. 191; **p. 203**; **p. 204**

Royal Collection Trust/© Her Majesty
  Queen Elizabeth II 2019, RL 14329: **p. 169**

© Victoria & Albert Museum,
  London, 4717-1901: **p. 88**; W.12-1994:
  p. 199

Wellcome Collection: **p. 19**; **p. 25**;
  p. 44; **p. 130**

Index

Page references in *italics* refer to illustrations

ale, 91–5, 142, 147
alecost (costmary), 26, *91*, 92, 112, 188–9
alehoof (ground ivy), *90*, 92, 112, 145, *147*
Alexanders, *i*, 13, *113*
all-heal, 113
angelica, 50, 113, 139, 142, 150
Apethorpe Manor, Northants, 135
Appleton Manor, Berks, 37, 176
apothecaries 41, 43–4, *47*, 48–50, 79
apple, 22, 29, 39, 65, 82, 87, 97–100, *101*, 142
apricot, 23, 39, 81–2, 107
artichoke (Jerusalem and globe), 25–6, *32*, 33–4, 68–9, *70–71*
Aubrey, John 93, 122, 153, 193
Austen, Rev. Ralph 98, *99*

Bacon, Sir Francis, 48, 93, 193
Barbados, 6, 43, 48
bay, 61, 65, 96, 102, 114, 143, 156, 168, 179, 189, 192, 197, 202
bayberry, 45, 196
Beale, John 9, 48, 100
bees, 27, 96–7
berries, 81, 85, 107
betony, 92, 114, *114*, 141, 142
Bettisfield, Flintshire, 35–6

Birkett, Elizabeth, 11, 14, 64, 65, 85, 158, 166
bog myrtle, 93
Boorde, Dr Andrew, 89, 93
borage 74, 78, 95, 107, 150
botanic gardens, 50
Bullein, William, *130*, 137, 139, 140, 142, 182, 185

calamint, 157
camomile, 26, 37, 78, 184
carduus Benedictus, 114–15, 135
carnation (gillyflower) 35, 72, 79, 102, 156, 193, 197, 198, 201, *203*
celandine (greater and lesser), 107, 117–18, 119, 139, 145, 157
Charles I, king of England, 5
Charles II, king of England, 5, 29, 43, 140, 144, 153, 185
Chelsea Physic Garden, 41, 49–50
cherry, 22, 35, 40, 81, *105*
chocolate, 110–11
cider, 29–32
clary, 104, 115
coffee, 108–9
coltsfoot, 108, 144
columbine, 202

comfrey, *ii–iii*, *115*, 115, 156
costmary *see* alecost
cowslips, 142
crab apples, 68, 94, 166
crown imperial, viii, 29, 36, *37*, 201
cuckoo pint (starchwort) 116, 174, *174*
Culpeper, Nicholas, 7–9, 32–3, 49, 112–29,
   135–7, 144, 154

daisy, *ii–iii*, 145–6, 184
Digby, Sir Kenelm, 10, 58, 96–7, 109–10,
   151–2, 153, 154
dill, 50, 74, 78
distilling, 50, *75*, 76–82
Dodoens, Rembert, 8, 12
Doggett, Mary, 11, 14, 61, 77, 111, 138, 190
dye plants (broom, rocket, greenweed,
   weld) *52*, 116, 128, 164–7
Dysart, Elizabeth, Duchess of
   Lauderdale, 18, 29, 76, 108, 135, 139, 150,
   155–6, 202

East India Company, 6, 44, 48
Elizabeth I, queen of England, 6, 8, 40, 47,
   54, 134, 166, 183, 193
Evelyn, John and Mary, 12, 17, 33, 38–41, 43,
   69, 72–4, 98–102, 108, 149, 154, 158, 168,
   182, 189, 201

Fanshawe, Lady Ann, 11, 12, 14–15, 77–8, 111,
   138, 140, 148, 151
fennel, 68, 92, 116, 138, 196
Fettiplace, Lady Elinor, 11, 15, 33–4, 64, 68,
   77, 79, 81, 86, 95, 97, 104, 107, 138, 148, 151,
   152, 154, 159, 176–7, 179, 194–5
feverfew, 33, *116*, 117, 159, 201
fig, 22, *22*, 144, 150
flax, 161–3
florists' flowers, 29, 35–6, 40, 201

Galen of Pergamon, 125, 132
galls, 164–5

Geffrye Museum, Hoxton, 49, *165*, 186
Gerard, John 6, 7–8, 22–3, 37, 52–3, 66, 92,
   112–29, 133, *135*–6, *137*, 138, 144, 145, 152,
   164, 175, 183, 196, 202
gillyflower *see* carnation
golden rod, 165, 202
Good King Henry, 58, 117, *117*
Goodyer, John, 25–6
grocers, 43–5, 49, 50–51, 52–3
ground ivy *see* alehoof

Ham House, Richmond, 18, 29, 73, 76, 80,
   156, 167, 170, 202
Hampton Court Palace, 41, 186, 205
Hanmer, Sir Thomas, 35–6, 136, *137*
Hardwick New Hall, Derbyshire, 60
hemp, 118, *160*, 161–3
henbane, *83–4*, 151
Henrietta Maria, 5, 10, *32*, 34, 68, 96
Hoby, Lady Margaret, 12, 20, 35, 77, 134
honey, 96–7
Hooke, Robert, 109, 171–2
houseleek, 27, 118, 143, 158
hyssop, 26, 68, 78, 118, 137, 141, 144–5, *145*,
   156, 158, 198

Jamaica, 6, 48
James I, king of England, 5, 6, 25, 40, 48,
   55, 186
James II, king of England, 5
Jinner, Sarah, 28–32, 58, 139, 141, 152–3
Jonson, Ben, 85, 104, 153, 155–6
Josselin, Ralph and Mary, 12, 77, 138, 140,
   142, 144, 146, 147, 148, 151, 158
Josselyn, John, 116, 145, 175, 184

Knole Park, Kent, 192, 197, 202–3

lavender, 26, 35, 118–19, *119*, 137, 143, 156, 157,
   178, 184, 186, 193, 202
Lawson, William, *19*, 20–22, 94, 193
Lemnius, Levinus, 182, 196, 197–8

lemon, 40, 80, 85, 97, 156, 173
lemon balm, 96, 184, 188, 190
lily, 142, 196, 198
liquorice, 22, 45, 53, *53*, 94, 106, 108, 142, 151, 157
liverwort, 108, 153
L'Obel, Matthias de, *25*, 49

maidenhair fern, 108, 120–21, *121*, 157
marigold, 52–3, 61, 74, 95, 120, *120*, 193, 196
marjoram, 27, 58, 97, 127, 141, 142, 156, 177–8, 184, 198
Markham, Gervase, 9, 26–7, 60–61, 86, 89, 131, 161, 164
marsh mallow, 120, 152
Mary II, queen of England, 5, 41, 205
Mayerne, Sir Theodore de, 48, 107
mead, 96–7
meadowsweet, 121, 183, *183*
Mildmay, Grace, Lady, 134–5
mint, 78, 107, 121, 142, 158, 188
mugwort, 92, 122, 141, *141*

New England, 6, 50, 115, 117, 145, 173, 175

Oglander, Sir John, 93
orange (and flower water), 40, *42*, 80–81, 156, 178, 192
orchard fruit, 22, 29, 39; *see also* apple, apricot, cherry, pear, quince
orpine, 122, *122*, 196, 198
orris root, 156, 177–8, *179*

Paracelsus, 132
Parkinson, John, 34–5, 49, 184
parsley, 26, 58, 60–61, *61*, 64, 69, 122–3, 137, 138
Partridge, John, 78, 175–6, 177
pear, 22, 29, 39, 102, *103*
peas, 28, 57
pellitory (of the wall/of Spain) 27, 33, 123, 142, 146, 148, 158

pennyroyal, vi, 26, 108, 123, 137, 178
Pepys, Samuel and Elizabeth, 5, 11–12, 58–9, 61–3, *62–3*, 65, 85–6, 94–5, 104, 106, 109, 140, 144, 146–7, 149, 152, 153, 155, 171, 179, 185–6, 187, 189, 194
perry, 29–32, 102
plantain, 124, *124*, 137, 142, 158
Platt, Sir Hugh, 54, 69, 79–80, 198–200
potato, 6, 23, 66–8, *66*
primrose, 74

quince, 22, 81

raspberry, 81, 85, 104, 106
rose, 29, 34, 37–8, 50, *76*, 78, 137, 141, 142, 156, 158, 176–8, 184 189, 192, 200, *203*
rose madder, 52, 119, 154, *164*, 164, 166
rose water 37–8, 54, 76, *76*, 80 106, 150, 152, 178, 190, 195, 198
rosemary, 26, 27, 35, 60, 69, 78, 82, 93, 96–7, 102, 104, 107, 124, 142, 146, 150, 156, 158, *159*, 168, 176, 178, 186, 192, 197, 202
Royal College of Physicians, London, 33, 131–2, 133–4
Royal Society, The, 108, 171–2
rue, 124–5, *125*, 139, 143, 144, 146, *149*, 149–50, 175, 184
rushes, for strewing, 181–6, 193, 197

saffron, 22, 46, 54–5, 107, 157, 165
sage, 60–61, 96, 125, 138, 140, 142, 143, 146
salad vegetables, 29, 33, 69–74
St John's wort, 125–6, *126*, 196
St Thomas' Hospital, London, 51, 147, 185
savory, 26, 64
Sayes Court, Deptford, *16*, 17
scabious, 151
Shakespeare, William, *40*, 45–6, 54, 61, 67, 79, 94, 96, 98, 102, 135, 168, 181
soapwort, 126, 173, *173*
sorrel, 26, 58, 96, 139, 166
southernwood, 157, 158, 175

spices, 6, 43–5
spirits, 107–8
strawberries, 27, *40*, 96, 104, 106
sugar, 6–7, 45–8
sweet briar, 93, 197, 200
sweet cicely, 126, 188
sweet flag (rush and *Calamus aromaticus*)
    126, 156, 175, 176, 184, 189
sweet gale, 92, 127
sweet grass (woodruff), 129, 183–4

tansy, 127, *127*, 153, 166, 184, 188
tea and tisanes, 108–10
thyme, 27, 58, 60, 85, 96, 128, 198
tobacco, 6, 23–5, *24*, *25*, 27, 138–9, 144, 149
tomato, 65–6
tormentil, 128, 151
tuberose, 40, 201–2
tulip, 29, 35, *199*, 201, *203*, 205
Turner, William, 7, 135, 173

Tusser, Thomas, 9, 27–8, *57*, 65, 168, 184

vegetables, 28, 29, 33–4, 50, 58
violets, 27, 38, 50, 61, 78–80, *79*, 96, 106, 156,
    159, 184, 192
Virginia, 6, 12, 23

Weald and Downland Museum,
    Singleton, 18–20, 28, 60, 91, 148, 162, 165
Wecker, Johann Jacob, 154, 157–8, 190–92
William III, king of England, 5, 41
willow, 196
wine, 102–4
woad, 128–9, *129*, 166
woodruff *see* sweet grass
Worlidge, John, 1, 36
wormwood, 51, 104, 129, 139, 143, 144–5, 175,
    176, 184
Wolley, Hannah, 10, 15, 32, *56*, 59–60, 116,
    150, 152, 154, 200